the weaver's
idea book
creative cloth on a rigid heddle loom

Jane Patrick

INTERWEAVE
interweavestore.com

editor ANN BUDD

technical editor JUDY STEINKOENIG

studio photography BRAD BARTHOLOMEW

step-by-step photography JANE PATRICK

chapter opening photography MICHAEL LICHTER STUDIO

weaving drafts LYNN TEDDER

art director and cover design LIZ QUAN

interior design CONNIE POOLE

production KATHERINE JACKSON

INTERWEAVE PRESS LLC
201 East Fourth Street
Loveland, CO 80537-5655 USA
interweavestore.com

Printed in China by Asia Pacific Offset, Ltd.

Library of Congress Cataloging-in-Publication Data
Patrick, Jane.
The weaver's idea book : creative cloth on a rigid-heddle
    loom / Jane Patrick.
        p. cm.
Includes bibliographical references and index.
ISBN 978-1-59668-175-0 (hardcover with concealed wire-o)
    1. Hand weaving--Patterns. I. Title.
TT848.P42 2010
746.1'4041--dc22
                                        2009039518

10 9 8 7 6 5 4 3 2 1

acknowledgments

While working on a book is mostly a solitary experience, making a book involves a good many folk. I'd like to thank the many individuals and companies who joined me on the journey that became this book:

First and foremost to my publisher, *Interweave*, without whose support this book would not have been possible. I'm sure many have contributed, and I thank them for their efforts, with special thanks to the creative and publicity team. I extend an additional and heartfelt thank you to my editor *Ann Budd.*

Thanks to the following; it would not have been possible without you:

- *Judy Steinkoenig*, my tech editor, who delved into the details and corrected and advised.
- *Lynn Tedder*, who did more than just make pretty drafts.
- *Angela Johnson*, my intern, who translated most of my rigid heddle patterns into computer drafts, as well as helped out in the Schacht office and wove samples in her spare time.
- *Sara Goldenberg White*, my weaving intern and seamstress who came to my house nearly every day during the summer to warp looms, weave samples and projects, and sew most of the pieces in the book.

- My weavers and designers: *Melissa Ludden Hankens, Betsy Blumenthal, Jessica Knickman, Stephanie Flynn-Sokolov, Gail Matthews, and Judy Steinkoenig.*
- To *Schacht Spindle Company* for generously giving me time off to work on this book, as well as hiring summer interns to assist me. I am especially grateful to the office staff who kept it all going: *Gail, Stephanie, Liz, and Christy.*
- To my husband, *Barry Schacht*, for his love and support.
- To my friends at my local weaving shop: *Shuttles, Spindles, and Skeins*—all that yarn in stock made designing so easy.
- To the following yarn companies who provided yarn for projects: *Brown Sheep Company, Berroco Yarns, Cotton Clouds, Crystal Palace Yarns, Louet North America, and SWTC.* Thank you to *Fiberworks* for providing me with an upgrade with their sketchpad feature, which helped making the drafts much, much easier. Thanks also to *Schacht* for providing all of the rigid heddle looms to weavers for this book.
- A special thank-you to *Betty Davenport* for her contributions to the field and for her book *Patterns and Textures on the Rigid Heddle Loom*, which has taught me volumes over the years.

All of the samples and weavings are by the author except where noted.

contents

Introduction 6

CHAPTER 1: There's Nothing Plain about Plain Weave 12
Designing with Plain Weave 15
Choosing Materials 16
Spaced Warps and Wefts 19
Weaving with Handspun 19
Color and Texture 21
Stripes and Plaids as Texture 22
Color-and-Weave 24
project: Felted Scarf in Beige 30
project: Pulled-Thread Scarf 32
project: Rag Bag Threesome 34

CHAPTER 2: Finger-Controlled Weaves 42
Loop Pile 45
Danish Medallions 47
Leno 53
Brook's Bouquet 59
Spanish Lace 64
Hemstitching 68
Conclusion 73
project: Shrug in Leno 74
project: Linen Placemats 76

CHAPTER 3: Pick-Up on the Rigid Heddle Loom 78
Pick-up Basics 80
Weft-Float Sampler 88
Warp-Float Sampler 96
Warp and Weft Floats 100
Exploring Weft Floats 103
Exploring Warp Floats 114
Exploring Color-and-Weave Plus Floats 120
Using Yarn and Structure 124
Conclusion 129
project: Felted Pin-Striped Wrap Skirt 130
project: Honeycomb Pillow Pair 132

CHAPTER 4: Weft- and Warp-Faced Fabrics 136
Weft-Faced Fabrics 138
Ghiordes Knot or Cut Pile 141
Loops 150
Soumak 155
Krokbragd 161
Clasped Weft 164
Weft-Faced Fabrics and Pick-Up Patterns 166
Warp-Faced Fabrics 169
Conclusion 173
project: Summertime Coasters 174

CHAPTER 5: More is More with Two Heddles 176
Indirect Warping for Two Heddles 178
Weaving with Two Heddles 180
Textures with Two Heddles 183
Exploring Twill 191
Two Heddles, Two Densities, and Two Structures 194
Two Heddles to Achieve the Proper Sett 196
Embroidery on the Loom 200
Doubleweave 203
Conclusion 221
project: Country Girl/City Girl Apron 222
project: Doubleweave Table Runner 226

Glossary of Weaving Terms 230
Direct, Single-Peg Warping 232
Project Record Sheet 235
Bibliography and Resources 236
Index 238

introduction

In 1978 or so I was asked by Robin Taylor Daugherty to take over teaching the rigid heddle weaving classes she'd been offering through the City of Boulder. I had taken a 4-shaft class from Deborah Chandler (then Debbie Redding) at the Weaving Shop in Boulder, and I was weaving every free moment. Even though I was pretty much a beginning weaver, I felt confident I could handle rigid heddle weaving. With a little tutorial from Robin, I was ready to teach my first class—thus commencing my involvement with the rigid heddle loom—little did I know . . .

Even though I was teaching rigid heddle weaving, I'm pretty sure that in my own mind I discounted it as "inferior" and not "real" weaving! This was just something to do before moving on to weaving on a floor loom. But as I wove on the rigid heddle loom, I found it increasingly surprised me.

A few years later when I applied for a job at Interweave Press, I was not a veteran weaver by a long shot. I'd been working in a federal CETA youth employment program and funding was running out. I didn't know what I was going to do next. I did know, though, that I wanted my next step to somehow involve weaving. I thank Deborah Chandler for steering me in that direction.

At Deborah's suggestion I called Linda Ligon, founder of Interweave Press, about a job. I polished up my resume and drove to Loveland. Our interview was more a lunch conversation, but in a few days I received a letter in the mail with a job offer. I was elated, thrilled.

As a new, enthusiastic weaver, working at Interweave Press was the best of all worlds. Every day I talked or corresponded with weavers, I saw loads of weaving and grew to appreciate the depth and breadth of weaving. When I look back, editing *Handwoven* taught me volumes about weaving, and it was in working on editorial material for the magazine that I began to truly appreciate the rigid heddle loom.

I am grateful to Betty Davenport, who was a frequent contributor during my tenure. Through the projects she submitted to *Handwoven*, I saw firsthand the broad capabilities of the rigid heddle loom. I learned also that you don't need sophisticated equipment to make super designs. Betty credits Suzanne Gaston-Voute for teaching her much of what she learned about the rigid heddle loom. Others, too, have contributed to the field, namely David B. McKinney and David Xenakis.

I should also mention that shortly after I began working for Interweave Press, I married Barry Schacht of Schacht Spindle Company. I had actually been teaching on the Schacht rigid heddle loom when I taught for the City of Boulder. Now, all aspects of my life were encompassing my passion for weaving. What more could a girl ask for?

I was also led down the rigid heddle path by my friends at Shuttles, Spindles, and Skeins, my local yarn shop in Boulder. They needed someone to teach rigid heddle weaving and recruited me to be part of their faculty. I have been teaching there for many years, as well as teaching rigid heddle workshops and classes throughout the United States.

I wanted to write this book because I kept hearing weavers—new and old alike—lament that they could only weave plain weave (over, under, over, under) on a rigid heddle loom. Every time, I'd reply that much, much more was possible. Even so, I begin my rigid heddle explorations with plain weave because it has more to offer than at first you might suspect. Though plain weave is simple in structure, it can be complicated in design. You'll see

in Chapter 1 that a simple structure is no deterrent to stunning fabric.

Chapter 2 includes the finger-controlled weaves, which involve manipulating threads by hand. I have a great affinity for these techniques because they can be employed at any time for an accent of color or texture. I also like that they, as in the case of leno, for example, bend yarns out of the woven grid.

In Chapter 3, I explore the vast possibilities the pick-up stick has to offer, including many pattern recipes and ideas. Then, in Chapter 4, I look at warp- and weft-faced fabrics, as these offer even more rigid heddle loom possibilities. Finally, in Chapter 5, I explain two-heddle weaving and include how to warp and weave with two heddles, including weaving double weave.

In writing this book, I've assumed that you have at least warped a loom and know something about throwing the shuttle back and forth. If you are new to weaving, please see page 230 for a glossary of terms. Although I've written this book for the rigid heddle loom, the truth of the matter is that many of these ideas and techniques apply to other types of looms. Therefore, I have also included drafts for shaft looms. As I wove the samples for this book, I always felt that that there was more to be explored in every category. There were times, such as when I was working on Danish medallions that I just had to tell myself it was time to move on.

My hope is that as you delve into the ideas and techniques in this book, you too will discover how much more there is to almost everything you find herein. Weaving, like most things, is like that.

The rigid heddle loom explained

Just what is a rigid heddle loom? On a continuum of looms, I'd put the rigid heddle loom in between a simple frame loom and a four-shaft loom. A rigid heddle loom, like a floor or table loom, has warp and cloth beams, which means that lengths of cloth can be woven. Where the rigid heddle loom has it over a simple frame loom is the clever slot-hole design of the heddle that gives this loom such powerful capabilities.

The rigid heddle serves multiple functions: it determines the sett (number of warp ends per inch), creates the spaces (sheds) for the weft to be woven through, and finally, beats the weft into place. Heddles come in a variety of "dents," such as 8, 10, and 12. "Dents" refers to the number of spaces, counting both slots and holes, per inch. To know what dent heddle you have, just place a ruler against the reed and count the slots and holes in an inch.

The heddle blocks assist in making the sheds. Most rigid heddle looms have a neutral position where threads are neither up nor down, an up position, and a down position. To weave, the heddle is placed alternately in the up and down positions to create the sheds for passing the shuttle through. When the heddle is in the up position, the threads in the holes are raised; when placed in the down position, the threads in the slots are raised. By alternately placing the heddle up and down, inserting a weft pick (row) each time, the simplest weave structure, plain weave, is woven.

The genius of the rigid heddle loom is the slot-hole configuration. Because the slot threads are free to move about, they can be manipulated with a pick-up stick to create weft- and warp-float patterns. I'll delve in to creating pick-up patterns in Chapter 3, as well as explore two-heddle weaving in depth in Chapter 5. For now, let's get weaving.

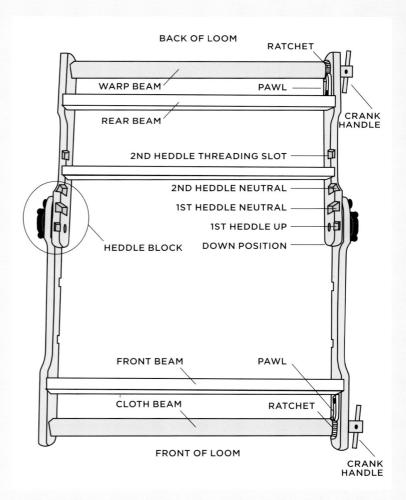

BACK OF LOOM

RATCHET

WARP BEAM

PAWL

CRANK HANDLE

REAR BEAM

2ND HEDDLE THREADING SLOT

2ND HEDDLE NEUTRAL

1ST HEDDLE NEUTRAL

1ST HEDDLE UP

DOWN POSITION

HEDDLE BLOCK

FRONT BEAM

PAWL

CLOTH BEAM

RATCHET

FRONT OF LOOM

CRANK HANDLE

What You Need

LOOM. For all of the samples in this book, I've used a rigid heddle loom that can accommodate two heddles. The Flip Loom by Schacht Spindle Co., Inc., has the spaces built right into the frame and makes using two heddles very easy. Although I've written this book specifically for the rigid heddle loom, you'll soon find that you can weave most of these fabrics on a table or floor loom as well. In the case of plain weave and the finger-controlled techniques, only a frame loom is required.

RIGID HEDDLE REED. Rigid heddle reeds come in a variety of dents depending on the requirements of a project. As a rule of thumb, thread worsted-weight yarn in an 8-dent reed and a sportweight yarn in a 10-dent reed. A fingering-weight yarn is best sett at 16 epi in two 8-dent reeds or 20 epi in two 10-dent reeds. You can thread 3/2 pearl cotton in a 10-dent or 12-dent reed.

Rigid heddle loom on stand.

SHUTTLES. Shuttles come in many styles and sizes. For rigid heddle weaving, I like to use a *stick shuttle*, which is a simple flat stick with slots in the end. Wind the weft around one side of the shuttle from end to end in a figure-eight path. You can wind yarn on just one side or both sides. Generally, I like to use a shuttle that is about the same length as my weaving is wide.

Some people like to use a slim *boat shuttle*, but check to see that the shed (the opening between the raised and lowered warp ends) is large enough on your particular loom to accommodate this type of shuttle. Keep in mind that you'll also need bobbins and a bobbin winder if you use a boat shuttle.

For warp-emphasis or warp-faced weaving, I like to use a *belt shuttle*, which has one beveled edge designed for beating in the weft.

HAND BEATERS. Hand beaters are helpful when extra beating is required. When weaving a thick or dense fabric, consider using a weighted hand beater.

THREADING HOOKS. These long hooks are necessary for threading the warp ends through the rigid heddle. I find a short heddle hook most comfortable to use.

WARPING PEG OR WARPING BOARD. Depending on the warping method you use, you'll need a warping peg or warping board to measure the warp.

PICK-UP STICKS. From time to time, you will need a pick-up (or shed) stick or two when weaving pick-up patterns. A pick-up stick dramatically increases the capacity of the rigid heddle loom and can be used to make patterns in both the warp and weft. I like a pick-up stick that's about 1½" (3.8 cm) wide, which makes a larger shed that is easier to weave through. You'll need a pick-up stick a couple of inches longer than the weaving width.

HEDDLE ROD AND STRING HEDDLES. These are helpful when weaving twill or when more than one pick-up stick is called for. Instructions for making and using a heddle rod are provided in Chapter 3, page 98.

From left to right: threading hook, stick shuttle, pick-up stick, weighted hand beater, warping peg with clamp, belt shuttle.

CHAPTER 1

There's Nothing Plain About
PLAIN WEAVE

I'm starting our weaving explorations with plain weave because it is the simplest and most basic of weaves. For plain weave, you lift every other warp thread, one up, one down, and so on. On the next pass of the weft, the ups and downs exchange places so that every thread that was raised on the previous pass is lowered on the next pass to create an over, under, over, under interlacement.

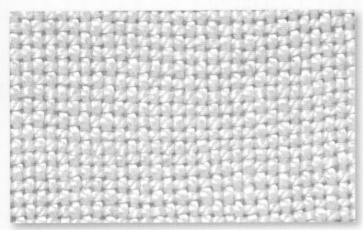
Plain weave is the simplest of structures.

The alternating warps and wefts of plain weave create the most stable of fabrics. The reason this is so is because plain weave—over, under, over, under—has the most interlacements possible per square inch. Where stability is desired, plain weave is your structure of choice.

But isn't over, under, over, under boring? Goodness, no. There's nothing plain about plain weave. Here are some reasons why:

Let's say you have a solid-colored warp. Even if you weave across it with the same weft, you don't have to have a ho-hum result. What if the yarn is a luscious variegated novelty, or a handspun natural merino wool, or a highly textured or handpainted yarn? Any of these materials have potential to create stunning results. What else could you do with this plain warp? The obvious choice is to change the weft by varying the colors or textures. By just choosing a contrasting weft color, you can create a whole new look. You could weave the entire piece with this weft or choose different colors or textures to create stripes.

Taking plain weave a step further, think about using more than a single warp yarn—either different colors or different textures—or both. Now you have even more possibilities! Weaving naturally lends itself to stripes. You can cross this warp with a single weft, or multiple ones. For a check or plaid, you can cross the striped warp in the same color or texture sequence, or vary it somewhat. If you know you want a striped fabric, think about putting the stripes in the warp instead of the weft—it'll make weaving faster because you don't have to stop and change shuttles. The disadvantage, of course, is that you'll have to be satisfied with your warp striping—once your loom is warped, there's no changing it.

All of this assumes that you are designing a balanced weave in which the number of warp threads in an inch equals the number of weft picks in an inch. In a balanced weave, the impact of warp and weft is about equal because they appear in the fabric more or less in the same amounts. The joy and challenge of working with balanced weaves is that you need to consider what is happening in both warp and weft. If your warp, for example, is a brilliant blue, and you cross it with another color, that brilliance will be minimized—because the saturation will not be as great. You could enhance the warp color by what you choose for weft. For example, if you want to brighten the blue, try crossing it with a bright green. Or, to dull the blue, cross it with its opposite color on the color wheel, orange.

You can purposefully design a fabric to blend colors. If you choose a blue warp and cross it with a red weft, your eyes will optically blend the two together to create purple—the impact will depend on the scale of your yarns, the relative value of the colors, and your viewing distance.

But what if you want to show off the warp more? Then you'll want to weave a warp-emphasis fabric where more of the warp is seen than the weft. You can do this by choosing a heavy warp yarn and a finer weft, or by beating the weft in looser to create longer warp floats, or by squishing the warp yarns closer together so as to minimize the impact of the weft.

The same applies to weft-faced fabrics where you can emphasize the weft by using a finer warp yarn than you've chosen for weft, spacing out the warp yarn, or beating in the weft to cover the warp. (Both warp- and weft-faced fabrics are discussed in Chapter 4.)

Designing with Plain Weave

So, where do you begin? The first step is to decide what it is that you want to weave. Let's say that you want to weave a scarf. You know that you must choose a yarn that is soft—no scratchy yarns around the neck! To test a yarn for comfort, brush the yarn along your cheek or neck to see if it feels soft. If not, better try another. You'll also want to seek out a yarn that has drape. A hard, twisted cotton, for example, probably won't give you the qualities you'll want in your finished piece, whereas a bamboo or soy silk yarn will.

Once you've decided on a yarn, how do you know how to sett it? That is, how close or far apart should you place the warp threads? What size dent should you use? For a balanced plain weave, you'll be aiming for a yarn that will weave up the same in warp and weft. Choosing the correct sett will help you achieve this.

The best way to begin is to wrap the warp yarn around a ruler for one inch. For the most accurate result, the wraps should be parallel and just touch each other with no spaces in between or crossed threads. Wind the yarn firmly but not so tightly that the yarn is compressed. The idea is to have the yarn in the wraps behave much like it will when woven. Count the number of wraps and divide by two for your warp sett. For example, if you wrap an inch on a ruler and it yields 20 wraps, divide by two to give you a warp sett of 10 ends per inch (2.5 cm), abbreviated epi. What if the yarn yields 9 or 11? Now you have to use a little judgment. Generally, if my wraps are 9, I'll round up, setting the yarn in a 10-dent reed, instead of an 8-dent one. If my wraps are 11, I would probably choose a 12-dent reed, but I might round down to a 10-dent reed if my yarn were fuzzy or textured.

Determining Sett

Warp sett (the number of warp ends in an inch) is much like gauge in knitting. Just as particular needles, yarn, and your own knitting style determine the number of stitches per inch (2.5 cm), the number of warp ends per inch (2.5 cm), called sett, is affected by the size of your yarn, how dense you'll pack in the weft, and how the fabric is finished.

For a balanced weave (the same number of warp ends per inch [2.5 cm] as weft picks per inch [2.5 cm]), the best way to determine your warp sett is to wrap a ruler for 1" (2.5 cm) with your warp yarn, then divide this number by two. Wouldn't wrapping just a half inch (1.3 cm) be just as good? Theoretically, yes, but wrapping a whole inch (2.5 cm), especially if it is a fat yarn, will give you a truer reading. Let's say, for example, that you wind your ruler with a sportweight yarn and it yields 20 ends in the inch (2.5 cm).

You then divide by two to get 10 warp ends per inch (2.5 cm). For a balanced weave, you'll weave the same number of picks per inch (2.5 cm), abbreviated ppi, as warp ends, in this case 10.

Wrapping gives you a good place to start, but weaving a sample can prevent disappointment later on. Here are my best practices guidelines:
- Wrap a ruler for an inch (2.5 cm) to determine the sett.
- Weave at least an 8" × 16" (20.5 × 40.5 cm) sample.
- Wash or finish the sample as you will your finished project.

Assess the sample for appearance and hand. Is the fabric what you expected? If not, you'll need to analyze why not. For example, if your fabric is too stiff, perhaps you beat the weft in too much, or perhaps the sett is too close. If at this point you feel that you have enough information to make the necessary adjustments, proceed with

To determine how to set a yarn, wrap it around a ruler for 1" (2.5 cm) and divide by two for your total ends per inch.

your project. If you can't proceed with confidence, weave another sample.

The only way to know for sure is to weave a sample. I almost always weave a sample, wash, and iron it to determine if the resulting fabric is what I'm after.

Choosing Materials

To illustrate how materials can influence the look of a simple plain-weave fabric, I chose a linen slub singles at about 2,500 yd [2,286 m]/lb of which I am particularly fond. I first crossed it with itself. Because the yarn itself has character—thick and thin spots and lighter-colored slubs accenting the natural honey-color—the surface is lively and interesting. For this first sample, I beat it in as I sett it, at 12 ppi. For the next sample, I beat very lightly, at about 6 ppi. Even though the weave is quite loose, the fabric is still quite stable, and the slubs are pronounced. The final sample, again using the same weft, was beat randomly with large areas left unwoven. I think this

Fabric from bottom to top: 2-ply natural linen alternated with heavy 2-ply linen, bleached white only, bleached white with heavy linen stripe accent, 2-ply natural linen combined with unspun flax.

A linen slub warp set at 12 epi is crossed with the same yarn and woven in a balanced weave.

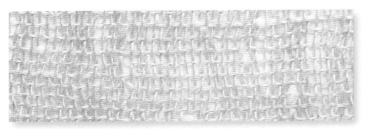

The same linen warp is woven with the same weft but packed in at just 6 picks per inch (2.5 cm).

The same warp with the same weft, but woven with a random and loose beat for an open and airy fabric.

sample, while not particularly stable, could make quite a lovely room divider or window screen.

For my next set of samples (at left), I tried contrasting wefts. Starting at the hemmed border, I alternated a 2-ply natural linen at 2,600 yd (2,377 m)/lb with a heavier 2-ply linen (950 yd [868 m]/lb). I continued with a bleached slub linen singles (1,500 yd [1,371 m]/lb), beating at about 10 picks per inch. I then accented this weft with the heavier 2-ply linen, weaving one row of this linen followed by three rows of white linen. And finally, I used the 2-ply natural linen for background and inserted unspun flax haphazardly. I rather like the resulting rustic look, and I find it fun to weave this way—watching what's happening in the fabric and inserting the accent intuitively.

Dramatic results are produced when single black weft picks are used.

For the next example, woven on the same warp as the above, I used black 5/2 pearl cotton (2,100 yd [1,920 m]/lb) for the hem and then one black pick after every five picks of linen to produce thin dotted stripes. I simply carried the

black up the selvedge instead of weaving it in. The little loops traveling up the selvedge, first on one side then the other do not bother me at all—I like the way they add a bit of interest at the selvedges. This is faster than weaving in the ends and doesn't mess with the lovely thin black line that would be disturbed if the ends were woven in.

Alternating stripes of slub linen and handspun nettles singles are separated with a single pick of white slub linen.

Subtle is good. Even though the sample above is rather quiet, I find its simplicity charming. It is particularly appealing because the materials used to create it are interesting and their proportions are just right. Here, I separated alternating stripes of linen slub (the same as the warp) and a handspun nettles singles (1,500 yd [1,371 m]/lb) with a single pick of white linen slub.

While the previous samples have a smooth elegance that is perfect for table linens, towels, or a summer jacket, the fuzzy swatches at left speak of blankets or warm wraps. The same warp is used for all three—a wool loop yarn (about 800 yd [731 m]/lb) sett at 8 epi. The first is crossed with a gray 2-ply wool at about 750 yards (686 m)/lb. The second swatch introduces two weft yarns—the dark gray used in the first swatch and the same wool loop used in the warp. Here, the white yarns seem to frame the gray to create a petite windowpane. The next example is woven with several strands combined as one: a fine multicolored slub and a 2-ply white wool (see Making Yarn on page 20). This weft becomes twisted around in the shed and, when combined with the wool loop warp poking out at intervals, makes a happily textured fabric. Because of the lofty yarns and light beat, these fabrics, though thick, are airy and lightweight.

In rigid heddle weaving, you are restricted to the available dents, such as 8, 10, or 12 (or the double of that number if two heddles are used—see Chapter 5). Sometimes I might have a yarn that I want to use, but it is too fine for my available setts, such as the bamboo yarn (2,100 yd [1,920 m]/lb) used on page 26. I really liked the feel and drape of this yarn, but it needed to be more closely sett than 10 or 12 dents per inch (2.5 cm). To achieve the proper sett, I doubled the yarn in warp and weft.

From bottom to top: A white wool loop warp is crossed with a dark gray 2-ply wool, alternating dark gray and white wool loop, and a combined-yarn weft to give a random effect.

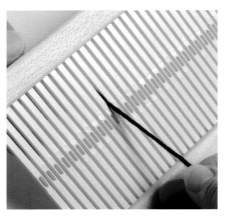

Run a potential warp yarn through both the slot and the hole of your reed to test it for excessive abrasion.

Spaced Warps and Wefts

An oh-so-simple and effective way to make deliciously wonderful fabrics is to just leave spaces in the warp and weft. I use spaced warps and wefts in a variety of ways. The first, as shown in this sample, is to just leave an inch or so unthreaded in the warp and likewise in the weaving. This curtain fabric provides a screen without blocking the out-of-doors. The spaces can be used to thread the fabric onto a curtain rod.

Handspun yarn on the loom with spaced warps and wefts.

Curtain with spaced warps and wefts.

Another spaced warp trick is to thread up a fine wool yarn, leaving spaces in the warp and weft and then felting the whole affair for a wonderfully textured scarf. The technique is so simple, and I love the random result of transforming a gauzy, loosely woven fabric into a very wearable scarf like the Felted Scarf in Beige on page 30.

Frequently, to add texture and to enhance drape, I leave spaces in the warp and/or weft. To do this, I thread an inch (2.5 cm) or so in the heddle as usual, but then I skip a few slots and holes, say, for example, a half inch (1.3 cm). In other words, I leave areas open in the heddle with no threads in them at all. I can weave this same pattern with a solid weft for warp-wise stripes of woven and unwoven areas, or I can weave it as a "check," weaving an inch (2.5 cm), leaving a half inch (1.3 cm) unwoven, and so on.

To leave spaces in my weft, I cut spacers out of thin cardboard, such as manila file folders. I weave an inch (2.5 cm), insert a spacer in the shed just as I would insert the shuttle, weave an inch (2.5 cm), and insert the next spacer. I then weave another inch (2.5 cm), take out the first spacer and insert it again into the shed, essentially playing leapfrog along the length of my warp. Over time, I've dispensed with the spacers and "eyeballed" my spaces with excellent results.

Weaving with Handspun

If you are a spinner, I encourage you to try out your handspun in woven fabrics. There is a belief that you can't use a singles in the warp. This is not necessarily the case. What you want is a strong singles that is not too large for the holes or slots of your rigid heddle. Give your yarn the "pull test" (you can use this test with commercial yarns, too). If the yarn pulls or drifts apart when you pull firmly on it, you'll know that it isn't suitable for the warp—reserve it for weft. If the yarn breaks with a snap, it should hold up as a warp yarn. To test for abrasion, run a piece back and forth in the slots and holes of your heddle. If you have trouble getting this yarn through the holes in your heddle, it's probably too large and will wear excessively during weaving.

Making Yarn

We are fortunate to have many yarns at our disposal. That said, sometimes you don't have just the yarn you need or you want a different look. Such was the case for the third swatch on page 18. I had a cone of very fine slub yarn (3,400 yd [3109 m]/lb) that I'd wanted to use for quite some time because I thought it would produce interesting results. The only problem was that it was quite fine, and I never found the right occasion to use it. As I worked on this project, I was looking for a yarn that had texture and perhaps a bit of variegation. Remembering this slub yarn, I decided to try using several strands of it together. Even tripled, the yarn didn't have the weight I wanted vis-à-vis the warp. But, by combining it with a fairly nondescript 2-ply wool (1,000 yd [914 m]/lb), I gained the size I wanted and produced an interesting result as the yarns twisted around each other in the shed—sometimes the wool appearing more prominently than the slub yarn; sometimes the other way around.

Fingering-weight handspun 2-ply mohair is used for warp and weft, accented by a handspun novelty yarn (threaded warpwise).

You can also combine handspun yarn and commercial yarns, or create yarns by plying two commercial yarns together to create a new one. This scarf sample is made of 2-ply handspun mohair, fingering-weight warp and weft with accents of a sparkly novelty yarn I plied from two different commercial yarns. I left spaces in the reed on each side of my handspun plied novelty yarn, allowing it a little extra breathing room.

Three fine ends of a variegated singles are combined with a 2-ply wool to make a new, custom yarn.

Randomly sleyed yarns in the warp are muted by a wooly handspun singles weft.

If you're afraid to plunge into using handspun yarn in the warp, use a commercial yarn for the warp and cross it with your handspun in the weft. For this swatch, I randomly sleyed several colors of 5/2 pearl cotton sprinkled with gold metallic thread in a 12-dent reed. I then crossed this with a heavier-weight handspun fuzzy wool singles.

Color and Texture

I wove the fabric shown below for a skirt. I call it my "dibby dabs" skirt because it contains so many yarns and colors. My colleague Stephanie Flynn-Sokolov picked out the yarns at my local weaving shop. Stephanie is a knitter (as well as a weaver and spinner) and loves the many textures and styles of yarns designed for knitting. She chose some of her favorites for this fabric, which I threaded randomly in my reed. This is an intuitive process. Mostly, I try to spread out the colors and textures and create some sort of visual rhythm as I thread. This is what sometimes is referred to as "designing in the reed." I begin by measuring all of the ends of a particular yarn on the warping board. Sometimes I might use the entire ball or skein,

other times I'll use as much of a color as seems correct. My rule of thumb, I suppose, is that I'll use less of a light-colored or highly contrasting yarn, and quite a bit of similarly toned colors for the bulk of the warp. I wove two fabrics on the same warp, one with a solid weft for a warp-striped fabric and my skirt fabric, which is crossed with the same warp yarns placed in the web intuitively. This is not the fastest way to weave, but it is interesting and fun to watch what happens in the fabric and respond with a new color or texture. This is truly a handwoven fabric—no two will ever, ever be the same. I like this idea—and the result—quite a lot.

A variety of textures and colors are used for warp stripes, which are crossed with a neutral solid weft yarn.

The same warp is crossed intuitively with the same yarns as used in the warp for a haphazard plaid I used for skirt fabric.

Stripes and Plaids as Texture

We naturally visualize stripes in color, but you also have texture at your disposal. For these four samples, threaded in a 10-dent heddle, I warped 1¼" (3.2 cm) stripes of sportweight 2-ply wool, sixteen doubled ends of 5/2 pearl cotton and separated these stripes with two single ends of wool loop (600 yd [548 m]/lb) separated by a pearl cotton warp threaded in a hole.

I threaded the wool loop in the slots because it was too tight in the holes; the slots gave it more space. For my first sample, I wove across with fine mohair loop. It provided a soft overall texture, accented by the more pronounced wool loop warp stripes. The softness of the wool contrasted with the shiny cotton creates subtle stripes.

For a plaid, I crossed the warp with itself, weaving as I threaded. Again, the result is a subtle plaid.

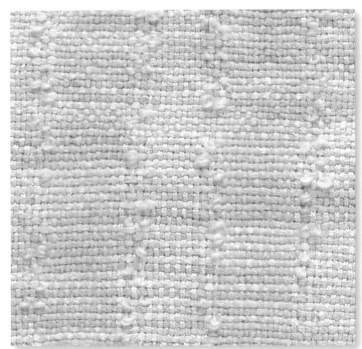

Using different textured yarns for stripes and plaids is another way to think about creating patterns in weaving.

A textured warp lends subtle surface variation when a variegated silk ribbon is used as weft.

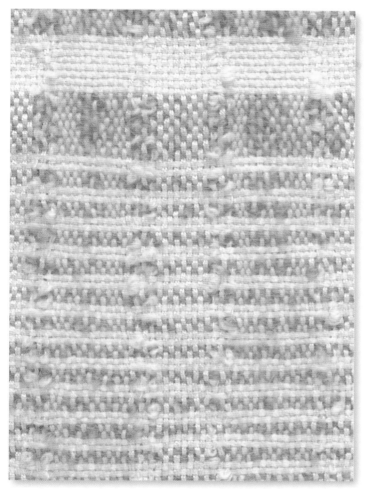

Trying out contrasting textures, as in this example, can produce interesting results.

On the same warp (at left), I used a subtle variegated silk ribbon (SWTC Amerah in Sandstone) for weft. The resulting fabric has a quiet texture that is, I believe, more interesting than if I'd just crossed a plain warp with the same yarn. The same could be said of the next sample, in which I alternated 2-pick stripes of fuzzy green mohair (Louet Brushed Mohair in Lichen) with a slippery and smooth rayon yellow ribbon (Crystal Palace Mikado Ribbon in solid yellow).

Sample! Sample! Sample!

Let me talk to you about sampling. I'm a big believer in it, and I always weave a sample if I'm not familiar with a yarn. Through sampling, I can feel confident that the yarn will give me the result I'm after—I'll not have any surprises when I'm finished weaving. Nothing discourages more than disappointment. Through samples, I explore sett and color and try out new ideas. Because I'm not creating a final product, I'm completely free to experiment—very often leading to new discoveries.

To sample for sett, I'll make a sample at least 8" (20.5 cm) wide; any narrower than that will not be a good test for sett because a narrow warp will beat in more than a wider one. If I'm just checking for color and/or structure, I might use a warp as narrow as 4" (10 cm). In general, a warp length of 2 yards (2 meters), which includes 28" (71 cm) of loom waste, is sufficient for a sample. As you sample, keep track of what you do. If you forget what you did, the sample is in vain. I know—I've lashed myself with a wet yarn many-a-time for "failure to report," "failure to completely record," "failure to write anything down at all!" It's hard, I know, to stop and write down what you've done as you excitedly weave along . . . but take it from a gal who knows, make yourself do it!

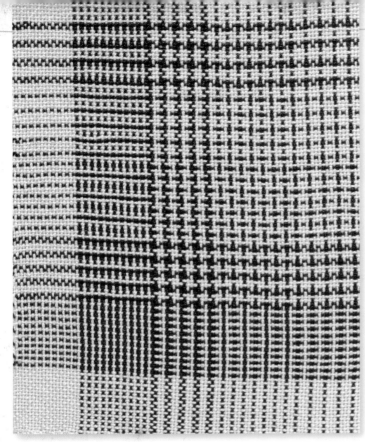

Color-and-weave sampler woven by Melissa Ludden Hankens.

Color-and-Weave

By using colors in different sequences, you can create an amazing number of color-and-weave effects. The sampler above illustrates just the tip of the iceberg of the vast possibilities when only two colors are used—and this is just plain weave! The structure is always the same: over, under, over, under. Only the color order changes. For example, just compare the solid white stripe with the next stripe of alternating ends of black and white. Use one sequence throughout a piece, or combine threadings and treadlings to create borders or accents, or even an all-over plaid-like design. If you are new to weaving or want to explore color-and-weave further, weaving this sampler would be a great exercise, as well as a useful reference for future projects.

COLOR-AND-WEAVE SAMPLER

Warp and weft: 3/2 pearl cotton set at 10 epi in a 10-dent reed and woven at 10 ppi. Colors: dark gray and natural white. Woven by Melissa Ludden Hankens.

BLOCK 1: 20 ends white (left bottom).
BLOCK 2: [1 dark, 1 light] 10 times—20 ends.
BLOCK 3: [2 dark, 2 light] 5 times—20 ends.
BLOCK 4: [1 dark, 2 light] 7 times—21 ends.
BLOCK 5: [1 dark, 3 light] 5 times—20 ends.

The sampler is woven as threaded: Weave 20 picks of white for Block 1, alternate 1 dark and 1 light ten times for Block 2, and so on. As you can see, this could go on and on and on . . . !

Check the reverse side. What you see on one surface is often different on the other side. This is due to the binary nature of weaving. For example, if a yarn travels over a warp yarn on the top, it travels under that same yarn on the reserve side. So, if a black warp is covered on the surface with a white weft, white will appear on the surface at that juncture. On the reverse side, though, the white weft travels under that black warp end so that black appears in that spot on the reverse.

On the following pages are some other swatches exploring color-and-weave. I've used two contrasting colors (melon and azure) of Harrisville Highland 2-Ply (900 yd [823 m]/lb) set at 7 epi on a Mini Loom (you could set it at 8 epi on a rigid heddle loom), but you could also use two different textures, such as a fuzzy wool loop yarn and a smooth worsted wool. Again, use these samples as springboards for your own designs. I wove these samples in a balanced weave on a small hand loom (Schacht's Mini Loom)—which is a wonderfully quick way to explore color combinations without committing to an entire warp.

SAMPLE 1: Warp: solid blue.
Weft: 1 orange, 1 blue.

SAMPLE 2: Warp: 1 blue, 1 orange.
Weft: 1 blue, 1 orange. Note: Horizontal stripes are on the front; vertical stripes will appear on the back.

SAMPLE 3: Warp: 2 blue, 2 orange.
Weft: 2 orange, 2 blue. Note: This forms houndstooth plaid.

SAMPLE 4: Warp: 2 blue, 1 orange.
Weft: 1 orange, 2 blue.

SAMPLE 5: Warp: 1 blue, 3 orange.
Weft: 1 blue, 3 orange.

SAMPLE 6: Warp: 4 blue, 4 orange.
Weft: 4 orange, 4 blue.

SAMPLE 7: Warp: 2 blue, 1 orange.
Weft: 1 orange, 1 blue.

SAMPLE 8: Warp: 3 blue, 3 orange.
Weft: 1 orange, 1 blue.

SAMPLE 8: Reverse. This example would make wonderful companion pieces in a garment—and all from the same fabric!

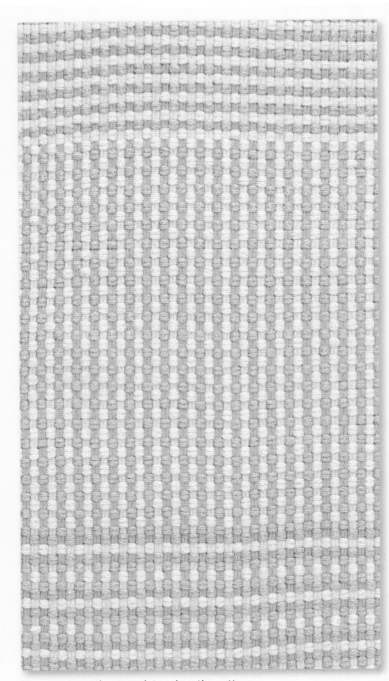
How you cross the warp determines the pattern.

An Exercise in Color-and-Weave

For the warp on this sampler, I alternated green and pink (doubled ends of Cotton Clouds Bamboo 7 in Blush and Willow) in a 10-dent reed. I then tried several weft sequences for different results. From top to bottom:

- I created horizontal stripes by weaving across with pink weft when my pink warps were up; I wove across with green when my green warps were raised.

- For vertical stripes, I wove across with green when the pink warps were raised, and I wove across with pink when the green threads were raised.

- For a color-and-weave pattern, beginning with the green warps raised, I wove 2 rows of green, 1 row of pink, 2 rows of green, 1 row of pink.

- For green dots, just weave with pink.

Log Cabin

Log cabin is a specific kind of color-and-weave effect. Generally, it involves two colors of yarns or two colors and sizes of yarns. Keeping in mind the sampler on page 26 where alternating colors produced vertical stripes and the reverse order produced horizontal lines, you can start to understand log cabin. The first time I saw log cabin it boggled my mind. There seemed to be much more to it than simply changing colors. Log cabin appears to be intricate in structure, but it's just over-and-under plain weave. Really! The structure never changes. It is always over, under. What does change is the color order. I like to think of threading and weaving log cabin as blocks, where block A is threaded dark, light, dark, light, and block B is threaded the opposite, that is, light, dark, light, dark. Just repeating a color so that two warp ends of the color are side by side shifts the interlacement enough to create color-and-weave patterning.

I particularly like log cabin woven as table textiles—mats or runners or placemats—where the yarns that are used are both contrasting in size and color. Often when designing a log cabin pattern, I use graph paper to draw out my two-block design. I then decide how wide I want the blocks and factor in my epi to make a threading guide. The samples here are all from one warp, which is a shame since there is much, much more to explore.

LOG CABIN SAMPLE 1

For the warp in these samples, I used 3/2 pearl cotton in medium gray and white Brown Sheep Cotton Fleece, which is a bit larger in size than the 3/2 pearl cotton. I used a sett of 10 epi and tried different wefts, illustrating the variety of looks that can be achieved.

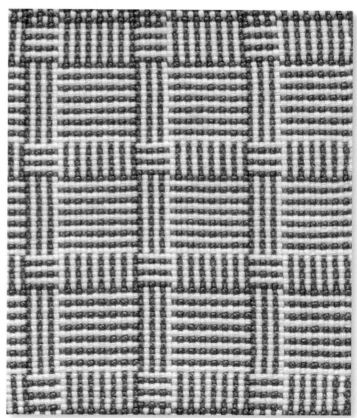

The warp is crossed with the same weft yarns.

For this sample, I used the same weft as warp and wove as I threaded. The result is crisp and pronounced.

Threading: *Block A:* Alternate [light, dark] 7 times (14 ends); *Block B:* Alternate [dark, light] 3 times (6 ends). The entire warp sequence is: Block A, Block B, Block A, Block B, Block A, Block B, Block A.

LOG CABIN SAMPLE 2

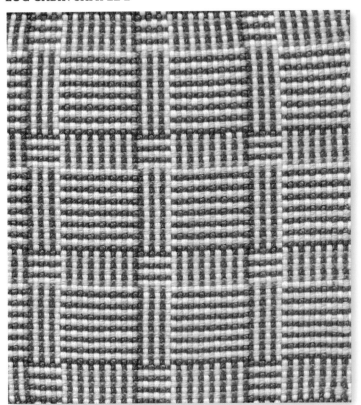

3/2 cocoa and off-white cotton are use for weft.

For this sample, I used the same weaving sequence as the first sample, but I changed the weft yarns, substituting 3/2 pearl in cocoa for the 3/2 gray and substituting off-white for the bleached white Cotton Fleece. The look is similar, but has more depth, which I find more interesting.

LOG CABIN SAMPLE 3

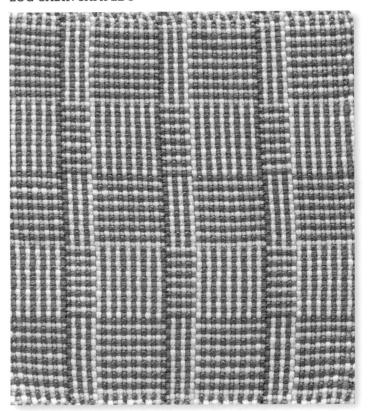

Equal blocks are woven in two shades of pink.

For this sample, I tried shades of pink for both wefts, a totally different color family from the first two samples, and I wove equal-size blocks. This sample is interesting, but I think I would like it better if I'd varied the sizes of the blocks as I'd done in the first two samples.

LOG CABIN SAMPLE 4

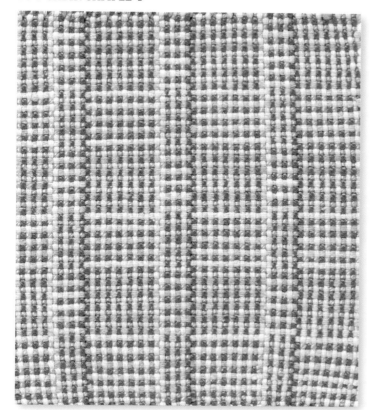

A subtle fabric results when a pale variegated silk ribbon is alternated with baby blue, woven in equal blocks.

This sample is subtle, but I think successful even so. The weft is a softly variegated silk ribbon yarn (SWTC Amerah in Sandstone) and a pale blue 3/2 pearl cotton. I wove equal blocks and, though the changes in the blocks are not as distinct as the previous samples, it could be quite effective as a jacket fabric where subtle patterning is called for.

LOG CABIN SAMPLE 5

A variegated sock yarn alternated with off-white cotton and woven in the same block sequence as the warp results in a lively surface.

Of all of the log cabin samples, this one has the most unique look, and it is completely due to the strong coloration of variegated sock yarn (Wildfoote from Brown Sheep in Lilac Desert). This color is alternated with the off-white Cotton Fleece.

Felted Scarf
IN BEIGE

For this felted scarf in plain weave, I threaded 1"
(2.5 cm) and then left the next 1" (2.5 cm) unthreaded
in the reed. I wove in the same manner, weaving 1"
(2.5 cm), then leaving 1" (2.5 cm) unwoven. The fabric
is very loosely woven, but during the felting process,
everything shrinks and felts together to stabilize it.

Finished Size

After felting: 8" (20.5 cm)
wide × 72" (183 cm) long, plus
8" (20.5 cm) fringe at each end.
Before felting: 14½" (37 cm)
wide × 108" (274.5 cm) long.

Yarn

Warp and Weft: 2/18 2-ply wool
at 5,040 yd (4,608 m)/lb: about
700 yd (640 m). This yarn is
Superfine Merino in Suede from
Jaggerspun.

Equipment

Rigid heddle loom with at least
a 15" (38 cm) weaving width;
12-dent rigid heddle reed; one
shuttle. Optional: two 1" (2.5 cm)
spacers a little wider than the
warp width.

Number of Warp Ends

96.

Warp Length

4 yards (3.6 meters), which
allows 28" (71 cm) loom waste,
part of which forms the fringe.

Warp Width

15"

EPI

12.

PPI

In woven areas—12.

Threading

Threaded	12		12		12		12		12		12		12		12
Open		12		12		12		12		12		12		12		12	

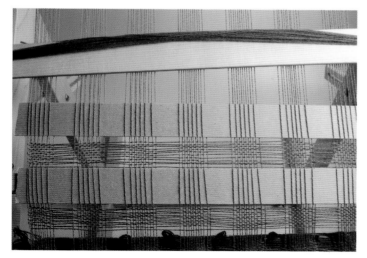

Use spacers to separate between each 1" (2.5 cm) of weaving. Use a gentle beat and try to achieve 12 ppi. It'll look loose, but this is as it should be.

Weaving

Weave a balanced weave (12 ppi) for 1" (2.5 cm), then insert a 1" (2.5 cm) spacer, weave the next 1" (2.5 cm), insert another spacer, and so on. I used two spacers, leapfrogging them as I wove. *Note:* The weave will be very open. This is as it should be.

Finishing

This fabric felted quickly by hand. I used very hot water and lots of soap and agitated the water and then the fabric for only a few minutes. Because my water was very hot, I wore rubber gloves. I inspected the progress often to avoid over-felting. When the fabric was sufficiently felted, I carefully hand-rinsed in cool water to prevent further felting, then I lay it flat to dry. I gave the fabric a light steam press. A few areas had felted on top of each other, which I corrected by gently pulling them apart.

Pulled-Thread
SCARF

Designed and woven by Stephanie Flynn-Sokolov

Soy silk and bamboo are wonderful yarns to use for scarves and shawls where drape and softness are desired. This project combines two yarns, a very fine soy silk used double and a fine bamboo, yielding three ends total used together for warp and weft. Though the overall fabric appears to be a solid color at a distance, up close you can see the two colors dancing about in the cloth. Stephanie was inspired by Jessica Knickman's Pulled Thread Pucker Shawl, which appeared in the Summer 2005 Schacht Spindle On-Line Newsletter.

Finished Size
About 8" (20.5 cm) wide and 56" (142 cm) long, plus 5" (12.5 cm) fringe at each end.

Yarn
Warp and Weft: SWTC Infinity (16/2 soy silk; 6,400 yd [5,852 m]/lb): #518 bronze, 2,100 yd (1,920 m). Cotton Clouds Bambu 12 (100% bamboo; 6,300 yd/lb [1,920 m]/lb): #393 Ginger, 1,050 (960 m).

Equipment
Rigid heddle loom with at least 10" (25.5 cm) weaving width; 12-dent reed; 12" (30.5 cm) stick shuttle.

Threading
To prepare for warping, make two separate balls of Infinity so that three yarns (two Infinity and one Bambu) can be measured at the same time.

Number of Warp Ends
120 working ends (2 Infinity and 1 Bambu used together).

Warp Length
3½ yards (3.2 meters); includes 28" (71 cm) for take-up and loom waste.

Warp Width
10" (25.5 cm) in reed.

EPI
12.

PPI
20.

Weaving

Use the same yarns (2 Infinity and 1 Bambu) wound together on a shuttle for the weft. Since this is slippery yarn, you'll need to carefully watch the selvedges during weaving. Pack in well at 20 ppi. Weave for about 94" (239 cm).

Finishing

Remove fabric from loom, untying the warp ends to leave enough warp length for making a twisted fringe after pulling the threads. Handwash in warm water, lay flat to dry, and steam-press. Finished fabric measures 90" (228.5 cm) before pulling.

Pull Selected Warps

About 2½" (6.5 cm) in from each selvedge, pull 4 warp threads to gather ruffles along the length of the scarf. Begin at one end of the scarf and start pulling, coaxing the ruffles along the length of the scarf. Gather to suit your fancy. To secure the weft, gather up the warp ends and make a twisted fringe at each end of the scarf. Wear with panache!

Fabric removed from loom.

Pull a group of four warp threads to gather the length.

Rag Bag
THREESOME

Designed by Jane Patrick and Sara Goldenberg White;
woven and finished by Sara Goldenberg White.

This Rag Bag Threesome is woven on one warp with varying
wefts. All of the cloth is woven in plain weave using doubled
bias-cut cotton fabric strips (or "rags") for the weft to create a
lively surface. Using two ½" (1.3 cm) bias-cut strips together
creates a dense fabric that beats in more tightly than a
single, 1" (2.5 cm) rag strip. The clutch fabric was woven with
alternating picks of two different fabrics. It is turned sideways
to construct the bag with the selvedges at the top.

Finished Size

Tote: About 15" (38 cm) wide
and 17" (43 cm) long, excluding
handles. **Purse with Shoulder
Strap:** About 7¾" (19.5 cm) wide
and 8¼" (21 cm) long, excluding
strap. **Clutch:** About 7" (18 cm)
wide and 6½" (16.5 cm) long with
5" (12.5 cm) flap with 1" (2.5 cm)
fringe.

Yarn

Warp: *8/4 Cotton Carpet Warp*
from Great Northern (1,600 yd
[1,463 m]/lb): Parakeet and Pear,
300 yd (274.5 m) each.
Weft: *45" wide 100% cotton
printed fabric, yellow floral, bias-*
cut into ½" (1.3 cm) strips: 1¾ yd
(1.6 m). 45" wide 100% cotton
printed fabric, green and blue
geometric, bias-cut into ½"
(1.3 cm) strips: 2 yd (1.8 m). 45"
wide 100% cotton printed fabric,
pink tie-dye, bias cut into ½"
(1.3 cm) strips: ¼ yd (0.22 m).
30 yd (27.4 m) of Parakeet warp
yarn is needed for the purse.
25 yd (22.8 m) of Pear for Tote
and Clutch headers.

Equipment

20" (51 cm) rigid heddle loom;
10-dent reed; two 16" (40.5 cm)
stick shuttles; one hand beater;
T-square; rotary cutter; self-

healing cutting mat; glue stick;
iron; sewing machine.

Notions

About 20 yd (18 m) of Parakeet
8/4 Cotton Cotton Warp for
purse handle; 3 yd (2.7 m)
¾" (2 cm) white cotton rope
(available at hardware stores) for
tote; Pellon non-woven fusible
interfacing for tabs on tote and
flap on purse.

Threading

Warp color order: Alternate 1 end
each of Parakeet and Pear.

Number of Warp Ends

200.

Warp Length

2¼ yd (2 m) for tote, includes 28"
(71 cm) for take-up and loom
waste; 3 yd (2.7 m) for the entire
Rag Bag Threesome.

Warp Width

20" (51 cm).

EPI

10.

PPI

Tote and clutch: 5 to 6.
Purse: 8.

TOTE

Prepare the Weft

Fold the cotton fabric lengthwise into quarters. Cut into ½" (1.3 cm) bias strips using a rotary cutter and T-square on a self-healing cutting mat. With the right sides of the bias-cut strips facing up, overlap the ends of the fabric ¼" to ½" (6 mm to 1.3 cm) and use a glue stick to glue them together. Wind two long strips together on the shuttle.

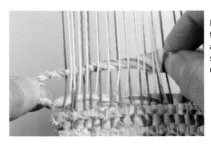

For a tidy selvedge, twist the rags as you go around the selvedge, snugging the weft loop up to the selvedge.

Weaving

Use cotton carpet warp to weave a 2" (5 cm) header (this will form the hem and won't show so either color is fine). Because the weft is so thick, you will need to beat down each pick with a hand beater. It is helpful to beat in the opposing shed to achieve a tighter pack, which is necessary to create a sturdy cloth suitable for a bag. This isn't as time-consuming or laborious as it sounds. To ensure a tidy selvedge, twist the weft at the edge before each pick; wet your fingers before you twist to help maintain the twist.

The tote fabric is woven in five sections. Begin by weaving 8¾" (22 cm) with the blue-green fabric (which allows for a 2" [5 cm] hem at the top). Next, weave alternate picks of blue-green and floral print for 6¾" (17 cm). Weave with the floral print only for 13½" (34.5 cm), then reintroduce blue-green fabric by alternating picks of floral print and blue-green for another 6¾" (17 cm). Finish by weaving 8¾" (22 cm) with blue-green, to end with 44½" (113 cm) of fabric, then weave 2" (5 cm) for a header as you did at the start.

Finishing

Secure the ends with knots or machine stitching. Wash the fabric by hand in hot soapy water until the glue joins rinse out and the cloth is fulled. Rinse with cool water and air or machine dry. The cloth, if packed tightly during weaving, will shrink about 2" (5 cm) in length and 1 to 1½" (2.5 to 3.8 cm) in width.

Assembly
bag body

Zigzag the hem header on each end of the cloth so that there is 1¾" (4.5 cm) of header remaining at the edges of the rag-woven cloth. Trim off the excess. Starting at the rag portion of the cloth, fold the top and bottom edges over 2" (5 cm). Then fold the header underneath the 2" (5 cm) rag flap, iron, and pin the cloth in place so that the edges are even and the header is concealed. Using a straight stitch, sew the flap ¼" (6 mm) from the bottom edge of the doubled cloth. This is going to become the top of your bag, so to ensure a nice crisp line, topstitch ¼" (6 mm) from the top edge of the fold.

Next, working with the bag inside out, pin the side seams together. Begin with a ½" (1.3 cm) seam allowance at the top of the bag and taper the allowance to 2" (5 cm) along the sides of the bag to the bottom. Stitch the seams in place so that they look like very long triangles. To form gussets at the bottom, turn the bag upside down and inside out. Sew a straight line across each corner to form a 3" (7.5 cm) triangle, then fold and tack the triangles outward to the sides.

Making Sewn Gussets

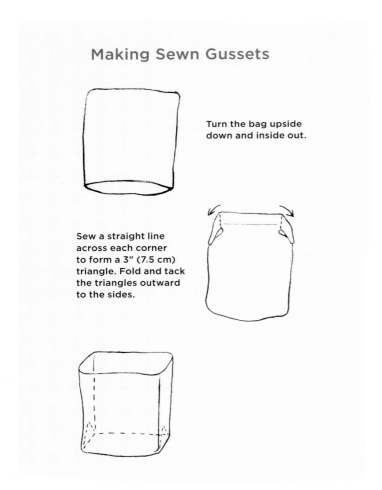

Turn the bag upside down and inside out.

Sew a straight line across each corner to form a 3" (7.5 cm) triangle. Fold and tack the triangles outward to the sides.

handle tabs

To make the handle tabs, cut the blue-green fabric along the grain into four 4" × 4¾" (10 × 12 cm) pieces. Cut four 3½" × 4½" (9 × 11.5 cm) pieces of fusible interfacing. Iron the interfacing onto the back side of the cloth so that the bottom edge of the fabric and interfacing are aligned and all other edges have a ¼" (6 mm) seam allowance. Iron the cloth seam allowance over the interfacing on the top and side edges. Next, fold the bottom edge of the fabric and interfacing up 1½" (3.8 cm), iron in place, then fold the top edge down 1½" (3.8 cm) to conceal the interfacing. Iron all four tabs, then topstitch ⅛" (3 mm) from the edge of the tabs on all four sides. Pin the tabs onto the front and back of the rag bag so that the top edge of each tab is 2" (5 cm) from the top and the outside edges are 2½" (6.5 cm) in from the sides of the bag. Stitch only the sides of the tabs to the bag. Stitch over the ⅛" (3 mm) tab topstitching as well as ¼" (6 mm) in from that line.

handles

Cut the rope in half. Tie a knot on one side of each piece, leaving a 3" (7.5 cm) tail of fringe. Insert one rope under a tab on one side of the bag so that the knot sits below the tab. Allow 8" to 9" (20.5 to 23 cm) of space between the top of the bag and the crest of the handle, then tie a knot under the other tab to secure the handle. Repeat on the other side of the bag, ensuring that both handles are the same length. Ravel the rope below each knot to create fringe, untwisting the rope with your fingers and combing it with a fine-tooth comb. Trim fringe to desired length.

Cut the rope in half.

Untwist rope below each knot, then comb it with a fine comb to create fringe.

PURSE WITH SHOULDER STRAP

Prepare the Weft

Prepare the weft the same as for the tote.

Weaving

The purse is woven basically the same as the tote, except that double fabric strips alternate with cotton carpet warp to create a lighter-weight fabric. Since the selvedge forms the top of the bag, take care to ensure a smooth tidy edge and be sure to twist the fabric strips at the selvedges.

With just Parakeet Cotton Carpet Warp, weave 2½" (6.5 cm), which can double as your header, then weave 8" (20.5 cm) alternating picks of carpet warp and cloth strips. Finish by weaving 2½" (6.5 cm) more with just the carpet warp.

Finishing

Finish as for the tote.

Assembly

bag body

Zigzag the carpet warp plain weave on both sides, leaving just shy of 1" (2.5 cm) of this cloth on each edge of the rag-weave section. Trim off excess. Fold both edges over ¼" (6 mm), iron, and pin in place. Stitch the fold into place using a straight stitch. Next, fold the cloth in half so that the carpet warp trim is on the sides of the bag and the selvedges of the cloth form the top of the bag. Pin the sides together and stitch on the right side about ⅛" (3 mm) in from the edge. At one lower edge, stop about 1" (2.5 cm) short of the bottom corner to leave space to insert the trim cord.

flap

Cut a rectangle on the grain from the same cloth used for the weft that measures 10½" × 5" (26.5 × 12.5 cm). Cut a piece of interfacing measuring 10" × 4½" (25.5 × 11.5 cm). Iron the interfacing onto the back side of the cloth so that ¼" (6 mm) of cloth extends beyond the interfacing on all four sides. Fold the cloth seam allowances over the top of the interfacing and iron in place. Fold the flap in half so that the interfacing is concealed and iron into place. Stitch the sides of the flap starting from the folded edge, then stitch along the bottom edge of the flap. The folded edge of the flap will lie over the front of the purse. Stitch the bottom of the flap to the back of the bag so that it is 2" (5 cm) from the top and centered at

Beginning and ending at one lower corner, pin the cord to the edge of the purse.

the top and side edges. Stitch the side edges of the flap to the top of the bag. Make buttonholes on the flap ½" (1.3 cm) from the bottom edge of the flap and 1" (2.5 cm) in from the sides. Make sure the buttonholes are long enough to accommodate the knot buttons (practice on a piece of scrap fabric first).

cord

The purse strap and knot buttons are made with twisted cord. To make the cord by hand, cut 6 strands of Parakeet Cotton Carpet Warp, each 55" (139.5 cm) long. Twist two groups of 3 strands each together in one direction, then hold the two groups together and let them twist back on themselves in the opposite direction. For quicker results, use the Incredible Rope Machine as shown on page 40. I made the purse handle with 18 strands and the buttons with 6 strands. The purse strap requires about 55" (139.5 cm), and each knot button requires

Bag assembly.

about 12" (30.5 cm) of rope. Expect about 40% take-up. Tie overhand knots in the ends of the cords to prevent raveling.

Beginning and ending at one lower corner and leaving 1" (2.5 cm) extra (to be inserted into the seam later), pin the edge of the cord along the sides and bottom of the bag. With matching thread, sew the cord in place, working between the plies of the cord to conceal the stitches. Tuck the cord ends into the hole at the corner and stitch the seam closed.

Make two Chinese knot buttons as described at right. Insert the cord ends of the button through the fabric from the right side of the bag, aligning the buttons with the buttonholes. Tie the ends in an overhand knot on the inside of the bag to secure the button. Leave enough "shank" so that there is sufficient length to use the button.

Chinese Knot Button

1. With the short end on the right, wrap the ends clockwise (right to left) to make a loop.

2. Continue moving clockwise and make a second loop, placing it under the first loop to make three cells. Both tails will be on the underside.

3. Insert the left (long) tail into the left-most cell from underneath. Place the end into the middle cell, underneath the next strand, and up into and exiting the right-most cell.

4. Moving clockwise, insert this end into the left cell from underneath.

5. Continue into the next cell and exit under the next two strands. Gradually tighten up the knot.

Making Rope on the Incredible Rope Machine

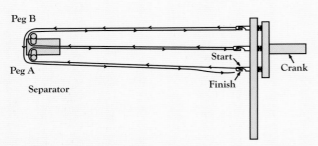

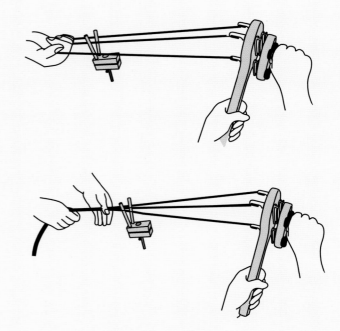

STEP 1. Clamp the separator to a table top. Determine the desired length of the rope and then tie the yarns to the first hook on the Rope Machine. Following the diagram, carry the yarns around Peg A, around the middle hook on the Rope Machine, around Peg B, then around the last hook on the Rope Machine, and finally return around the outside of Pegs B and A, ending where you began. There should be two lines of yarn from each peg. For a thicker rope, repeat the process as many times as desired (I repeated the process three times) for the bag handle and two times for the button rope.

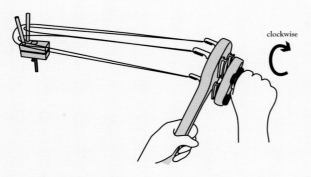

STEP 2. Turn the handle crank to add twist to the strands. Turn the handle crank in the direction of the twist in the yarn (clockwise for most yarns) to add twist, keeping the yarns taut as you crank. The more turns, the tighter the finished rope will be. As the yarns become more twisted, they will "take up" and shorten the rope strands. Crank until the twist is so tight that when tension is released, the yarns kink back on themselves.

STEP 3. Pull the three strands slowly away from the separator to twist them back onto themselves to make the rope. Take hold of the yarns at the back of the separator and pull them slowly, evenly, and smoothly, allowing them to twist together in a counterclockwise direction (opposite what you did in the first step). It is helpful to have a second person hold the Rope Machine while you pull the yarn through the separator. Add more twist, if needed, by cranking clockwise.

As the Rope Machine moves closer to the separator, crank a few clockwise turns to keep the strands tightly twisted. When the Rope Machine reaches the separator, slip the three strands off the hooks and tie an overhand knot in the end to secure them.

CLUTCH

Weaving

For this variation, a third, tie-dye pink print fabric was alternated with the floral print fabric used in the tote. The weaving for the clutch is basically the same as for the Tote. Weave 2½" (6.5 cm) of Pear Cotton Carpet Warp in plain weave, then weave 7" (18 cm) alternating picks of tie-dye print and floral print bias-cut fabric strips, and finish by weaving another 2½" (6.5 cm) of Pear Cotton Carpet Warp.

Finishing

Finish as for the tote.

Assembly

Fold the fabric widthwise so that the selvedge forms the bag flap. Sew the side seams as for the purse. Next, fold the selvedge edge up about 6" (15 cm) to form the bag (the flap should end 2" [5 cm] from the bottom edge of the bag). Lift the flap portion of the bag and iron the pocket section, pin the sides, and stitch on the right side as close to the edge as possible. If desired, add a snap to secure the flap to the body of the bag.

Fringe Trim

Using Parakeet thrums (warp waste) from your loom, create bundles of 4 threads. Fold the bundles in half. Insert the crochet hook into a weft loop along the selvedge and pull through a loop, then insert the ends of the bundle through the loop and pull to tighten. Trim fringe to desired length.

Make fringe with bundles of 4 warp waste threads.

CHAPTER 2

Finger-Controlled
WEAVES

Because you can add finger-controlled weaves anywhere anytime, they are a great resource to tuck into your bag of weaving tricks. Add a highlight, accent, or special border without re-threading or re-warping. Plan an entire project around a special finger technique, or ad lib when your piece needs a special little touch. These techniques are so versatile and effective that I'm surprised they aren't employed more often. Perhaps because—and this is the only drawback that comes to mind—they are slow to weave and must be done by hand. Instead of tossing the shuttle to and fro, finger-controlled weaves involve twisting, wrapping, gathering, or laying in. And this takes time.

Making Loops

STEP 1. Open the shed and insert the pattern (loop) weft from one side of the weaving to the other, leaving the weft from the shuttle hanging. Beginning (with the shed open) at the side in which you inserted the weft (being right-handed, I always start at the right side), slide your finger into the opening between 2 raised warps and pull up on the pattern weft and place this loop over the knitting needle (Figure **1**). Continue in the same manner until you've reached the other selvedge. In this example, I used a doubled weft and picked up a loop between every other space.

STEP 2. Beat as best you can before removing the knitting needle (Figure **2**).

STEP 3. Remove the knitting needle and press the loops firmly into place (Figure **3**).

STEP 4. With background weft, weave across in the opposite shed (if you made the loops with the heddle in the up position, weave across in the down position). For this example, I used a separate background weft, a single strand of the same yarn I used for the loops (instead of the doubled strands). I wove two rows of plain weave before commencing with the next row of loops (Figure **4**).

I urge you to re-think time. Yes, adding a leno border or bodice accent takes longer than, say, changing shuttles, but if this little detail takes a piece from "unremarkable" to "wow," it's oh, so worth it. I think of finger-controlled weaves like the forgotten stepchild—ready and waiting for attention.

The following examples highlight the basics of these techniques woven on a balanced weave. I've also included the loop pile in Chapter 4 because it is primarily a weft-faced technique.

Loop Pile

Loop pile is an easy way to create texture. Use it for allover loops (see Chapter 4) or for random accent spots on the surface of your fabric. Loop pile is worked on an open shed and has a plain-weave background that holds everything together.

To form loop pile, simply insert a row of the yarn into the shed for the loops (usually a heavier yarn than used for the warp and weft), then use a knitting needle to pick up the loops as desired. Beat the loops into place, packing firmly so that they are securely fastened, and anchor them with a row or two of plain weave. Depending on the yarn you choose, the loops can be soft and fuzzy yarn or rough and crisp (see the Country Girl/City Girl Apron on page 222). You can work the loops from selvedge to selvedge, in isolated areas, or as individual "spots" on a plain-weave ground.

Because loops do not contribute to a stable fabric structure, you'll need to weave one or more rows of plain weave after every row of loops. If, for example, you pick up loops with the heddle in the up position, you'll need to weave a row of plain weave in the down shed. If weaving a large piece with allover loops, weave at least two rows of plain weave between each row of loops. The number of rows you weave will also depend on the look you want. If you think of each space between warps as a square on graph paper, you can plan a design based on the number of spaces between warps. You'll notice also that the spaces shift depending on whether the heddle is in the up or down position. Therefore, as you design your pattern, keep in mind whether or not you want to create loops that will line up vertically. If you do, then you'll always need to make loops in the same shed, say, for example, the up shed. If this is the case, then you will need to weave an odd number of rows between each row of loops. Look at the candlewick example below. For this pattern, I counted 39 spaces between warps when my heddle was in the down position. I then used graph paper to plot out a design that would fit in those confines. Then, because I wanted the loops to stack up, I wove three rows of plain weave in between each row of loops. The warp in this sample is 3/2 pearl cotton sett at 10 epi, the background weft is 10/2 pearl cotton, and the pattern (loop) weft is Phoenix Soysilk from SWTC.

CANDLEWICK

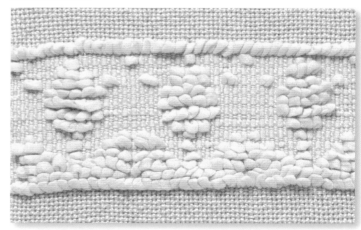

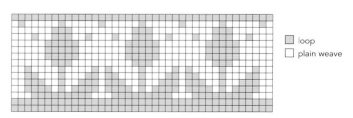

☐ loop
☐ plain weave

Chart of candlewick pattern.

LOOP NOTES

Because loops are not tied knots, they can be pulled out. Beat well after placing a row of loops to help hold them in place. Washing the fabric after weaving will full the fabric and "lock in" the loops.

Work loops from the selvedge, beginning at the same side in which the shuttle enters the shed.

It is easiest to work from your dominant side when picking up loops, although your design may dictate that you work the loop weft in both directions.

Generally, the weft is inserted selvedge to selvedge. If there are spaces between loops, the yarn will be visible between the loops. You'll want to incorporate this into your design.

Loops can be cut for a cut-pile look, though I recommend washing the fabric prior to cutting the loops to ensure that they do not pull out. Loops should be long enough to stay put; yarns too short may work their way out of the ground fabric.

The bigger the knitting needle, the larger the loop. If you want to make giant loops, use a dowel or flat stick. The loops will be easier to pick up if you make a point at the end of the dowel or stick.

loop ideas

REGULARLY SPACED LOOPS

Stripes of soy silk ribbon with petite loops accent the surface of this sample. I inserted the ribbon every 6th row and picked up a loop on a size U.S. 10 (6 mm) knitting needle in every 8th space between raised warps.

RANDOM CUT LOOPS

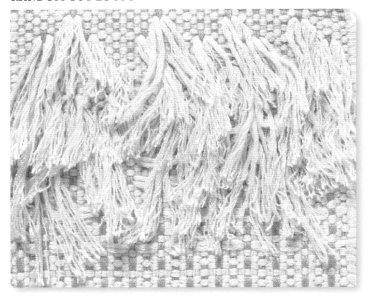

This shaggy effect is fun to do and would make a great accent on a bag or skirt. I used the same yarn for the loops that I used for the background weaving, and, as I wove along, I just pulled out huge loops randomly. I cut the loops after weaving and washing.

DOTS

In this sample, I pulled out loops every 6th space. I wove 3 rows of plain weave between each row of loops and then offset the loops in the next row.

FRINGE

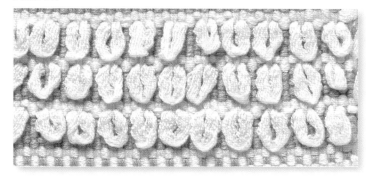

These loops have a fringe-like look because they are fairly large and worked in every other space.

DENSE LOOPS

Here, I used several strands of yarn together and picked up loops in every other space to create a dense pile. Wouldn't this make a nice hat trim?

Danish Medallions

To make Danish medallions, sections of warp and weft are grouped together to create a pattern. The result can be lacelike or textured, depending on how you execute the medallions. Generally, Danish medallions are worked on a plain-weave ground, as shown here.

danish medallion ideas

ALTERNATING GROUPS FOR ALLOVER TEXTURE

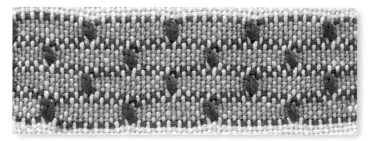

For this example, I used a contrasting gray background weft and chose a yarn twice as large as my warp and weft for the outlining weft in a slightly darker color. By offsetting the groupings in each row of medallions and not pulling the outline weft taut, an allover spot effect is created. For the first row, I carried the shuttle under 8 raised warp threads for all of the groupings except for the final group, in which I traveled under 4 raised warps. I offset the second row of medallions by starting at the right selvedge with a group of 4 raised warp threads and then groups of 8 raised warps thereafter. In this example, I wove 4 rows of gray background weft between each row of medallions.

STACKED MEDALLIONS

In this example, I've made all of the medallions the same size and stacked them one on top of the other. I used a heavy wool for the outlining weft and, even though this sample had a light hand washing in very warm water, the wool shrank enough for the cotton background to pucker. Heavy felting could create a richly textured fabric with wool outlining cells.

DANISH MEDALLION NOTES

Tightly cinch up the outline yarn to make a rounder shape and create more holes in the weaving.

The thicker the outline yarn, the more pronounced the design. Using the same yarn to make the medallions will create a subtle texture.

Work a single row for a border or repeat rows for an allover pattern.

For a tidy edge, even when weaving multiple rows of medallions, start and stop the outline, or contrasting, weft after each row of medallions.

Weaving Danish Medallions

STEP 1. Open the shed and weave in the outline weft (typically heavier than the background weft) from selvedge to selvedge. If you are right-handed, work the first shot of medallion weft from left to right. I leave a tail at the left side and weave it into the same shed at this time, inserting it into the shed under only a few warp threads and letting the tail hang out the back (Figure **1**). I'll cut this flush with the fabric after I've washed and pressed the fabric.

STEP 2. Weave from selvedge to selvedge as many picks with the background weft for as many picks as desired. The more picks, the taller the medallion. In this example, I wove 8 picks (Figure **2**).

STEP 3. Now its time to create the medallions. Change sheds, and, with the shed open, pick up the shuttle with the outline weft. (To carry the outline weft up the selvedge to complete the medallion, make sure that this weft is over the background weft at the selvedge when you insert it into the shed.) Insert the shuttle into the shed as far as your medallion will be wide. In this example, I counted 4 raised warps and exited the shed with my shuttle between the 4th and 5th raised warp thread (Figure **3**).

STEP 4. Poke a crochet hook through the web in front of and underneath the first row of outline weft (Figure **4**).

STEP 5. Grab the second outline weft and pull it up through the hole, drawing out a loop (Figure **5**).

STEP 6. Insert the shuttle into the loop from right to left (Figure **6**) and pull as taut as desired (Figure **7**). Repeat for rest of the row.

STEP 7. To finish off the medallions, cut off the yarn from the shuttle, leaving a tail that is about 3 times as long as the height of the medallion. Insert the crochet hook into the front edge of the first outline weft and one warp thread in from the edge (Figure **8**). Grab the tail with your hook and draw it all the way through this hole. Next, bring the tail up the selvedge and into the open shed, leaving the tail hang out on the back side (Figure **9**).

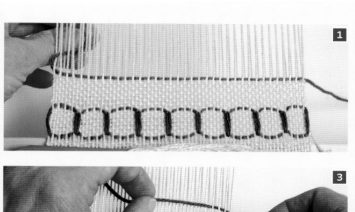

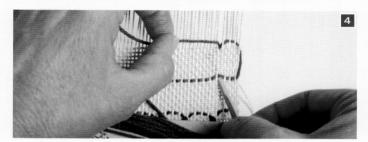

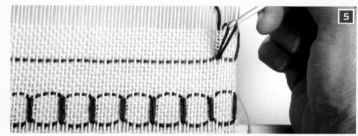

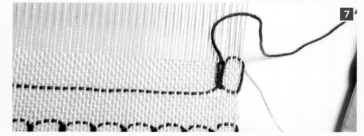

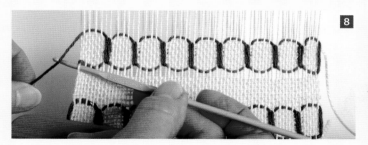

ADDING BEADS

Think of adding a beaded accent to the end of a scarf, curtain, or jacket cuff. Beads are easy to insert as you make your medallions, and they rest securely on the surface of the fabric. To add beads, begin by bringing the loop to the surface in the usual way when you form the medallions (Figure 1). Before inserting the shuttle through the loop, thread a bead onto the loop (Figure 2), drawing the loop through the bead until it is long enough to insert the shuttle. Pull the outlining weft taut and continue on to the next group (Figure 3).

FIGURE 1

FIGURE 2

FIGURE 3

PLAY WITH COLOR

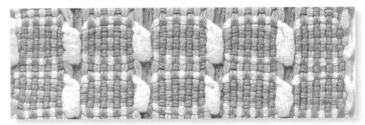

For this sample, I used bleached white rayon ribbon as an outline on a background of green and pink.

TEXTURED MEDALLIONS

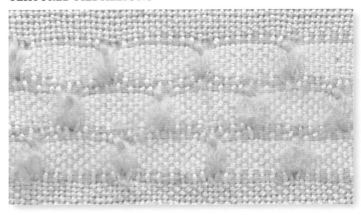

For this example, I used a shiny yellow rayon ribbon for the background weft and a fuzzy mohair for the outline. I offset the medallions brick fashion. These medallions form skinny rectangles, but small squares would be interesting as well.

DOUBLE DANISH MEDALLIONS

CROW'S FEET

When I was researching Danish medallions, I found a drawing in Shirley Held's book *Weaving, a Handbook for Fiber Craftsmen* that I thought was intriguing. Here, I present my version of this idea. The variegated ribbon adds a perky touch. To work double Danish medallions, weave 2 outline wefts,

following each outline row with the desired amount of background. Work the medallions on the 3rd pass of the outline weft. To work the medallions from my dominant side, I started weaving the outlining weft from the right selvedge. For this example, weave the outline right to left, followed by 7 rows of background, then weave the outline weft left to right (**Figure 1**), followed by 7 more rows of background. Use the outline weft to make the medallions on the next pass. Begin the first grouping by traveling under 4 raised warp

FIGURE 1

FIGURE 2

threads. Poke the crochet hook in front of and underneath the first outline weft and draw a loop all the way to the top. Create the next grouping by traveling under 4 raised warps and then draw up the loop from the closest (the 2nd) outline weft (**Figure 2**). Alternate these two medallions to create a scalloped motif.

Crow's feet are worked just like regular Danish medallions, except instead of drawing up a single loop, you make three loops that all radiate from the same point to form "feet." For this example, I inserted an outline weft from left to right, wove 8 picks of background, and then inserted the outline weft, counting 5 raised warps for each medallion. I inserted my crochet hook at this point to make the first loop (**Figure 1**) and then made additional loops by moving 2 raised warp threads on each side of the first loop (**Figures 2 and 3**).

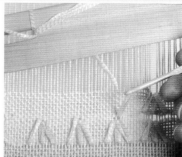

FIGURE 1

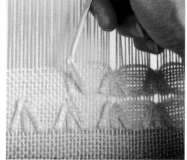

FIGURE 2

FIGURE 3

SIZE AND MATERIALS

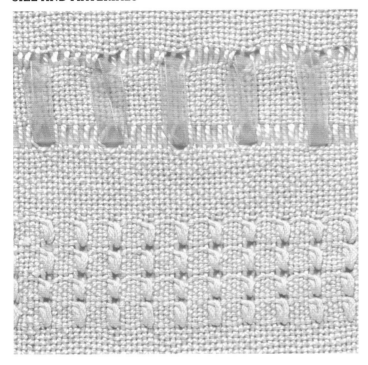

Danish medallions can be pushed both in scale and materials. For the bottom example, I used a heavier-weight outline weft, stacked my medallions, and made quite small medallions, weaving just 4 picks of background weft and counting just 3 raised warp ends for each medallion. For the upper example, I used a sheer golden ribbon to outline a single row of giant medallions. For these, I wove 12 picks of background and made each medallion 6 raised warps wide.

MEDALLIONS AND SPACED WARPS

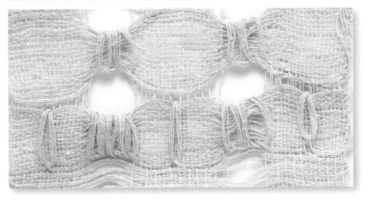

In this sample, I sleyed 16/2 hemp at 10 epi for an open-weave fabric. I threaded 2" (5 cm) in the reed, then skipped 1" (2.5 cm). I chose the same yarn for weft, tripling it for the outline weft. For the first row (top), I made the medallions between each woven area, loosely winding around the exposed wefts as I traveled from one medallion to the next. For the next row, I repeated what I did in the previous row but added a second medallion in the center of each woven area. I like the big medallions best.

Leno

Leno creates a lacelike structure that is quite stable. Any time you want holes in a fabric, even quite large ones, leno is worth exploring. Simply put, leno is made by twisting warp threads around each other before the weft is inserted. The crossed warp threads create holes that produce the lacey effect as well as stabilize the fabric.

Leno can be worked on an open shed or on a closed shed and with a variety of twisted thread combinations—1:1 leno is created by twisting 1 warp end over its neighbor, 2:2 leno is created by twisting 2 warp ends over 2 warp ends. Other combinations, such as 1:2 leno, can also be worked. Work leno from selvedge to selvedge or as a motif or border within the fabric.

Like most finger techniques, it is easiest to work from your dominant side (in my case that's from right to left). For step-by-step instructions for how to make leno, see page 54.

Leno Ideas

1:1 LENO ON AN OPEN SHED

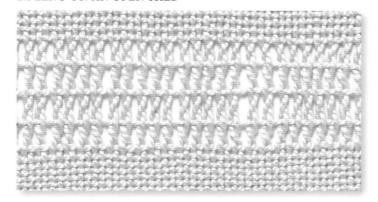

Here, I've worked 2 rows of 1:1 leno. Even though there are three lines of weft in this pattern, there are just 2 rows of leno twists. The reason it looks like more is that on the return trip, the weft locks the twists into place. I like to think of the return trip as my "free" row, because a twist is created without my having to manipulate any threads. In essence, the twists locked into place with my weft yarn on the first pass must twist back on the return trip.

2:2 LENO ON AN OPEN SHED

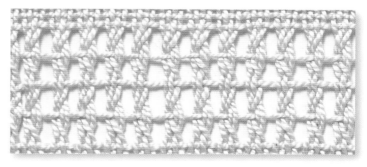

In this sample, 2 rows of 2:2 leno are worked on an open shed.

LENO WITH SPLIT GROUPS ON OPEN AND CLOSED SHEDS

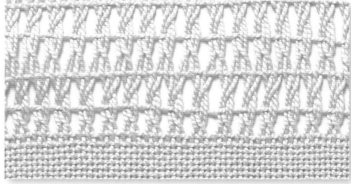

STEP 1. Beginning at the right with the shed open and ready for the next pick and the selvedge thread up, work 2:2 leno holding the twists on a pick-up stick. Turn the pick-up stick on edge and weave across in front of the pick-up stick as usual.

STEP 2. With a closed shed (heddle in neutral—neither up nor down), work 1:1 leno. Just follow the twist down to the fell of the cloth—odd-numbered and even-numbered warp threads will naturally twist together. Hold these twists on the pick-up stick and weave across.

STEP 3. Open the shed and, for the final row, work 2:2 leno, offsetting the twists by beginning with one group of 1:1 leno. Weave across as before.

Making Leno on an Open Shed

STEP 1. Open the shed so that the right outside-most thread is an up thread and ready for the next shot of plain weave.

STEP 2. Using the fingers of your left hand, pull the top right warp thread slightly to the left. With a pick-up stick held in your right hand, dip down to the bottom of the shed and pick up the bottom selvedge thread and hold it on the pick-up stick (Figure **1**). Let the raised warp thread slide under the pick-up stick.

STEP 3. Repeat all the way across the warp. As you bring the top thread over and pick up the bottom thread on the pick-up stick, the threads will twist around each other.

STEP 4. When you reach the left selvedge, turn the pick-up stick on its edge (you can check the twist here).

STEP 5. Insert the weft in front of the pick-up stick (Figure **2**).

STEP 6. Remove the pick-up stick and beat (Figure **3**).

STEP 7. Change sheds and weave back to the right selvedge, locking the twist into place (Figure **4**).

You can immediately make another row of leno as before or weave several rows of plain weave before making another row of leno.

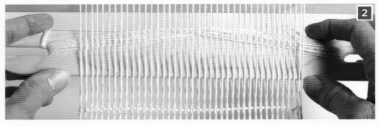

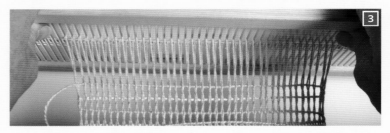

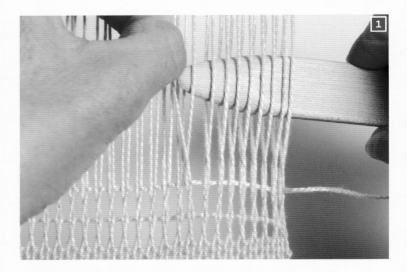

3-GROUP LENO ON A CLOSED SHED

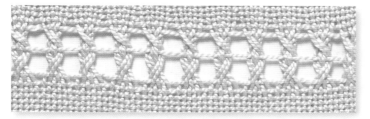

This leno variation uses three elements—the outer groups cross each other and the center is brought up between and held on the pick-up stick. It is worked on a closed shed (see page 57). For this example, I used 6 threads per group. I lifted threads 1 and 2 and 5 and 6, leaving 3 and 4 down (**Figure 1**). I then twisted 1 and 2 over 5 and 6 (**Figure 2**) and brought 3 and 4 up between them and placed them on my pick-up stick (**Figure 3**).

FIGURE 1 **FIGURE 2**

FIGURE 3

3-GROUP LENO VARIATION

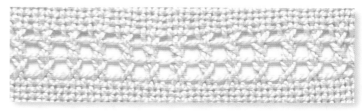

This sample is worked like the previous one, but with fewer threads. Here I used groups of 4 threads, first twisting the 4th thread over the 1st, then bringing the 2nd and 3rd threads up through the center of the twist and onto my pick-up stick. This could be quite effective if the 2 center threads were a contrasting color.

2:2 LENO WITH SPLIT GROUPS ON A CLOSED SHED

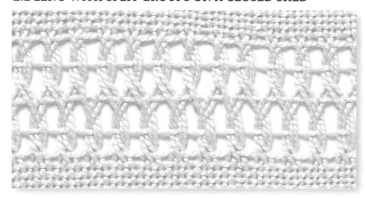

STEP 1. On a closed shed, work 2:2 leno from selvedge to selvedge.

STEP 2. Open the shed and weave across to lock in the twist.

STEP 3. Again, on a closed shed, work 1:1 leno for the first 2 warp ends, then 2:2 thereafter to shift the groupings. For example, on the first row, threads 1 and 2 twist with threads 3 and 4; when the groupings shift, threads 3 and 4 will twist with threads 5 and 6.

STEP 4. Weave back on the next shed (if you wove across in the up position, weave back in the down position) to lock in the twist.

MEXICAN LACE

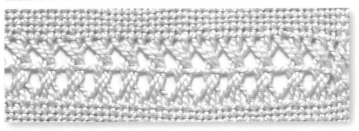

This 2:2 leno is worked on an open shed with the outermost warp thread in the down position. Working right to left, in the first group only, twist 3 top threads to the right (**Figure 1**) and pick up the bottom 2 threads with the pick-up stick. Thereafter, twist groups of 2:2 (**Figure 2**). Because the threads are shifted over by one, the lace is more open and delicate at the edges. At the end of the row, you'll end with 1 top thread and 2 bottom threads.

FIGURE 1

FIGURE 2

2:2 LENO TWISTS IN DIFFERENT DIRECTIONS

Here, I twisted 2 over 2, but I twisted adjacent sets in opposite directions, first to the left, the next set to the right, the next the left, then right, and so on. This sample was worked on a closed shed (see page 57).

LENO, THE JANE VARIATION

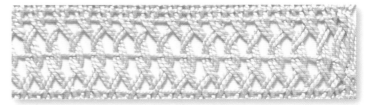

In this variation woven on a closed shed (see page 57), I twisted warp threads 1 and 2 over warp threads 5 and 6, skipping threads 3 and 4. In the next group, I twisted warp threads 3 and 4 over threads 9 and 10, essentially skipping a pair of warp threads in each group.

COMBINING TWO FINGER TECHNIQUES

Here, two bands of 1:1 leno frame a border of rayon ribbon of stacked Danish medallions. This could be used for an allover pattern repeat for a table runner or borders at each end of a placemat.

RANDOM GROUPS

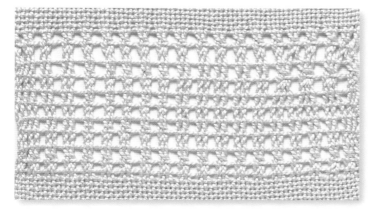

I worked the leno band in this sample on a closed shed (shown at right). I made 2: 2 leno on the first pass, then I combined areas of 1:1 and 2:2 leno in the next 2 rows, followed by a row combining 3:3, 1:1, and 2:2 leno, then I finished with a final row of 2:2 leno. I like the effect of these different twists, and I think this has great pattern potential. It would be especially effective in fine threads—something I'll try one of these days.

Leno on a Closed Shed

The process of making leno on a closed shed is quite similar to that of leno created on an open shed, except that instead of picking up the thread with the pick-up stick, you'll use your fingers to create the twists. For 2:2 leno, begin by twisting the second set of warp threads (threads 3 and 4) over the first set (**Figure 1**). Bring 1 and 2 to the top to form the twist and place over your finger. When you have several twists on your fingers (**Figure 2**), transfer them onto a pick-up stick or just insert your shuttle every few twists as you go.

FIGURE 1

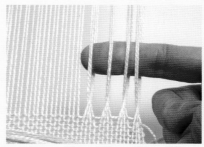

FIGURE 2

LENO AND A STRIPED WARP

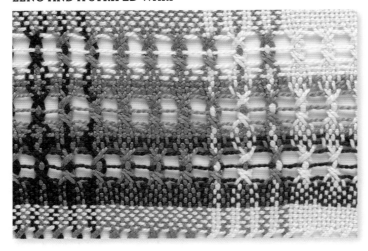

We generally think of leno worked with a single color, but I encourage you to consider adding other colors. In this example, 2-end warp stripes create interesting patterning for 2:2 leno. Woven by Melissa Ludden Hankens.

2:2 LENO WITH END-ON-END STRIPED WARP

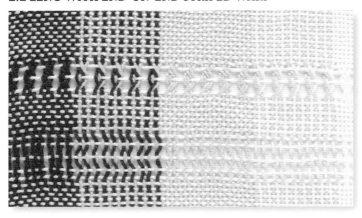

Compare the previous striped example with this one in which two colors alternate in the warp. When worked in both 2:2 and 1:1 leno on a closed shed, a shadow effect is created.

IDEA FOR A HANGING

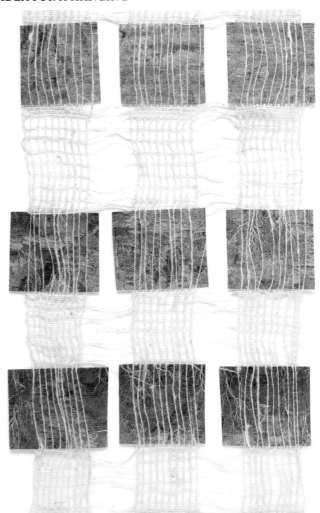

A spaced warp separates each vertical line of 1:1 leno and is accented with paper squares. The spaces between the squares create a negative space to give the piece a three-dimensional look.

Brook's Bouquet

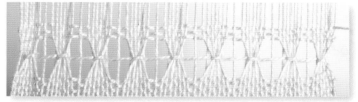

Brook's bouquet is another way to make spaces, or lace, in a fabric. The technique involves wrapping a weft yarn around groups of warp threads on an open shed (see page 60). The shed is changed and the weft is returned from whence it came through a plain-weave shed, thus "locking" the bouquets in place. Brook's bouquet is characterized by little 4-pane windows that separate each bouquet. These "incidentals" are warp threads on the bottom of the shed that reveal themselves when the bundles are made. I find them rather charming, enhancing the lace quality of this technique.

As with all finger-controlled techniques, it is easiest to work from the side of your dominate hand.

STACKED BOUQUETS

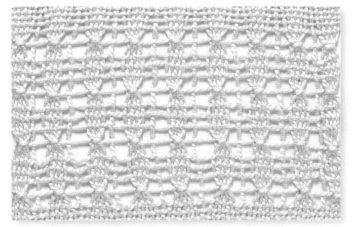

Here bouquets stand one on top of the other in a linear fashion. Four raised warps are used for each bouquet. I first worked bouquets from right to left, then wove 3 picks of plain weave to end up on the right side for the next row of bouquets.

ALTERNATING BOUQUETS

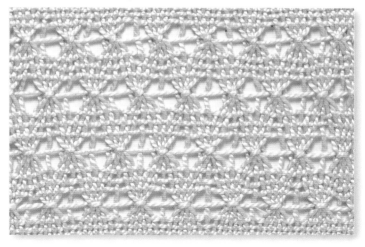

Because each row of bouquets is offset in this sample, you'll find that using even numbers of warp ends for your bundles will give the most pleasing result. In this sample, I made 4-raised-warp groups for each bundle. To offset the next row of bouquets, I began the next row with a 2-raised-warp bundle and then 4-raised-warp bundles thereafter, ending with a 2-raised-warp bundle. The 3rd row is worked like the 1st row, the 2nd like the 4th, and so on.

USING COLOR AND MULTI-WRAPPINGS

Here, for a bright accent that shouts for attention, I used a hot pink yarn of the same size as the background. I used 4-raised-warp groupings, but instead of just encircling the bundle once, I wrapped 4 times, being careful to not cross my wrappings so as to create a tightly wound column. This causes the bundles to tip playfully to one side. The more wraps, the more enhanced the effect.

Making Brook's Bouquet

STEP 1. Open the shed.

STEP 2. Working from right to left (or from the direction of your dominant hand), insert the shuttle into the shed as far as your bouquet is big.

STEP 3. For this sample, I counted 4 raised warp threads before bringing my shuttle out of the shed (Figure **1**).

STEP 4. Bring the shuttle from left to right over this same group of 4 raised warp threads (Figure **2**), then reinsert the shuttle into the shed from right to left, bringing the shuttle out of the shed just as you began (Figure **3**).

STEP 5. Pull tight to cinch up the bundle (Figure **4**).

STEP 6. Keep moving right to left, repeat from Step 2 for each subsequent group (Figure **5**).

For uniform bundles, maintain even tension on the working end. I sometimes pinch the previous knot with one hand as I bring the shuttle out of the shed for the next bundle, thus preventing the previous bouquet from loosening up.

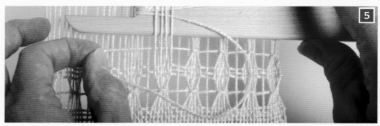

SPOTS

To create a subtle texture, make single bouquets at intervals. On an open shed, insert the shuttle for about 1" (2.5 cm), make a bouquet, insert the shuttle into the shed for 1" (2.5 cm) more, make another single bouquet, and so on. The bouquets prevent the weft from packing in as much as it would normally, creating a lacelike line in the cloth.

BORDER

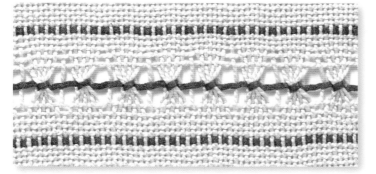

Here, I've used a contrasting rayon ribbon for a border. I inserted the ribbon from left to right so it would be in position to work the bouquets from right to left. I wove 5 rows of background weft (carrying the ribbon up the selvedge), then a row of bouquets (4-raised-warp groups) with the ribbon, then 5 rows of background weft, then finished with a final row of ribbon.

CENTRAL MOTIF

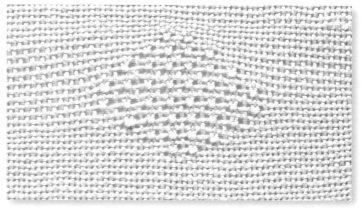

In this sample, I made tiny 2-end bouquets to create an accent within a field of plain weave. Keep in mind that the bouquets prevent the background weft from beating in as firmly. To prevent a loosely woven background, plan your entire project with this condition in mind. Working a sample before commencing on the final project is well worth the time (there goes my mantra again).

BOUQUETS ON A CLOSED SHED

When you make bouquets on a closed shed, the windowpane effect is eliminated. With the shed closed, wrap any number of ends for the bouquets. For this example, I used 5 warp threads for each bundle.

SPLIT GROUPS ON A CLOSED SHED

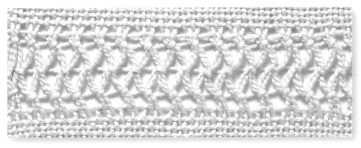

Here, 4-thread groups are made on the first pass. On the second pass, the row begins and ends with 2-thread groups. The 3rd row is worked like the 1st.

STEPPED BROOK'S BOUQUET

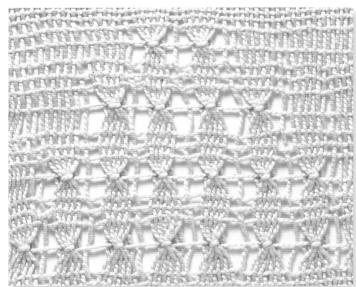

To add a variety of textures, I began this sample on an open shed with 5-raised-thread bouquets from selvedge to selvedge, followed by 3 rows of plain weave. For the next row of bouquets, I omitted a bouquet at either selvedge. I repeated the sequence, eliminating a bouquet on each side until just two bouquets remained. Be aware that the areas void of bouquets will not beat in as tightly and will result in an open weave.

BOUQUETS BOTH WAYS

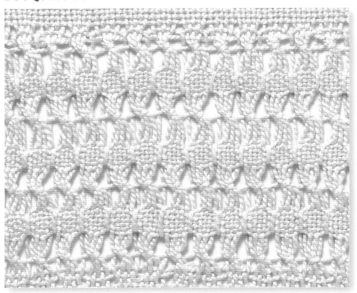

For this variation, I first worked bouquets both weft-wise and warp-wise. First, I worked 4 rows of 5-thread bouquets on a closed shed separating each row of bouquets with 7 rows of plain weave. When all 4 rows of horizontal bouquets were completed, I worked vertically (warp-wise).

For the vertical bouquets, you'll need a tapestry needle threaded with a long length of the same yarn (the longer the wrapping yarn, the fewer joins you'll have). Secure the tail by weaving it into the fabric at the selvedge for about ½" (1.3 cm).

For the first vertical row, I started at the bottom (first horizontal row of bouquets) between the first and second bouquets. I wrapped around the plain-weave area between bouquets and then traveled up on the back side to the next plain-weave area between bouquets (**Figure 1**). This

FIGURE 1

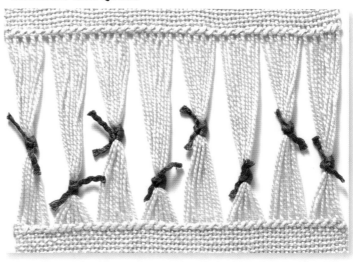

creates a long float on the back side—okay for curtains but a potential problem in a garment. After completing the 4th horizontal row (top row) of bouquets **(Figure 2)**, I carried the wrapping thread across on the back to in between the second and third bouquets and wrapped down this vertical column to the bottom (1st

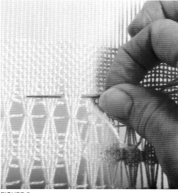

FIGURE 2

row of bouquets) as I did for the first pass. I repeated this to the other selvedge and wove the tail into the fabric to secure it.

"CHEATER" BOUQUETS

ANOTHER USE OF COLOR

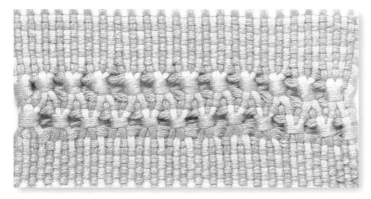

In this sample, end-on-end warp color is accented with wrapped bouquets made on a closed shed.

This sample of little tied groups illustrates that, really, there are no rules. Here, I've simply tied little bows of rayon ribbon around groups of warp threads. You could have a lot of fun with this idea in a curtain, for example. A little weight in the hem or rod along the edge will ensure that the warps are taut for maximum impact. I secured the weft along the edge at the top and bottom with overcast stitches using the weft tail.

Spanish Lace

Spanish lace is made simply by weaving back and forth in small sections, changing the shed with each pass, and then moving onto the next section and repeating for that section (see opposite page). Make Spanish lace as open or as tightly packed as you desire.

SPANISH LACE IN VERTICAL ALIGNMENT

Using the same weft as warp, I counted 5 raised warps and wove 4 rows in this section, then advanced to the next section on the 5th row, continuing to the selvedge. I then wove 3 rows of plain weave from selvedge to selvedge before repeating a row of Spanish lace, followed by 3 more plain-weave rows and another row of Spanish lace.

EXTRA LARGE SPANISH LACE

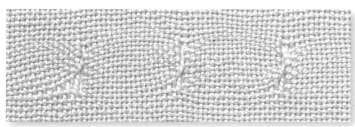

In this variation, I used groups of 10 raised warps for each section and wove for 10 rows, advancing to the next section on the 11th row to create rather long slits.

RANDOM GROUPS

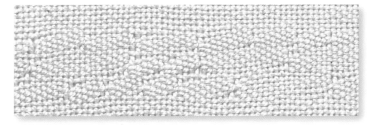

For each row of lace in this sample, I chose different-sized groupings, but wove the same number of weft picks in each group to maintain an even horizontal weft line. After each row of Spanish lace, I returned to the other side, always working Spanish lace from the same direction. I find the difference between large and small groups rather interesting.

HEAVY WEFT

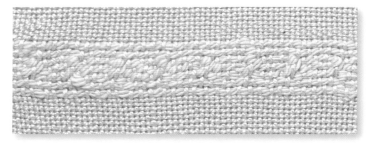

Here, a thick soft weft is used to create a textured border.

CINCHED GROUPS

For this sample, I pulled the weft as tightly as I could after each pick to draw in each group and accentuate the open spaces between groups. The diagonal line where the weft travels from one group to the next lends a charming design element. In this sample, I used 5 raised warps and 5 weft rows in each group.

Weaving Spanish Lace

STEP 1. Open the shed and, beginning at one edge (right selvedge shown here) insert the shuttle into the shed and weave under 5 raised warp threads.

STEP 2. Bring the shuttle out of the shed and change sheds.

STEP 3. Weave back to the selvedge. Change sheds.

STEP 4. Weave under the same 5 raised warps and continue on to weave the next group, counting another 5 raised warps for a total of 10 warp threads in the same shed (Figure **1**), then exit the shed.

STEP 5. Change sheds and weave back under the second group of 5 raised warp ends (Figure **2**). Change sheds and weave back across this group and onto the next 5 raised warps.

STEP 6. Continue across the warp in this manner. When you reach the other (left) side, you can weave another row of Spanish lace to return again to the right side, or just weave across (Figure **3**). Press this row into place with the rigid heddle (Figure **4**) or use a hand beater.

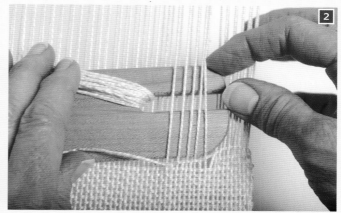

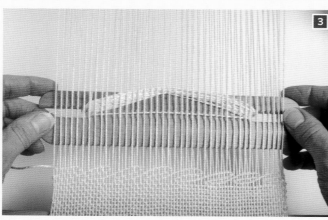

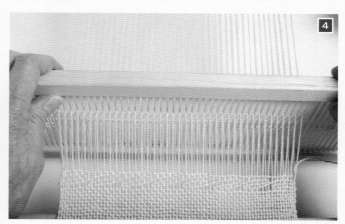

UNUSUAL MATERIALS

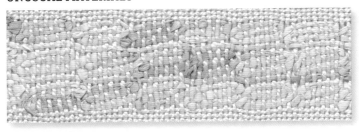

Here, hand-dyed Kasuri bamboo tape creates a fabric with an irregular surface. The slight dye variation creates visual interest.

GOING AND COMING SPANISH LACE

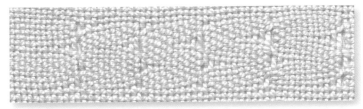

For this sample, I worked groups of 6 raised warps in the middle from right to left, 5 weft picks per group. After completing this row, I worked the same groupings from left to right to return to the other selvedge.

GOING AND COMING, VARIATION

Here's the same idea, only with larger groupings of the same size across the warp (8 raised warps with 9 wefts per group). Keep in mind that as the groups increase in height, they will tip one way and the other in the direction the weft travels between groups. You can enhance this phenomenon by increasing the height of your groups even more.

SPANISH LACE NOTES

Pull the weft tight as each section is woven to enhance the lacelike effect.

Always change sheds with each pass of the shuttle. If the weft is in the same shed, you've made a mistake.

Each group is distinct. That is, no warp ends are shared between groups.

Returning to the other selvedge after weaving a row of Spanish lace creates a horizontal weft line after the row of lace.

Because small areas are built up at a time, it can be difficult to use the heddle for beating in the weft. A belt shuttle—a shuttle with one beveled edge—works well for pressing the weft in as you go. You can also use a hand beater.

VARIEGATED RIBBON

The soft colors of silk ribbon move from group to group across this sample.

SPANISH LACE VARIATION

Using soy silk ribbon, I first wove a group of 8 raised warps for 5 weft picks. I then wove under the next 8 raised warps with 1 weft pick (skipping Spanish lace in this group) and wove the next group of 8 for 5 picks, and so on (**Figure 1**). On the return trip, I skipped over the areas woven with Spanish lace on the first pass and filled in with 5 weft rows in the previous skipped sections (**Figure 2**).

FIGURE 1

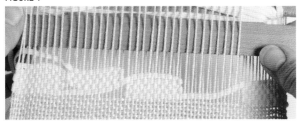

FIGURE 2

Weaving a Header

Many weavers use thick yarn or rags to begin a weaving, but I like to use the same yarn that I plan to use for the weft. I find that larger yarns spread out the warp differently than the project weft does and, when I begin weaving with the project yarn, the first 1" (2.5 cm) or so ripples. The ripples don't form if I use the project weft yarn, or a yarn similar in size (which you might want to do if your weft is in short supply or expensive), for the header.

SIZE VARIATION

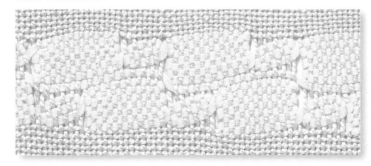

With soy silk ribbon, I varied the size of my groups both warp-wise and weft-wise. Thinking of this variation as blocks, weave as follows:

Block A: 8 raised warps, 7 weft repeats.
Block B: 4 raised warps, 3 weft repeats.
STEP 1. Weave A, B, A, B, A, B, A (the final group is just 4 raised warps).
STEP 2. Weave 1 pick of plain weave all the way back to the other side.
STEP 3. Weave the blocks in the opposite order: B, A, B, A, B, A, B.

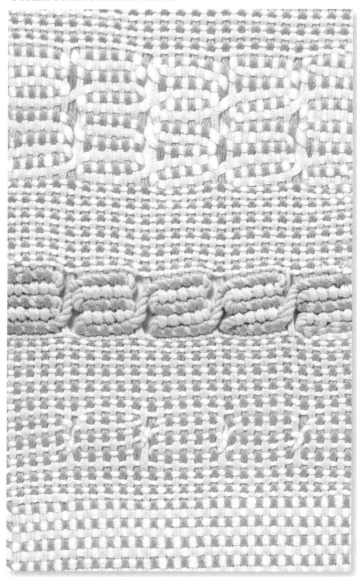

Think about scale and materials when you choose your weft for Spanish lace. From bottom to top: 3/2 pearl cotton (same yarn as background), thick cotton string, rayon ribbon. The end-on-end colored warp adds interest to these samples.

Hemstitching

It's hard to know exactly where to place hemstitching—it forms a nice edge finish and is also quite effective for creating spaces, or lacelike effects, in a woven cloth. For this reason, I've included it here with other finger-controlled techniques. In addition to instructions for the basic stitch, I've provided some examples of how it can be used as an accent along a hem, to make a border on a table runner, or for an airy accent on the edge of a curtain.

If you like to embroider, you'll take to hemstitching. It relates to drawn-thread work in that a set of threads is missing in the area to be hemstitched. In drawn-thread work, you pull out yarns in the fabric. In weaving, the same effect is created by simply leaving areas (usually warps) unwoven instead of pulling out threads to create spaces. The advantage of hemstitching in weaving is that threads don't have to be removed. Also, because the warp is under tension on the loom, it is easy to hemstitch the taut threads.

hemstitching as a weft protector

In general, you need to finish the edges of weaving to prevent the weft from raveling. Hemstitching is a great technique to prevent raveling at the beginning and end of a piece—it acts as a weft protector, if you will. Hemstitching allows you to finish a piece of weaving and be done with it—no need to sew a hem or tie a fringe later.

I like hemstitching, particularly for fabrics such as runners or coasters that need to lie flat on a table. Hemstitching is free of bulky knots, is a great way to finish samples, and is faster than tying the warp ends into knots. It also requires that less space be left between individual projects on a single warp—at least 5" to 6" (12.5 to 15 cm) is required for tying knots; hemstitching allows you to leave just the fringe you need. Hemstitching can be quite elegant, and you'll see from the variations presented here that it can be employed for many special effects.

Hemstitching at the Beginning of a Piece

Even though the results at each end of the fabric are the same, hemstitching is worked slightly differently—at the beginning of a piece, you're working up into the fabric; at the end, you're working down into the fabric. When I first started hemstitching, all went smoothly at the beginning, but I could never seem to translate the movements at the other end of the cloth. I'm sure I'm not alone in this. Therefore, I've shown the same stitch at the start and at the end of my sample.

When I begin a project, I tie onto the loom and then, to create a header to spread the warp to the weaving width, I weave back and forth 3 times, changing the shed with each pass but not beating between picks. I then press these 3 picks into place and repeat again. Usually two repeats produce enough header to even out the warp for weaving. These beginning picks are pulled out after the weaving is complete.

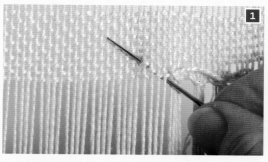

Working from right to left, I begin hemstitching by leaving a tail of weft yarn 4 times the width of my weaving and then weave 5 to 10 picks before beginning the hemstitching. I decide on the size of the grouping, then thread the tail on a tapestry needle. In this case, I counted over 4 warps threads and up 3 weft picks. The groupings are arbitrary and depend completely on the effect I want. For more impact and bigger bundles, I might count up 5 weft picks and over 6 warps. Sometimes, I'll try a few stitches to see if I like the look. If not, I'll take it out and begin again. Even the simplest detail of your hemstitching can make a big result in the final look of a piece.

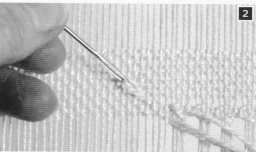

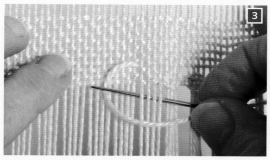

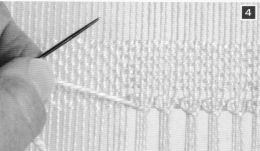

STEP 1. Working right to left (or from your dominant side), insert the needle at the bottom edge of your project, traveling underneath the fabric and bringing it to the surface the desired number of warps and weft picks away—in this case, 4 warp threads and 3 weft picks (Figure **1**). Exit at this juncture and pull the thread through (Figure **2**).

STEP 2. Again, working right to left, insert your needle along the bottom edge under 4 warp threads. Exit, keeping the needle on top of the loop (Figure **3**).

STEP 3. Pull the yarn through and tighten the knot (Figure **4**).

STEP 4. Repeat Steps 1 to 3 to the opposite edge.

To secure the end, I weave the tail into the last bundle, leaving the end hanging off the back. I'll trim this tail flush with the fabric after I've washed the fabric.

Hemstitching at the End of a Piece

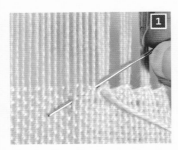

STEP 1. Leaving a tail 4 times the width and working right to left (or from your dominate side), insert the threaded needle from the fell (the edge closest to the reed) of the cloth diagonally underneath the fabric. In this case, I counted across 4 warp threads and 3 weft picks (Figure **1**). Exit at this juncture, pulling the thread through.

STEP 2. Make a loop to the left. Again, working right to left, insert the needle horizontally under 4 warp threads along the fell of the cloth (Figure **2**).

STEP 3. Pull the thread through and pull tight (Figure **3**).

Repeat Steps 1 to 3 to the opposite edge, then secure the end in the same manner as the beginning hemstitching.

ladder hemstitching

Ladder hemstitching makes a delightful detail. Use it as a base for lacing ribbons through at the top of a bag, for example. Think of a skirt with a broad border of several rows of ladder hemstitching and a colorful lining peeking through the holes.

In ladder hemstitching, you will work the first edge in hemstitching as though you're at the end of the piece (in this example, 4 ends per group), then leave between ½" (3.2 cm) and 1" (2.5 cm) of unwoven warp. Weave 5 to 10 picks before beginning the corresponding hemstitch along this edge just as you would at the beginning of a piece. A narrow spacer can be used to "hold" the space.

Place a spacer in the shed to leave a uniform space across the width when working ladder hemstitching. See page 72 for a nifty way to cut paper spacers.

LADDER HEMSTITCHING, VARIATION

When fewer threads are used in a bundle, the result is more delicate. Here, I used 2 warps per grouping and left about 1" (2.5 cm) of warp exposed between the two hemstitched edges.

Italian Hemstitching

This variation of hemstitching is a little more time consuming, but the square shape makes an effective highlight, such as at the edge of a table mat. I worked this example in a contrasting yarn. You'll need a length of yarn about 5 times the width of your weaving.

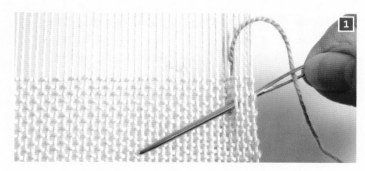

STEP 1. Insert the needle along the fell line, 4 threads in from the selvedge. Travel over these 4 warp threads left to right, then, working from right to left, insert the needle from the fell of the cloth (reed side) diagonally across the underside of the fabric. In this example, I counted across 4 warp threads and 4 weft picks (Figure **1**).

STEP 2. Draw the thread through.

STEP 3. Insert the needle horizontally at the first warp of the 4 from right to left and back into the same hole, keeping the needle on top of the thread (Figure **2**), and pull tight.

STEP 4. Carry the thread straight up to the fell and insert the needle horizontally from right to left under the next 4 warp threads along the fell of the cloth (Figure **3**).

STEP 5. Returning from left to right, insert the needle diagonally under the fabric for the next group (Figure **4**).

STEP 6. Repeat Steps 2 to 5 as desired.

Note that the stitch is not complete at the right selvedge of the first grouping. Catch this edge with the tail of the yarn after you've removed the fabric from the loom, stitching the tail into the back of the fabric to secure it.

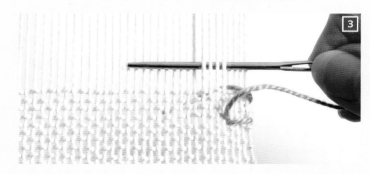

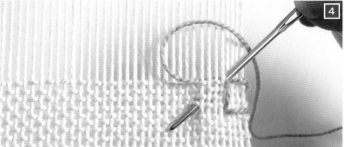

ZIGZAG HEMSTITCHING

Begin as for ladder hemstitching, working a row of hemstitching (in this case 4 warps per group). Leave some warp exposed (about ½" [1.3 cm] shown here), weave a few rows of plain weave, then begin hemstitching as for at the beginning of a piece. To offset the groups, begin with a group of 2 warps and work groups of 4 from there on, ending with a group of 2 at the other edge. Generally, you'll want to work in even numbers of warp threads so you can divide the first group of the second hemstitching in half.

HEMSTITCHED TRIM

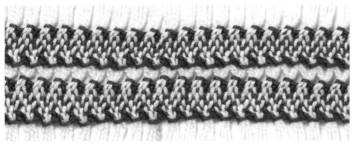

Bright blue yarn creates a bold accent in this hemstitched trim. Woven by Judy Steinkoenig.

Nifty Tool

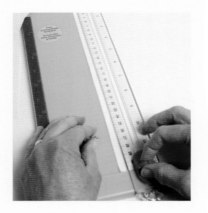

I use a small paper cutter designed for scrapbooking to cut strips of manila file folder for spacers. It's a fast and easy way to cut perfectly straight strips in almost no time.

NEEDLE WEAVING

Use hemstitching (see page 69) or soumak (see page 157) as I've done on this sample to secure the warps on either side of a broad band of exposed warps. This illustrates a technique that, in a way, is a weaving within a weaving. With a nod to embroidery, needle weaving offers a whole new world of embellishment. I've worked the needle weaving in this sample in the same color as the cloth, as it might be traditionally worked, but it could be exciting worked in a color pattern, à la tapestry fashion.

Needle weaving is simply weaving back and forth in sections to create a pattern. Here I wove over 2, under 2 to contrast with the background cloth. Though my pattern is geometric, you can be as free as you want with your design. Who says you have to weave over the same number of warps and threads for the entire band? Play with different interlacements and sizes of motifs. Again, if you have a penchant for embroidery or tapestry, needle-woven accents can be quite a blast.

To begin, use a strip of cardboard to create the unwoven warp space for needle weaving and pull the cardboard out when the edges are secured. Needle-weave back and forth in small sections (**Figure 1**). Secure the ends after removing the fabric from the loom, stitching the ends up through the weaving warp-wise (**Figure 2**), and trimming the ends flush after washing.

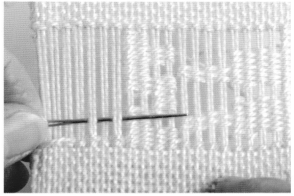

FIGURE 1

FIGURE 2

Conclusion

Perhaps my affinity for the finger-controlled weaves is due to my penchant for fiddly things. I think it's more than that, though. I believe I'm drawn to these weaves because of the complete freedom they offer the handweaver. You can create whole textiles with any of these techniques or use them just for a border or accent. Truly, there are no rules. I like this. I like playing around, trying this idea and that, developing a look, a feel, making something that is completely unique. Last but not least, the finger-controlled weaves are in their very nature worked by hand. There may be machines that can create leno, but certainly there's no machine that can create Brook's bouquet or Danish medallion or a lovely zigzag hemstitched border. I hope you'll forgive the finger-controlled weaves for the time it takes to create them, and explore them to discover your own unique variations and applications.

I've explored several finger-controlled techniques and their applications in this chapter. And even though I've shown numerous variations and ideas, I must say I feel that I've only just begun. As I was working on the samplers for this chapter, I never seemed to be lacking for the next "what if." Almost every technique, whether leno or Brook's bouquet or Danish medallions, can provide rich material for its own slim volume.

SHRUG
in Leno

Designed by Jane Patrick
and Sara Goldenberg White;
woven by Sara Goldenberg White

Oh-so-soft alpaca yarn and 2:2 leno combine
to create an elegant accessory for most
any time. Even with this finger-manipulated
weave, you'll be surprised at the pace in
which this lovely piece weaves up. The
construction is easily accomplished.

Finished Size
About 10½" (26.5 cm) wide and
20" (51 cm) long, plus 3" (7.5 cm)
fringe at each end.

Yarn
Warp and Weft: *Berroco Ultra
Alpaca Fine* (50% wool, 30%
alpaca, 20% nylon; 433 yd
[400 m]/100 g): #1214 Steel
Cut Oats, 2 skeins.

Equipment
Rigid heddle loom with at least
12" (30.5 cm) weaving width;
12-dent reed; 16" (40.5 cm) stick
shuttle; 20" (51 cm) pick-up stick.

Notions
Tapestry needle; straight pins;
sharp-pointed sewing needle;
three ½" (1.3 cm) antique
buttons.

Number of Warp Ends
144.

Warp Length
2⅔ yards (2.4 meters), which
allows 28" (71 cm) loom waste,
part of which forms the fringe.

Warp Width
12" (30.5 cm).

EPI
12.

PPI
3 picks plain weave, 1 row leno,
3 picks plain weave are woven in
1" (2.5 cm).

Weaving

First Half

Leaving a 40" (101.5 cm) tail, weave 4 picks of plain weave. Thread the tail on a tapestry needle and hemstitch (see page 69) 4 ends per bundle. Weave in pattern as follows: weave 2:2 leno, returning to the initiating selvedge row, then weave 2 picks of plain weave (3 picks of plain weave total). Repeat this sequence for 24" (61 cm). Hemstitch the last row, working 4 ends per bundle as before.

Center

With scrap yarn, weave 6" (15 cm) of plain weave to become fringe.

Second Half

Leaving a 40" (101.5 cm) tail, weave 4 picks of plain weave, hemstitch, weave 24" (61 cm) of 2:2 leno with plain weave in between as for first half. Hemstitch end to finish.

Finishing

Remove fabric from loom. Cut the two halves apart in the center of the 6" (15 cm) section worked in scrap yarn, leaving 3" (7.5 cm) on each side. Remove scrap yarn to expose fringe. Trim the other 2 warp ends to 3" (7.5 cm) as well. Gently handwash the two pieces in lukewarm soapy water, being careful not to agitate (and felt) the fabric. Gently squeeze out the excess water and lay flat to dry.

Assembly

Lay both pieces flat. Pin the two pieces together along the selvedges for 4½" (11.5 cm) from each fringe end. Handstitch one side along the 4½" (11.5 cm) to the fringe. Handstitch the other side for just 1" (2.5 cm), then leave the remaining 3½" (9 cm) open to the fringe. Attach three antique buttons along the short seam as shown in photograph. Wear the buttons in front or on the shoulder.

LINEN PLACEMATS
with Leno and Spanish Lace Borders

Designed and woven by Betsy Blumenthal

These mats are a good way to start exploring linen.
To help maintain a tight tension on my warp yarns,
I like to weave fairly close to the heddle block.
Advancing the warp after every 2" (5 cm) of weaving
helps maintain an even beat and tidy selvedges—
something you want in a placemat.

Finished Size
Four mats, each measuring
13½" × 18¼" (34.5 × 46.5 cm).

Yarn (for four mats)
Warp and Weft: *Louet Euroflax
Sport Weight* (100% wet-spun
linen; 1,300 yd [1,189 m] lb;
270 yd [247 m]/100 g): #44
Sandlewood, 755 yd (690 m;
used in warp and weft); #34
Pewter, 315 yd (288 m; used in
warp only).

Equipment
Rigid heddle loom with at least
a 15" (38 cm) weaving width;
12-dent reed; two stick shuttles,
12" or 16" (30.5 or 40.5 cm) long;
pick-up stick for leno (optional).

Threading
Alternate 1 end Sandlewood,
1 end Pewter.

Number of Warp Ends
180; 90 each of Sandlewood
and Pewter.

Warp Length
3½ yards (3.2 meters) for 4
mats. *Note:* 2¼ yards (2 meters)
are needed for 2 mats. These
measurements allow for 28"
(71 cm) loom waste.

Warp Width
15" (38 cm).

EPI
12.

PPI
12.

Weaving

Using Sandlewood for weft, weave 2" (5 cm) plain weave for hem.

Beginning Border

Make 1 row of 2:2 leno on a closed shed (see page 57). Weave 8 picks of plain weave.

Weave 3 rows of Spanish lace (see page 64), weave across using 1" (2.5 cm), or 12 warp ends, per group, 5 picks high on the first row. On the return row, make the first group 18 warp threads wide to offset the groups from the previous row. Work the third row the same as the first.

Weave 8 picks of plain weave.

Make 1 row of 2:2 leno on a closed shed.

Center

Weave 10" (25.5 cm) of plain weave.

End Border

Repeat border.

End with 2" (5 cm) of plain weave for hem.

Repeat this sequence for each mat, marking the row between mats with a contrasting yarn. Each mat will measure 22" (56 cm) long on the loom.

Finishing

Remove fabric from loom. Machine zigzag between the ends of each mat on each side of the contrasting yarn, then cut between mats to separate. Handwash in warm water, line dry, and press. Turn under the raw edges about ¼" (6 mm), then fold again to meet the leno border for a ¾" (2 cm) hem, then handstitch in place. Steam-press with a press cloth.

CHAPTER 3

PICK-UP
on the Rigid Heddle Loom

It's easier than you think.

Because of the unique design of the rigid heddle loom, it is especially suited to pick-up patterns. Therefore, I consider this chapter the heart and soul of this book. I've talked about how each thread holds its own individual possibility. You as a weaver have control over that one thread, and for that matter, each and every thread. But it's not particularly practical to control the path of individual threads, and that's why you have a loom to help you manage them in groups. Using a pick-up stick (or two) to control warp threads increases the possibilities and expedites the process of creating patterns. This is where the rigid heddle loom shows its true colors.

Pick-up Basics

Before going any further, I invite you to examine your heddle and how it works on the loom. Notice that when it is in the up position, the slots threads are down; when the heddle is in the down position, the slot threads are up. When the heddle is in the neutral position, no threads are raised or lowered. In short, the slot threads are where the action is. Because they are free to move around (unlike the threads in the fixed holes), the slot threads can be manipulated. You do this with the aid of a pick-up stick.

Whenever I teach pick-up techniques on the rigid heddle loom, I see lightbulbs flashing in my students' eyes as they start to realize the possibilities—and also see that pick-up on the rigid heddle loom is simple and dramatically enhances the potential of this little loom.

To explore pick-up, warp your rigid heddle loom with a 2-yard (1.8-meter) warp of 60 ends of 3/2 pearl cotton sett at 10 epi for a 6" (15 cm) weaving width. You'll be surprised at how easy this is!

weaving pick-up

Weaving pick-up patterns requires a pick-up stick or two, even three or four (more on this later). I use two pick-up sticks and sometimes a strip of paper to separate the raised and lowered warp threads when I weave pick-up patterns. The pick-up stick must be at least as long as the weaving width. It's a good idea to use a pick-up stick that's a little wider than the weaving width to have space at each end to manipulate it. For example, use a 25" (63.5 cm) pick-up stick for a weaving width of 20" (51 cm). In addition to different lengths, pick-up sticks come in a variety of widths. I like ones that are at least 1" (2.5 cm) wide with tapered points at each end and a flat, not curved, edge. The tapered points help to negotiate picking up the threads; one at each end means you don't have to worry about which end of the stick you use. The flat edge helps to keep the pick-up stick upright in the shed.

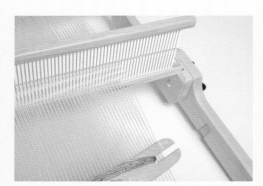

Heddle in the up position.

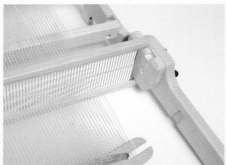

Heddle in the down position.

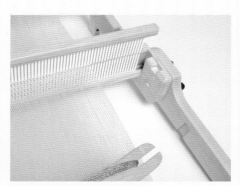

Heddle in the neutral position.

How to Weave Pick-up

STEP 1. Begin by putting the heddle in the down position (see page 80). This places the slot threads on top where they can be easily manipulated.

STEP 2. Insert a pick-up stick (or strip of paper) into the shed in front of the heddle to separate the raised and lowered warp threads. As you gain confidence, you may find this isn't necessary. Now you're ready to pick up the pattern. Even though the pick-up stick is used behind the heddle, picking up the warp threads in front of the heddle makes it easier to see what you're doing.

STEP 3. Pick up the raised warp threads according to your pattern. Here, I've picked 1 up, 1 down. To pick up the raised (slot) threads, begin at the selvedge and pick up the desired threads (1 up, 1 down, or 2 up, 2 down, or 1 up, 3 down, and so on), using an up and down dipping motion with the pick-up stick. When the pattern says "up," place a warp thread on the pick-up stick; when the pattern says "down," place a

warp thread underneath the pick-up stick. For a 2-up-2-down sequence, there will be 2 wrap threads on the pick-up stick, 2 underneath, and so on (Figure **1**).

STEP 4. After you've picked up all of the desired threads, remove the separator. Then place the heddle in neutral (Figure **2**).

STEP 5. Turn the pick-up stick on edge (Figure **3**).

STEP 6. To transfer the picked-up threads to behind the heddle, first place the heddle in neutral, and then turn the pick-up stick on edge. Transfer this pattern to behind the heddle by inserting a second pick-up stick behind the heddle into the shed created by the first pick-up stick. Remove the pick-up stick that's in front of the heddle—it has done its job. Now, slide the pick-up stick behind the heddle to the back of the loom. You'll bring this stick forward when it's needed to create a shed (Figure **4**).

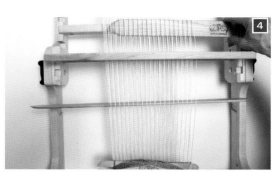

For weft floats, place the heddle in neutral and place the pick-up stick on edge to create a new shed.

For warp floats, place the heddle in the up position and slide the pick-up stick forward to behind the heddle. Leave it flat (do not turn it on edge).

You can use the same pick-up stick to create weft or warp floats. For weft floats, leave the heddle in neutral, bring the pick-up stick up behind the heddle, and turn it on edge to create a new shed. For warp floats, place the heddle in the up position and slide the pick-up stick forward, leaving it flat. The bottom threads rise to the top to create warp floats. You can use these simple techniques to create literally hundreds, if not thousands of patterns.

note: In pick-up weaving notation, "pick-up stick" means turn the pick-up stick (heddle in neutral) on edge (to create a weft float); "up and pick-up stick" means to place the heddle in the up position and slide the pick-up stick forward, leaving it flat (to create a warp float).

Side view of the shed in the up position behind the heddle.

Side view of the shed in the up position as the pick-up stick is slid forward, raising threads from the bottom of the shed to the top where they will form warp floats.

Weft Floats

To begin exploring pick-up patterns, I want to start with a series of exercises, beginning with weft floats. I suggest you try these techniques on a sample warp to familiarize yourself with the sequences and motions.

With the heddle in the down position (picking up only the raised-slot-warp threads), use the pick-up stick to pick up one warp end, skip the next, pick up the next, and so on so that every other raised warp thread is on the pick-up stick. There are several ways to weave these weft floats.

First, weave 2 rows of plain weave (one pick in the up shed and one in the down shed). To weave the pattern row, place the heddle in neutral. Next, slide the pick-up stick close behind the heddle and turn it on edge to create a new shed. Insert the weft—it will travel over 3 warps, under 1, and so on. Lay the pick-up stick flat and slide it to the back of the loom until you need it. The weaving notation looks like this:

3/1 FLOATS

Pick-up stick pattern: *1 up, 1 down; repeat from *.
STEP 1. Up (heddle in up position).
STEP 2. Down (heddle in down position).
STEP 3. Pick-up stick (heddle in neutral, pick-up stick turned on edge).
Repeat these 3 steps for pattern.

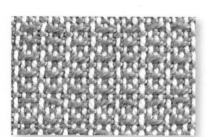 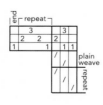

That's all there is to it. There will be 2 rows of plain weave, followed by 1 row in which the weft travels over 3 warps and under 1 warp. Weave this pattern with the same weft or accent the pick-up row by using a thicker weft, called a pattern or supplementary weft.

To create a denser pattern, sandwich the pick-up rows between plain weave, as shown in the next exercise.

3/1 FLOATS ALTERNATING WITH PLAIN-WEAVE PICKS
Pick-up stick pattern: *1 up, 1 down; repeat from *.
STEP 1. Up.
STEP 2. Pick-up stick.
STEP 3. Down.
STEP 4. Pick-up stick.
Repeat these 4 steps for pattern.

 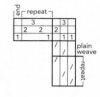

If you repeat the pick-up row between 2 rows made in the up position, you will create more space for the yarns to move around in the float area, thus creating a lace structure. Try this:

3/1 LACE
Pick-up stick pattern: *1 up, 1 down; repeat from *.
STEP 1. Up.
STEP 2. Pick-up stick.
STEP 3. Up.
STEP 4. Down.
Repeat these 4 steps for pattern.

 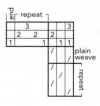

You can increase the effect by repeating the sequence, but eventually you'll need to weave a row in the down position to tie it all down. Try this variation:

3/1 LACE VARIATION
Pick-up stick pattern: *1 up, 1 down; repeat from *.
STEP 1. Up.
STEP 2. Pick-up stick.
STEP 3. Up.
STEP 4. Pick-up stick.
STEP 5. Up.
STEP 6. Down.
Repeat these 6 steps for pattern.

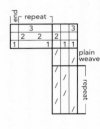

About Floats

A float, warp-wise or weft-wise, is any time a yarn travels over another group of yarns. In plain weave (over, under, over, under) a yarn floats over one thread and under the next—not much of a float at all. But, when a weft float travels over, for example, three warps and then is tied down by the fourth warp, a new interlacement is created.

Warp Floats

Without changing the pick-up stick used for weft floats, you can make warp floats by using the stick a little differently. Instead of making another shed by putting the heddle in neutral, place the heddle in the up position (hole threads are raised) and slide the pick-up stick close behind the heddle. Leave the pick-up stick flat (don't turn it on edge) and draw up warp (slot) threads from the bottom of the shed to the top.

1/3 WARP FLOATS
Pick-up stick pattern: *1 up, 1 down; repeat from *.
STEP 1. Down (heddle in down position).
STEP 2. Up and pick-up stick (heddle in up position, pick-up stick slid up to behind heddle but left flat).
STEP 3. Down (heddle in down position).
STEP 4. Up (heddle in up position).
Repeat these 4 steps for pattern.

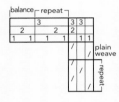

Increase the length of the warp float just by adding additional repeats. Weave as follows:

1/5 WARP FLOATS

Pick-up stick pattern: *1 up, 1 down; repeat from *.
STEP 1. Down.
STEP 2. Up and pick-up stick.
STEP 3. Down.
STEP 4. Up and pick-up stick.
STEP 5. Down.
STEP 6. Up.
Repeat these 6 steps for pattern.

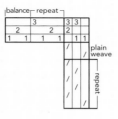

Just as with weft floats, you can create many different combinations by changing which warp threads you pick up. Try 2 up, 2 down; or 2 up, 1 down; or 3 up, 3 down. Who says you have to repeat the same sequence all the way across the warp? Try 1 up, 1 down for a few repeats, then switch to 3 up, 3 down, and so on.

Supplementary Weft

A supplementary weft (also referred to as a pattern weft) is an additional weft yarn used to create a woven pattern. Generally, a supplementary weft is larger in size than the background yarns and is used just for the pick-up pattern row. The greater the size difference between the ground and supplementary weft yarns, the more the supplementary weft will obscure the background.

Use supplementary wefts on a plain-weave ground, weaving one or two rows of plain weave with the background yarn in between each supplementary pattern row. The pattern will be denser if just one row of plain weave is woven between each supplementary weft pattern row.

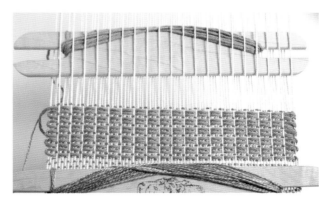

Two shuttles are alternated, one with a supplementary weft that weaves the pick-up row and another with a lighter-weight yarn that weaves plain weave. The pick-up pattern is 1 up, 1 down.

Creating Spots

What if you want to create spots rather than horizontal and vertical lines of floats? For this, you'll need two pick-up sticks, one to weave the first sequence and another to weave the second sequence. The first pick-up stick can stay in place when you use the second one, but in most cases, the second pick-up stick will need to be removed to weave the first sequence again. This takes a little more time, but it goes fairly quickly if you use the first pick-up stick as a guide.

A Note about Lace Structures

Lace structures may not be fully revealed until the fabric is removed from the loom and allowed to relax. This brings up a point about yarn behavior. The over-under-over-under arrangement of weaving provides structure that captures and keeps yarns in place. But each yarn in a weaving wants to escape—and will—if given a chance to do so. When you create floats, you provide opportunities for the yarns to move (which is perfectly illustrated by honeycomb, which I'll talk about a little later). When you sandwich a pick-up row between two up-shed rows, you introduce space in the structure that allows the yarns to bend, or escape, from the structure of the cloth.

SPOT LACE

To weave a spot lace, for example, you'll pick up the spots for the first sequence, leaving spaces between the spots for the next set of spots. Generally, you'll want the 2nd row of spots centered between the spots of the previous row.

Pick-up stick pattern A: *4 up, 2 down; repeat from *.

Pick-up stick pattern B: Pick up the first warp thread, *2 down, 4 up; repeat from *.

STEP 1. Up.

STEP 2. Pick-up stick A.

STEP 3. Up.

STEP 4. Pick-up stick A.

STEP 5. Up.

STEP 6. Down.

STEP 7. Up.

STEP 8. Pick-up stick B (slide pick-up stick A to the back of the loom and insert pick-up stick B).

STEP 9. Up.

STEP 10. Pick-up stick B.

STEP 11. Up.

STEP 12. Down.

Repeat these 12 steps for pattern.

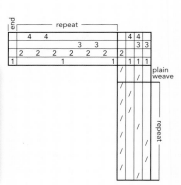

If you are weaving yards and yards of fabric, you'll find that taking the second pick-up stick in and out becomes a bit tedious. That's where string heddles and a heddle rod come to the rescue. See page 98 for instructions for making and using a heddle rod.

Combined Warp and Weft Floats

It's easy to combine both warp and weft floats in the same cloth, and often you can leave the pick-up stick in place for both. Just weave weft floats with your pick-up stick on edge (heddle in neutral) and create warp floats by sliding the pick-up stick forward with the heddle in the up position.

Pick-up stick pattern: *1 up, 2 down; repeat from *.

STEP 1. Up.

STEP 2. Pick-up stick (heddle in neutral, pick-up stick on edge).

STEP 3. Up.

STEP 4. Down.

STEP 5. Up and pick-up stick (heddle in up position, pick-up stick flat slid forward behind heddle).

STEP 6. Down.

STEP 7. Up and pick-up stick (heddle in up position, pick-up stick flat slid forward behind heddle).

STEP 8. Down.

Repeat these 8 steps for pattern.

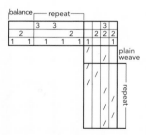

Managing Edges

You may notice that the weft yarn doesn't always catch at the edge of the weaving, especially when you use two weft yarns. When this happens, you can intentionally bring the weft thread around the edge warp thread or you can secure the working weft by twisting it around the resting weft.

Depending on the pattern, you may also be able to adjust the threading so that the last few threads at each edge are woven in plain weave. For example, when making warp floats, begin and end the pick-up pattern 2 or 3 warp ends from the selvedge.

To catch the selvedge warp thread on this pattern row, insert the shuttle over the selvedge warp end in order to catch the weft at the edge.

To catch the weft at this selvedge edge, insert the shuttle under the selvedge warp end.

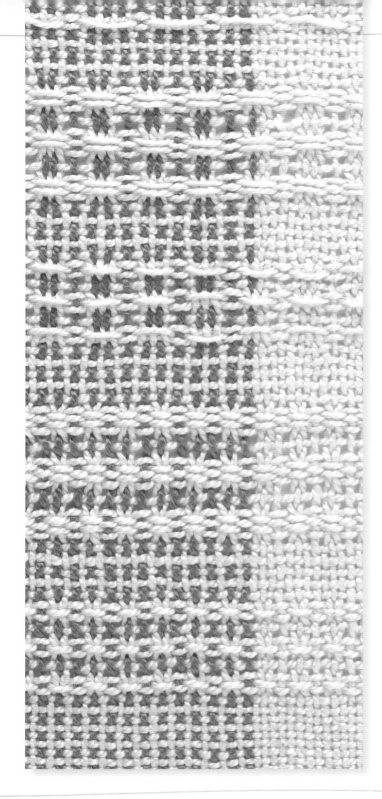

Weft-Float Sampler

The following samples illustrate many of the patterns possible on the rigid heddle loom. You'll see that many patterns can be woven on a single warp—and this is one of the wonderful advantages of rigid heddle pattern weaving: you can pick up and weave a 3/1 lace for awhile and then just take out your pick-up stick and try a 5/1 lace or a combination of the two. By contrast, unless you have a loom with many shafts, you would need to rethread for a new structure each time. This is what I mean about the power of the rigid heddle loom. It's simple and complicated at the same time.

I've included a draft with each of the following pick-up patterns so that you can translate them to shafts on a floor or table loom. All drafts are written for rising shed looms and are read from right to left and top to bottom. Many of the drafts require three and four shafts, although there is a sprinkling of patterns requiring five or more (but you can do them all with a lowly pick-up stick or two on a rigid heddle loom!). Keep in mind that it's not the sophistication of your equipment that creates stunning results, it is the sophistication of how you use yarn and color and structure and finishing that turns raw material into magnificent cloth.

These samples were woven with 3/2 pearl cotton threaded in a 10-dent reed. The right edge was threaded with natural; the left side was threaded with alternating gray and natural (gray in slots). Natural is used for weft. Brown Sheep Cotton Fleece in off-white is used for the supplementary weft float samples.

Sampler woven by Melissa Ludden Hankens.

3/1 LACE

Pick-up stick pattern: *1 up, 1 down; repeat from *.

STEP 1. Up.

STEP 2. Pick-up stick.

STEP 3. Up.

STEP 4. Down.

Repeat these 4 steps for pattern.

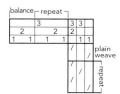

3/1 LACE, VARIATION

Pick-up stick pattern: *1 up, 1 down; repeat from *.

STEP 1. Up.

STEP 2. Pick-up stick.

STEP 3. Up.

STEP 4. Pick-up stick.

STEP 5. Up.

STEP 6. Down.

Repeat these 6 steps for pattern.

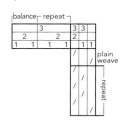

5/1 LACE

Pick-up stick pattern: *1 up, 2 down; repeat from *.

STEP 1. Up.

STEP 2. Pick-up stick.

STEP 3. Up.

STEP 4. Down.

Repeat these 4 steps for pattern.

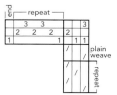

5/1 LACE, VARIATION

Pick-up stick pattern: *1 up, 2 down; repeat from *.

STEP 1. Up.

STEP 2. Pick-up stick.

STEP 3. Up.

STEP 4. Pick-up stick.

STEP 5. Up.

STEP 6. Down.

Repeat these 6 steps for pattern.

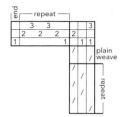

7/1 LACE

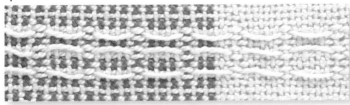

Pick-up stick pattern: *1 up, 3 down; repeat from *.

STEP 1. Up.

STEP 2. Pick-up stick.

STEP 3. Up.

STEP 4. Down.

Repeat these 4 steps for pattern.

7/1 LACE, VARIATION 2

Pick-up stick pattern: *1 up, 3 down; repeat from *.

STEP 1. Up.

STEP 2. Pick-up stick.

STEP 3. Up.

STEP 4. Pick-up stick.

STEP 5. Up.

STEP 6. Pick-up stick.

STEP 7. Up.

STEP 8. Down.

Repeat these 8 steps for pattern.

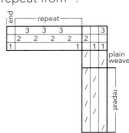

7/1 LACE, VARIATION

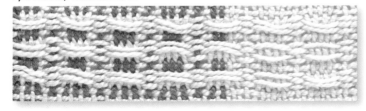

Pick-up stick pattern: *1 up, 3 down; repeat from *.

STEP 1. Up.

STEP 2. Pick-up stick.

STEP 3. Up.

STEP 4. Pick-up stick.

STEP 5. Up.

STEP 6. Down.

Repeat these 6 steps for pattern.

WEFT FLOATS SEPARATED WITH PLAIN WEAVE

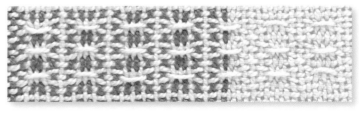

Pick-up stick pattern: *2 up, 2 down; repeat from *.

STEP 1. Up.

STEP 2. Pick-up stick.

STEP 3. Up.

STEP 4. Down.

Repeat these 4 steps for pattern.

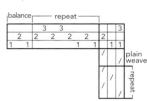

WEFT FLOATS SEPARATED WITH PLAIN WEAVE, VARIATION

Pick-up stick pattern: *2 up, 2 down; repeat from *.

STEP 1. Up.
STEP 2. Pick-up stick.
STEP 3. Up.
STEP 4. Pick-up stick.
STEP 5. Up.
STEP 6. Pick-up stick.
STEP 7. Up.
STEP 8. Down.
Repeat these 8 steps for pattern.

Planning Patterns

Because the same warp was used for many of the pick-up patterns in this section, not all of them work out evenly at the left selvedge. This is something you'll want to take into account when you plan a project. For example, if you weave a table runner, you'll want to make sure to balance the pattern across the weaving width so that the pattern is symmetrical between the right and left edges. I usually work out a pick-up pattern on a sample warp to determine the number of warp ends in each pattern repeat. From this I figure out the number of warp ends necessary for a particular project. When balancing a pattern, you may find it helpful to have each selvedge thread in a slot or in a hole. In other words, for a 1-up, 1-down threading, you may want to end with 1-up at the other selvedge to balance the pattern.

5/1 SPOT LACE

Pick-up stick pattern A: *4 up, 2 down; repeat from *.
Pick-up stick pattern B: 1 up, *2 down, 4 up; repeat from *.

STEP 1. Up.
STEP 2. Pick-up stick A.
STEP 3. Up.
STEP 4. Pick-up stick A.
STEP 5. Up.
STEP 6. Down.
STEP 7. Up.
STEP 8. Pick-up stick B.
STEP 9. Up.
STEP 10. Pick-up stick B.
STEP 11. Up.
STEP 12. Down.
Repeat these 12 steps for pattern.

3/1 AND 5/1 WEFT FLOATS

Pick-up stick pattern: *1 up, 1 down, 1 up, 1 down, 2 up, 2 down; repeat from *.

STEP 1. Up.
STEP 2. Pick-up stick.
STEP 3. Up.
STEP 4. Pick-up stick.
STEP 5. Up.
STEP 6. Down.
Repeat these 6 steps for pattern.

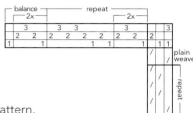

9/1 SPOT LACE

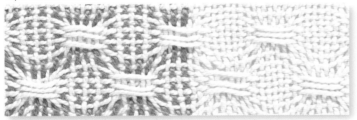

Pick-up stick pattern A: *4 up, 4 down; repeat from *.
Pick-up stick pattern B: *4 down, 4 up; repeat from*.
STEP 1. Up.
STEP 2. Pick-up stick A.
STEP 3. Up.
STEP 4. Pick-up stick A.
STEP 5. Up.
STEP 6. Pick-up stick A.
STEP 7. Up.
STEP 8. Down.
STEP 9. Up.
STEP 10. Pick-up stick B.
STEP 11. Up.
STEP 12. Pick-up stick B.
STEP 13. Up.
STEP 14. Pick-up stick B.
STEP 15. Up.
STEP 16. Down.
Repeat these 16 steps for pattern.

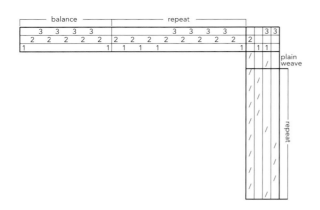

3/1 FLOATS WITH SUPPLEMENTARY WEFT

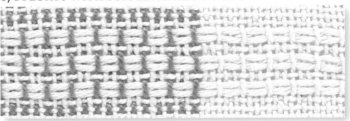

Pick-up stick pattern: *1 up, 1 down; repeat from *.
STEP 1. Up.
STEP 2. Pick-up stick, supplementary weft.
STEP 3. Down.
STEP 4. Pick-up stick, supplementary weft.
Repeat these 4 steps for pattern.

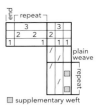

3/1 FLOATS WITH SUPPLEMENTARY WEFT, VARIATION

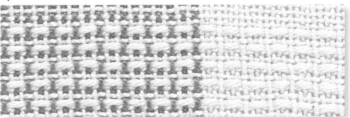

Pick-up stick pattern: *1 up, 1 down; repeat from *.
STEP 1. Up.
STEP 2. Down.
STEP 3. Pick-up stick, supplementary weft.
Repeat these 3 steps for pattern.

5/1 FLOATS WITH SUPPLEMENTARY WEFT

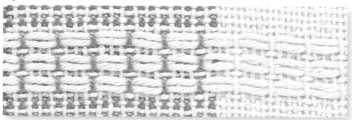

Pick-up stick pattern: *1 up, 2 down; repeat from *.
STEP 1. Up.
STEP 2. Pick-up stick,
supplementary weft.
STEP 3. Down.
STEP 4. Pick-up stick,
supplementary weft.
Repeat these 4 steps for pattern.

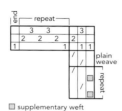

5/1 FLOATS WITH SUPPLEMENTARY WEFT, VARIATION

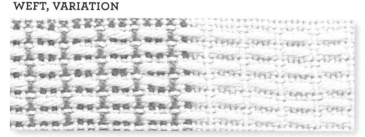

Pick-up stick pattern: *1 up, 2 down; repeat from *.
STEP 1. Up.
STEP 2. Down.
STEP 3. Pick-up stick,
supplementary weft.
Repeat these 3 steps for pattern.

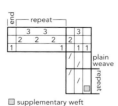

7/1 FLOATS WITH SUPPLEMENTARY WEFT

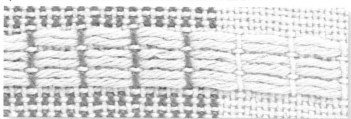

Pick-up stick pattern: *1 up, 3 down; repeat from *.
STEP 1. Up.
STEP 2. Pick-up stick,
supplementary weft.
STEP 3. Down.
STEP 4. Pick-up stick,
supplementary weft.
Repeat these 4 steps for pattern.

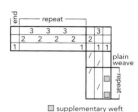

7/1 FLOATS WITH SUPPLEMENTARY WEFT, VARIATION

Pick-up stick pattern: *1 up, 3 down; repeat from *.
STEP 1. Up.
STEP 2. Down.
STEP 3. Pick-up stick,
supplementary weft.
Repeat these 3 steps for pattern.

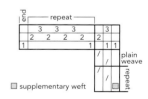

Multiple Pick-up Sticks

I wanted to show you just how far you can push pick-up. Here, I've used three pick-up-stick sequences to create a diamond motif. I could create even more intricate designs by adding additional pick-up patterns. As I've said before, there are few limitations to exploring the power of the pick-up stick. Shaft loom weavers should take note that this pattern requires 5 shafts. If you have just a 4-shaft loom but have a pattern that requires more, you can warp up your trusty rigid heddle loom and create it with pick-up sticks.

5/1 SPOT LACE DIAMONDS

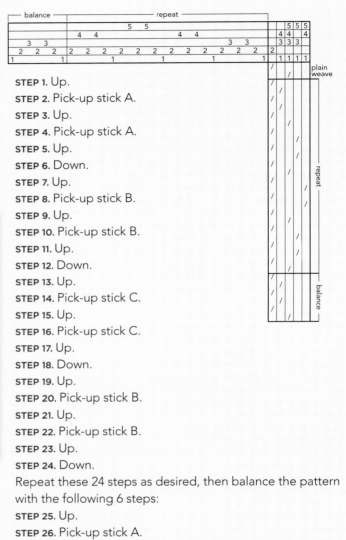

STEP 1. Up.
STEP 2. Pick-up stick A.
STEP 3. Up.
STEP 4. Pick-up stick A.
STEP 5. Up.
STEP 6. Down.
STEP 7. Up.
STEP 8. Pick-up stick B.
STEP 9. Up.
STEP 10. Pick-up stick B.
STEP 11. Up.
STEP 12. Down.
STEP 13. Up.
STEP 14. Pick-up stick C.
STEP 15. Up.
STEP 16. Pick-up stick C.
STEP 17. Up.
STEP 18. Down.
STEP 19. Up.
STEP 20. Pick-up stick B.
STEP 21. Up.
STEP 22. Pick-up stick B.
STEP 23. Up.
STEP 24. Down.

Repeat these 24 steps as desired, then balance the pattern with the following 6 steps:

STEP 25. Up.
STEP 26. Pick-up stick A.
STEP 27. Up.
STEP 28. Pick-up stick A.
STEP 29. Up.
STEP 30. Down.

Pick-up stick pattern A: 1 up, *2 down, 10 up; repeat from *.
Pick-up stick pattern B: *4 up, 2 down; repeat from *.
Pick-up stick pattern C: 7 up, *2 down, 10 up; repeat from *.

SUPPLEMENTARY WEFT FLOATS, VARIATION 1

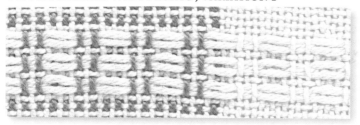

Pick-up stick pattern: *2 up, 2 down; repeat from *.

STEP 1. Up.

STEP 2. Pick-up stick, supplementary weft.

STEP 3. Down.

STEP 4. Pick-up stick, supplementary weft. Repeat these 4 steps for pattern.

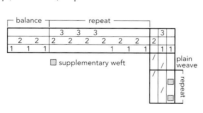

SUPPLEMENTARY WEFT FLOATS, VARIATION 2

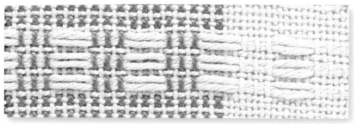

Pick-up stick pattern: *3 up, 3 down; repeat from *.

STEP 1. Up.

STEP 2. Pick-up stick, supplementary weft.

STEP 3. Down.

STEP 4. Pick-up stick, supplementary weft. Repeat these 4 steps for pattern.

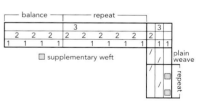

SUPPLEMENTARY WEFT FLOATS, VARIATION 3

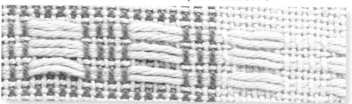

Pick-up stick pattern: *4 up, 4 down; repeat from *.

STEP 1. Up.

STEP 2. Pick-up stick, supplementary weft.

STEP 3. Down.

STEP 4. Pick-up stick, supplementary weft. Repeat these 4 steps for pattern.

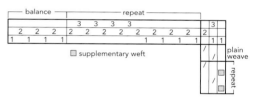

SUPPLEMENTARY WEFT DOTS

Pick-up stick pattern: *4 up, 1 down; repeat from *.

STEP 1. Up.

STEP 2. Pick-up stick, supplementary weft.

STEP 3. Down.

STEP 4. Pick-up stick, supplementary weft. Repeat these 4 steps for pattern.

This is just the beginning of what you can do with pick-up. Add in plaids, stripes, textured yarns, and variations of the above ideas, and you have a lifetime—or more!—of weaving ahead of you. And be reminded that there's a whole new world on the reverse side—any time you've produced a weft float on one side, there's a warp float on the other!

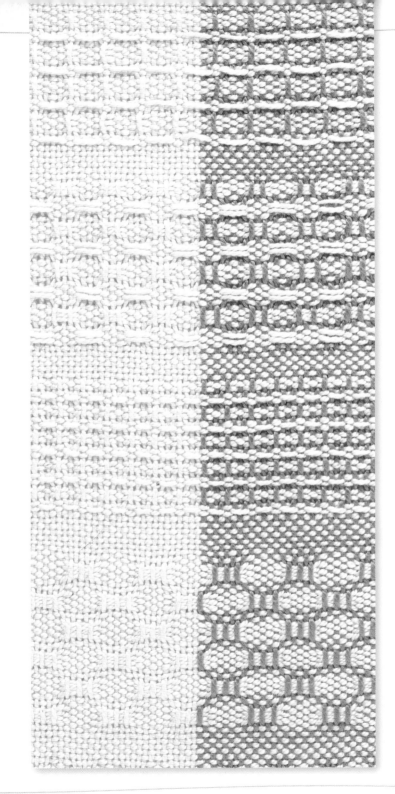

Warp-Float Sampler

warp-float samplers

For the following samples of warp-float weaves, two broad stripes of 3/2 pearl cotton, one in gray and the other in natural, are used for warp. The weft is 3/2 pearl cotton in natural. The warp is sett at 10 epi with 4" (10 cm), or 40 ends, each of gray and white for an 8" (20.5 cm) weaving width. It is woven at 15 ppi to create a weft-emphasis fabric. I like the way the warp floats show to good advantage in contrast to the weft. Sampler woven by Melissa Ludden Hankens.

SINGLE-WARP FLOATS

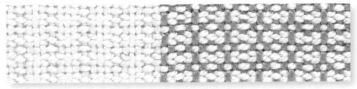

Pick-up stick pattern: *1 up, 1 down; repeat from *.

STEP 1. Down.
STEP 2. Up and pick-up stick.
STEP 3. Down.
STEP 4. Up.
Repeat these 4 steps for pattern.

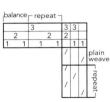

WARP FLOATS IN PAIRS

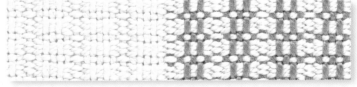

Pick-up stick pattern: *2 up, 1 down; repeat from *.

STEP 1. Down.
STEP 2. Up and pick-up stick.
STEP 3. Down.
STEP 4. Up and pick-up stick.
STEP 5. Down.
STEP 6. Up.
Repeat these 6 steps for pattern.

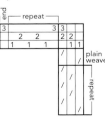

WARP FLOATS IN GROUPS OF THREE

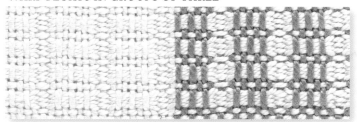

Pick-up stick pattern: *3 up, 1 down; repeat from *.

STEP 1. Down.

STEP 2. Up and pick-up stick.

STEP 3. Down.

STEP 4. Up and pick-up stick.

STEP 5. Down.

STEP 6. Up and pick-up stick.

STEP 7. Down.

STEP 8. Up.

Repeat these 8 steps for pattern.

balance		repeat						
		3	3	3			3	3
	2					2	2	
1	1	1	1	1	1	1	1	1

SPACED AND PAIRED WARP FLOATS

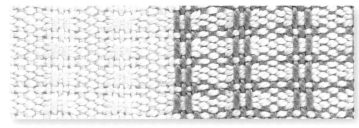

Pick-up stick pattern: *2 up, 2 down; repeat from *.

STEP 1. Down.

STEP 2. Up and pick-up stick.

STEP 3. Down.

STEP 4. Up and pick-up stick.

STEP 5. Down.

STEP 6. Up.

Repeat these 6 steps for pattern.

balance		repeat					
		3		3		3	3
2	2			2	2	2	
1	1	1	1	1	1	1	1

PAIRED WARP FLOATS IN ALTERNATING BLOCKS

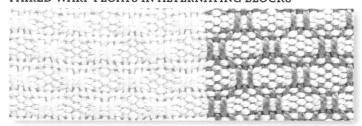

Pick-up stick pattern A: *2 up, 2 down; repeat from *.

Pick-up stick pattern B: *2 down, 2 up; repeat from *.

STEP 1. Down.

STEP 2. Up and pick-up stick A.

STEP 3. Down.

STEP 4. Up and pick-up stick A.

STEP 5. Down.

STEP 6. Up.

STEP 7. Down.

STEP 8. Up and pick-up stick B.

STEP 9. Down.

STEP 10. Up and pick-up stick B.

STEP 11. Down.

STEP 12. Up.

Repeat these 12 steps for pattern.

balance		repeat							
		3		3			3	3	
2	2			2	2	2			2
1	1	1	1	1	1	1	1	1	1

WARP FLOATS IN GROUPS OF THREE, ALTERNATING BLOCKS

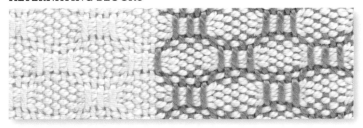

Notice how the line between the blocks curves. This is what happens when sets of threads woven in blocks alternate to produce a structure called honeycomb (more on this later).

Pick-up stick pattern A: *3 up, 3 down; repeat from *.
Pick-up stick pattern B: *3 down, 3 up; repeat from *.

STEP 1. Down.
STEP 2. Up and pick-up stick A.
STEP 3. Down.
STEP 4. Up and pick-up stick A.
STEP 5. Down.
STEP 6. Up and pick-up stick A.
STEP 7. Down.
STEP 8. Up.

Repeat Steps 1–8 with pick-up stick B; repeat 8-step blocks of A and B for pattern.

Again, check the reverse to see what's happening on the other side in the way of weft floats. Because the floats are in the warp, you'll find that they take a bit more planning—especially if you want to introduce color. If you want your warp floats to be an accent color or different texture, be sure to thread them in the slots.

Making and Using a Heddle Rod

When using two pick-up sticks that don't slide past each other, you need to remove one after each pick and replace it when it's needed again. If you need to do this only occasionally, it feels doable, but if you need to re-pick every 3rd or 4th row, it becomes tedious and slow. A wonderful solution is to make string heddles and attach them to a heddle rod to lift the necessary threads.

To make reusable heddles, use your rigid heddle as a template. First, measure 18" (45.5 cm) lengths of cotton carpet warp (any strong smooth cotton string will do) for as many warp ends as will be lifted. For efficiency sake, measure all the lengths at once. Tie each length of cotton around the rigid heddle in a good, hard square knot. It is important to try to tie all the heddles tightly (so they don't come undone) and of consistent length (so all the warp ends raise to the same height). Cut all of the tails to less than ¼" (6 mm) so they don't get in the way. Remove the loops from the rigid heddle template.

To install the heddles on the loom, insert the pick-up stick in the pattern that the heddles will be lifting. Leave the pick-up stick in place, flat, so you can easily see which warp threads need heddles. Then, slip a string loop under the desired warp thread, fold it in half, and insert both loops over the heddle rod. Continue across the warp until all threads on the pick-up stick are installed on the heddle rod.

To prevent the string heddles from sliding off the rod and to hold them in place, cover the top of the heddle rod with masking tape. I like to use painter's masking tape because it isn't very sticky and can be easily removed at the end of the project.

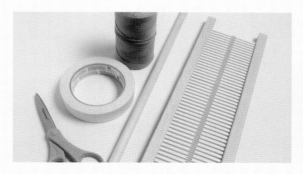

1. You'll need a heddle rod or stick, strong string such as cotton carpet warp, your rigid heddle as a template for tying the heddles, and masking tape.

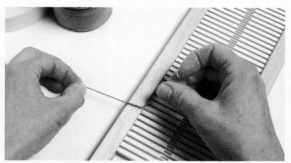

2. Use your rigid heddle reed as a template for tying string heddles the proper length.

3. Insert the pick-up stick in the shed, leaving it flat. Fold the string heddle in half and place it under the warp thread.

4. Slip the doubled string heddle over the heddle rod.

5. After all the string heddles have been installed, lift up the heddle bar so that the loops are taut.

6. Cover the string loops with masking tape to keep them in place and to prevent the rod from slipping out.

Warp and Weft Floats

It is fun to use the same pick-up stick pattern to create warp and weft floats. Here are a few of what I call mock waffle weave or windowpane floats. (*Note:* A true waffle weave, characterized by deep cells, isn't easily created on the rigid heddle loom. This type of weave is more suitable for a harness loom—the more shafts the better.)

SINGLE WARP AND WEFT FLOATS IN A DELICATE, LACELIKE EFFECT

Pick-up stick pattern: *1 up, 1 down; repeat from *.

STEP 1. Up.
STEP 2. Pick-up stick.
STEP 3. Up.
STEP 4. Down.
STEP 5. Up and pick-up stick.
STEP 6. Down.
Repeat these 6 steps for pattern.

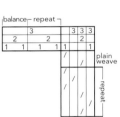

DOUBLE WINDOWPANE, MOCK WAFFLE WEAVE

Pick-up stick pattern: *2 up, 2 down; repeat from *.

STEP 1. Up.
STEP 2. Pick-up stick.
STEP 3. Up.
STEP 4. Pick-up stick.
STEP 5. Up.
STEP 6. Down.
STEP 7. Up and pick-up stick.
STEP 8. Down.
STEP 9. Up and pick-up stick.
STEP 10. Down.
Repeat these 10 steps for pattern.

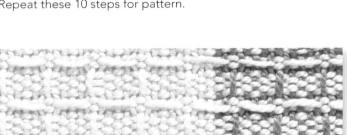

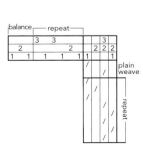

SINGLE WINDOWPANE

Pick-up stick pattern: *1 up, 2 down; repeat from *.

STEP 1. Up.
STEP 2. Pick-up stick.
STEP 3. Up.
STEP 4. Down.
STEP 5. Up and pick-up stick.
STEP 6. Down.
STEP 7. Up and pick-up stick.
STEP 8. Down.
Repeat these 8 steps for pattern.

3 × 3 × 2 × 2 SQUARES

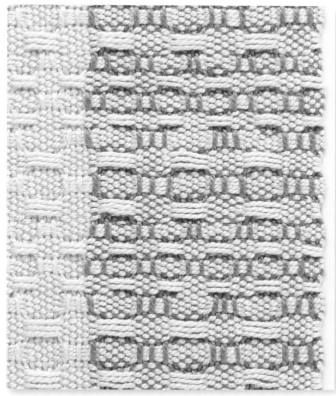

This sample has a very long treadling sequence. Here the aim was to create an irregular pattern by changing the pick-up stick sequence between sections.

Pick-up stick pattern A: *2 up, 2 down; repeat from *.

Pick-up stick pattern B: *3 up, 3 down; repeat from *.

STEP 1. Up.

STEP 2. Pick-up stick A.

STEP 3. Up.

STEP 4. Pick-up stick A.

STEP 5. Up.

STEP 6. Down.

STEP 7. Up and pick-up stick A.

STEP 8. Down.

STEP 9. Up and pick-up stick A.

STEP 10. Down.

Repeat Steps 1–10 once more, then work pattern B as follows:

STEP 1. Up.

STEP 2. Pick-up stick B.

STEP 3. Up.

STEP 4. Pick-up stick B.

STEP 5. Up.

STEP 6. Pick-up stick B.

STEP 7. Up.

STEP 8. Down.

STEP 9. Up and pick-up stick B.

STEP 10. Down.

STEP 11. Up and pick-up stick B.

STEP 12. Down.

STEP 13. Up and pick-up stick B.

STEP 14. Down.

Repeat Steps 1–14 once more, then repeat the entire sequence for pattern.

LARGE DOUBLE WINDOWPANE

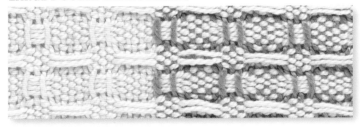

Pick-up stick pattern: *2 up, 3 down; repeat from *.

STEP 1. Up.
STEP 2. Pick-up stick.
STEP 3. Up.
STEP 4. Pick-up stick.
STEP 5. Up.
STEP 6. Down.
STEP 7. Up and pick-up stick.
STEP 8. Down.
STEP 9. Up and pick-up stick.
STEP 10. Down.
STEP 11. Up and pick-up stick.
STEP 12. Down.
Repeat these 12 steps for pattern.

Spots

Just as in the weft-float spot weaves, warp-float spots are created with two pick-up sticks by alternating which floats are lifted, block fashion.

TINY ALTERNATING WARP SPOTS

Pick-up stick pattern A: *2 up, 2 down; repeat from *.
Pick-up stick pattern B: *2 down, 2 up; repeat from *.

STEP 1. Down.
STEP 2. Up and pick-up stick A.
STEP 3. Down.
STEP 4. Up.
STEP 5. Down.
STEP 6. Up and pick-up stick B.
STEP 7. Down.
STEP 8. Up.
Repeat these 8 steps for pattern.

TEXTURE WITH WARP AND WEFT FLOATS

A textured float surface with small warp and weft single-end floats creates a subtle allover texture. I especially like the white-on-white sample for its delicate texture.

Pick-up stick pattern A: *3 up, 1 down; repeat from *.
Pick-up stick pattern B: *1 up, 3 down; repeat from *.

STEP 1. Up.
STEP 2. Pick-up stick A.
STEP 3. Up.
STEP 4. Down.
STEP 5. Up and pick-up stick B.
STEP 6. Down.
Repeat these 6 steps for pattern.

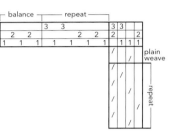

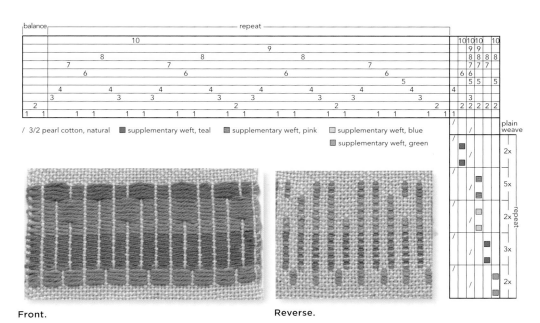

Exploring Weft Floats

The following samples illustrate ways to interpret basic threadings/interlacements in design. Many of these involve 3/1 weft float patterns (1 up, 1 down) woven in a variety of manners. They illustrate how you can use a variety of pick-up floats to create designs that might require ten shafts on a shaft loom. This is an example of the power of the rigid heddle loom—so much can be accomplished with just a pick-up stick!

Warp: 3/2 pearl cotton in natural, threaded 6" (15 cm) wide in a 10-dent reed.

Weft: 3/2 pearl cotton background or plain weave; Brown Sheep Cotton Fleece for supplementary weft, except where noted.

SOLID BANDS

For this sample, I used different pick-up patterns and several supplementary wefts to create a solid band of floats. I like the way the solid vertical lines between the horizontal weft floats add dimension to the pattern. The reverse is quite different—light and airy with a pointillist feel.

Pick-up stick pattern A: *1 up, 2 down; repeat from *.

STEP 1. Up.

STEP 2. Pick-up stick, supplementary weft, teal.

STEP 3. Down.

STEP 4. Pick-up stick, supplementary weft, teal.

Repeat these 4 steps once more.

Pick-up stick pattern B: *1 up, 1 down; repeat from *.

STEP 1. Up.

STEP 2. Pick-up stick, supplementary weft, pink.

STEP 3. Down

STEP 4. Pick-up stick, supplementary weft, pink.

Repeat these 4 steps 4 more times.

Pick-up stick pattern C: *1 up, 1 down; repeat from *.

STEP 1. Up.

STEP 2. Pick-up stick, supplementary weft, blue.

STEP 3. Down.

STEP 4. Pick-up stick, supplementary weft, blue.

Repeat these 4 steps once more.

Pick-up stick pattern D: 1 up, *3 down, 1 up, 1 down, 1 up, 1 down, 1 up; repeat from *.

STEP 1. Up.

STEP 2. Pick-up stick, supplementary weft, teal.

STEP 3. Down.

STEP 4. Pick-up stick, supplementary weft, teal.

Repeat these 4 steps 2 more times.

Pick-up stick pattern E: *1 up, 1 down, 1 up, 3 down; repeat from *.

STEP 1. Up.

STEP 2. Pick-up stick, supplementary weft, green.

STEP 3. Down.

STEP 4. Pick-up stick, supplementary weft, green.

Repeat these 4 steps once more.

Reverse: Spots of color appear on the reverse side. To me, this example looks like reflections on water—an effect that could be enhanced with color choices.

Front.

Reverse.

WEFT FLOATS AND PLAIN-WEAVE DOTS

Front.

Reverse.

In this example, rows of supplementary weft floats are divided with a single pick in a contrasting color of supplementary weft woven in a plain-weave shed. I like the contrast of scale created by the single plain-weave weft dots and the longer supplementary floats. 5/2 pearl cotton is used for background.

Pick-up pattern: *1 up, 1 down; repeat from *.

+ ** **STEP 1.** Pick-up stick, supplementary weft, blue.

STEP 2. Up.

STEP 3. Down.

Repeat these 3 steps 2 more times+, then weave:

STEP 4. Up, pattern weft, green or pink.

STEP 5. Down.

STEP 6. Up.**

Repeat from ** to ** 2 more times, ending with the first sequence (+ to +), being sure to always alternate the plain weave background. For example, on the next repeat, Step 2 will fall in the down shed.

Reverse: Where a bolder pattern appears on the face of the cloth, there is a subtle and equally pleasing pattern on the other side.

WEFT FLOATS AND PLAIN-WEAVE DOTS, VARIATION

Front.

Reverse.

Here, 3 wefts are used: 5/2 in Wisteria (pink) and Bleached White (white) contrast with the fluffy Nymph (blue) Cotton Fleece supplementary weft. The contrast of scale gives this sample a lighthearted feel that would not be possible had yarns of all the same size been used.

Pick-up stick pattern: *1 up, 1 down; repeat from *.

STEP 1. Pick-up stick, supplementary weft, blue.

STEP 2. Up, 5/2 pink.

STEP 3. Pick-up stick, supplementary weft, blue.

STEP 4. Down, 5/2 white.

STEP 5. Up, 5/2 white.

STEP 6. Down, 5/2 white.

Repeat these 6 steps for pattern.

Reverse: I like the delicate quality of this face. On this side, you can see the interaction of the natural 3/2 pearl cotton warp and the 5/2 white weft.

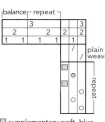

☐ supplementary weft, blue
◉ 5/2 pearl cotton, pink
○ 5/2 pearl cotton, white

TAPESTRY EFFECT

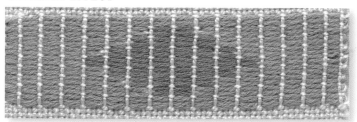

For an allover pattern with a tapestry-like effect, I wove a diamond by inserting colors according to a diagram. Each float area equals one square on the graph paper. Three butterflies of yarn are required—1 pink (Tea Rose Cotton Fleece) and 2 blue (Nymph Cotton Fleece)—in the areas where the diamond is bordered on each side.

Pick-up stick pattern: *1 up, 1 down; repeat from *.

STEP 1. Pick-up stick, supplementary wefts, following diagram below for color placement.

STEP 2. Up.

STEP 3. Pick-up stick, supplementary wefts.

STEP 4. Down.

Repeat these 4 steps for pattern.

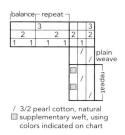

/ 3/2 pearl cotton, natural
▢ supplementary weft, using colors indicated on chart

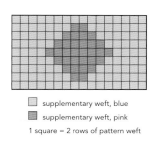

▢ supplementary weft, blue
▨ supplementary weft, pink

1 square = 2 rows of pattern weft

COMBINING ELEMENTS

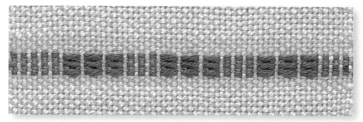

Front.

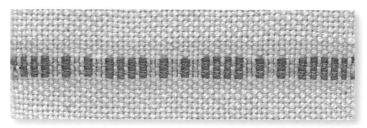

Reverse.

By combining several elements, this dainty border has a lot going on. 3/2 pearl cotton in Daffodil (yellow) on each side frames the supplementary-weft border; the block pick-up pattern enhances the textural appeal.

Pick-up stick pattern: *4 up, 1 down, 1 up, 1 down, 1 up, 1 down; repeat from *.

STEP 1. Weave 3 rows of plain weave in 3/2 pearl cotton, yellow.

STEP 2. Pick-up stick, supplementary weft, teal.

STEP 3. Weave 2 rows of plain weave in 5/2 cotton, pink.

STEP 4. Pick-up stick, supplementary weft, teal.

STEP 5. Weave 2 rows of plain weave in 5/2 cotton, pink.

STEP 6. Pick-up stick, supplementary weft, teal.

STEP 7. Weave 3 rows of plain weave in 3/2 pearl cotton, yellow.

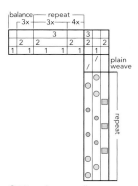

◎ 3/2 pearl cotton, yellow
▢ supplementary weft, light blue
◉ 5/2 pearl cotton, pink

COLUMNS

Front.

Reverse.

In this sample, columns form along the areas of pick-up. The thick supplementary weft creates a thick line of floats.

Pick-up pattern: 4 up, *2 down, 1 up, 2 down, 5 up; repeat from *.

STEP 1. Up, 3/2 pearl cotton, yellow.

STEP 2. Down, 3/2 pearl cotton, yellow.

STEP 3. Up, 3/2 pearl cotton, yellow.

STEP 4. Pick-up stick, supplementary weft, blue.

STEP 5. Up, supplementary weft, blue.

STEP 6. Pick-up stick, supplementary weft, blue.

Repeat these 6 steps for pattern.

Reverse: Columns of pale warp floats contrast with the horizontal color stripes.

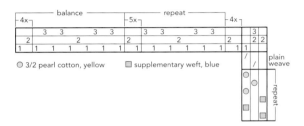

SUPPLEMENTARY WEFT WITH LACE

Front.

Combine weft supplementary floats with weft lace for a border that could be used at an edge or as an allover pattern motif. Again, different sizes of yarn contribute to the tactile quality of this sample.

Pick-up stick pattern: *1 up, 1 down; repeat from *.

Border:

STEP 1. Pick-up stick, supplementary weft, pink.

STEP 2. Up, 5/2 pearl cotton, light blue.

STEP 3. Down, 5/2 pearl cotton, light blue.

STEP 4. Repeat these 3 steps 3 times, end with pick-up stick, supplementary weft, pink.

Lace (3/2 pearl cotton in natural):

STEP 1. Up.

STEP 2. Pick-up stick.

STEP 3. Up.

STEP 4. Down.

STEP 5. Repeat these 4 steps 5 times, then weave the border again.

SUPPLEMENTARY WEFT WITH LACE, VARIATION

Front.

Reverse.

Blue dots and dashes are framed by a pink and green border. There's nothing fancy about this sample, yet it has a delightful quality about it.

Weft: Lime Light (green) Cotton Fleece for supplementary weft; Wisteria (pink) 5/2 pearl cotton for the border; Natural and Mineral (blue) 3/2 pearl cotton for spot lace.

Pick-up stick pattern A (for border): *1 up, 1 down; repeat from *.

Pick-up stick pattern B: *5 up, 1 down; repeat from *.

Pick-up stick pattern C: 2 up, 1 down, *5 up, 1 down; repeat from *.

Border:

STEP 1. Up, 3/2 pearl cotton, natural.

STEP 2. Pick-up stick A, supplementary weft, green.

STEP 3. Up, 5/2 pearl cotton, pink.

STEP 4. Pick-up stick A, supplementary weft, green.

STEP 5. Up, 3/2 pearl cotton, natural.

STEP 6. Down, 3/2 pearl cotton, natural.

Spot lace:

STEP 1. Up, 3/2 pearl cotton, natural.

STEP 2. Pick-up stick B, 3/2 pearl cotton, blue.

STEP 3. Up, 3/2 pearl cotton, natural.

STEP 4. Pick-up stick B, 3/2 pearl cotton, blue.

STEP 5. Up, 3/2 pearl cotton, natural.

STEP 6. Down, 3/2 pearl cotton, natural.

STEP 7. Repeat the 6-step spot-lace sequence using pick-up stick C. Then repeat both spot-lace sequences again, then repeat the border.

Reverse: I like the single warp float separating the blue weft lines, lending texture and creating ovals instead of straight lines.

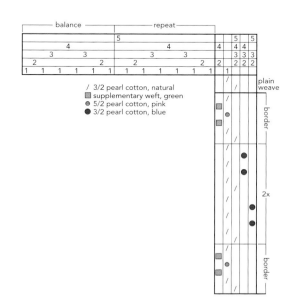

/ 3/2 pearl cotton, natural
▫ supplementary weft, green
● 5/2 pearl cotton, pink
● 3/2 pearl cotton, blue

INLAID PATTERN

For this example, I inlaid the supplementary weft in my pick-up rows into three areas of 4 floats each. Inlaying sections separately serves to isolate the blocks, resulting in a bolder statement. I placed the pick-up stick all the way across the warp and then chose sections for the picked-up blocks. You'll need a separate butterfly of supplementary weft for each block—I used Rue (teal) and Petal Pink (pink) Cotton Fleece for the supplementary wefts, 3/2 pearl cotton in natural and Pistachio (green) for the background, doubling it for the single rows of green, and 5/2 pearl cotton in Mineral (blue) between the two pink supplementary weft rows of the border.

Pick-up stick pattern: *1 up, 1 down; repeat from *.

STEP 1. Pick-up stick, supplementary weft, pink.

STEP 2. Up, 5/2 pearl cotton, blue.

STEP 3. Down, 5/2 pearl cotton, blue.

STEP 4. Pick-up stick, supplementary weft, pink.

STEP 5. Up.

STEP 6. Down.

STEP 7. Up, green doubled.

STEP 8. Down.

STEP 9. Up.

STEP 10. Down.

STEP 11. Pick-up stick. Inlay row with supplementary weft in teal, each block is 4 floats wide; 2 float spaces were skipped before the next block.

STEP 12. Up.

STEP 13. Repeat Step 11.

STEP 14. Down.

STEPS 15–22. Repeat Steps 11–14 two more times.

STEP 23. Repeat Step 11.

STEP 24. Up.

STEP 25. Down.

STEP 26. Up.

STEP 27. Down, green doubled.

STEP 28. Up.

STEP 29. Down.

STEP 30. Pick-up stick, supplementary weft, pink.

STEP 31. Up, 5/2 pearl cotton, blue.

STEP 32. Down, 5/2 pearl cotton, blue.

STEP 33. Pick-up stick, supplementary weft, pink.

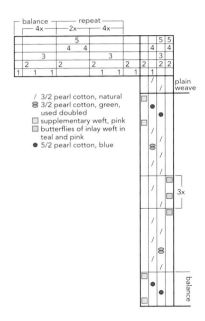

/ 3/2 pearl cotton, natural
8 3/2 pearl cotton, green, used doubled
☐ supplementary weft, pink
☐ butterflies of inlay weft in teal and pink
● 5/2 pearl cotton, blue

INLAID BLOCKS, VARIATION

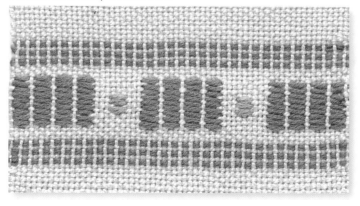

In this sample, I handstitched a little blue dot in the center between the blocks (you can weave the blue dot in on a shaft loom—which is reflected in the draft). On a closed shed, I placed blue weft over 3 warps, repeating between plain-weave rows 3 times while doing my inlay rows. For the border of this sample, I alternated a smaller 3/2 pearl cotton with a heavier-weight Cotton Fleece so the blue predominates.

Weft: Cotton Fleece in Rue (teal), Petal Pink (pink), and Nymph (blue); 3/2 pearl cotton in Daffodil (yellow) and Natural.

Pick-up stick pattern: *1 up, 1 down; repeat from *.

Border:

STEP 1. Up, 3/2 pearl cotton, yellow.

STEP 2. Down, Cotton Fleece, teal.

Repeat these 2 steps 2 more times, then weave another pick of yellow—7 rows total.

Pick-up pattern area (use 3/2 natural for plain-weave background):

STEP 1. Down.

STEP 2. Up.

STEP 3. Down.

STEP 4. Pick-up stick, supplementary weft, inlay pink.

STEP 5. Up.

STEP 6. Pick-up stick, supplementary weft, inlay pink.

STEP 7. Repeat Steps 3–6 three more times; on the 4th, 5th, and 6th rows of supplementary inlay, stitch a blue dot in the center in between each inlaid area, traveling over 3 warp ends.

STEP 8. Down.

STEP 9. Pick-up stick, supplementary weft, inlay pink.

STEP 10. Up.

STEP 11. Down.

STEP 12. Up.

Border:

STEP 1. Down, 3/2 pearl cotton, yellow.

STEP 2. Up, Cotton Fleece, teal.

STEP 3. Repeat Steps 1 and 2 two more times.

STEP 4. Down, 3/2 pearl cotton, yellow.

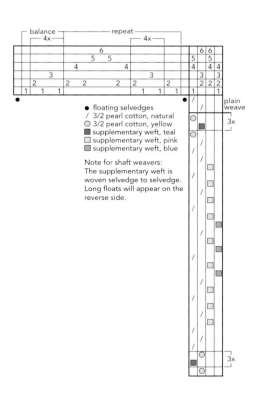

FLOATS FOR FRINGY EFFECTS

Front.

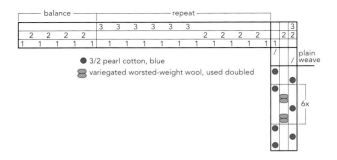

Reverse.

You can create little fringes in your fabric by weaving long floats and then cutting them after the fabric is washed. I like how the colors in the yarn produce soft color changes in the pattern areas. The floats in this example are too long to be practical for most uses—but when cut, they produce a fun, fringy detail.

Weft: 3/2 pearl cotton in Mineral (blue) for background; worsted-weight Cascade Paints #9863, doubled, for the supplementary wefts.

Pick-up stick pattern: *4 up, 6 down; repeat from *.

To begin, weave 1 row in the up shed and 1 row in the down shed. Weave pattern as follows:

STEP 1. Up.

STEP 2. Pick-up stick, supplementary weft (doubled weft).

STEP 3. Down.

STEP 4. Pick-up stick, supplementary weft (doubled weft). Repeat these 4 steps 6 times.

STEP 5. Up.

STEP 6. Down.

STEP 7. Up.

Reverse: The blocks of supplementary weft that appear on the reverse side almost look like doubleweave blocks. Inlay sections of different colors to increase the complexity of this design.

balance					repeat											
					3	3	3	3	3							3
2	2	2	2							2	2	2	2		2	2
1	1	1	1	1	1	1	1	1	1	1	1	1	1	1	1	

/ plain weave

● 3/2 pearl cotton, blue

◙ variegated worsted-weight wool, used doubled

6x

BOWS

Front.

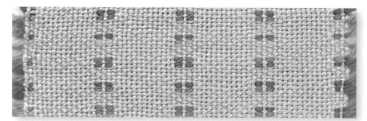

Reverse.

If you repeat each pattern row just 2 times and then weave plain weave between each set, you can isolate the pattern rows to create a light, delicate pattern after the floats are cut. Again, variation in the pattern yarn makes for subtle variations in color, contributing to the general appeal of these motifs.

Weft: 3/2 pearl cotton in Petal Pink (pink) for the background; Cascade Paints #9863 for the supplementary pattern weft.

Pick-up stick pattern: *2 up, 6 down; repeat from *.

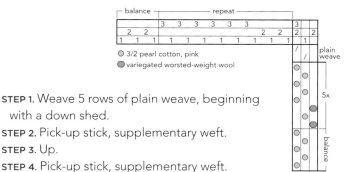

balance			repeat								
		3	3	3	3	3	3			3	
2	2							2	2	2	2
1	1	1	1	1	1	1	1	1	1	1	1

○ 3/2 pearl cotton, pink
● variegated worsted-weight wool

STEP 1. Weave 5 rows of plain weave, beginning with a down shed.

STEP 2. Pick-up stick, supplementary weft.

STEP 3. Up.

STEP 4. Pick-up stick, supplementary weft.

STEP 5. Repeat Steps 1–4 four more times, ending with 5 rows of plain weave.

Reverse: Columns of dots appear on the reverse side where the floats on the front are tied down by warp.

EXPLORING CUT WEFTS

Front.

Reverse.

In this sample, I offset the blocks to create a lattice pattern of floats on the surface—great for a pillow top.

Weft: 3/2 pearl cotton in Pistachio (green) for the background; Cascade Paints #9863, tripled, for the supplementary pattern weft.

Pick-up stick pattern A: *2 up, 6 down; repeat from *.

Pick-up stick pattern B: 4 down, *2 up, 6 down; repeat from *.

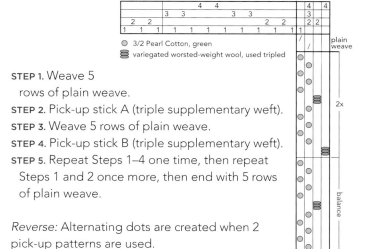

balance			repeat							
			4	4					4	4
		3	3			3	3		3	
2	2						2	2	2	2
1	1	1	1	1	1	1	1	1	1	1

○ 3/2 Pearl Cotton, green
▨ variegated worsted-weight wool, used tripled

STEP 1. Weave 5 rows of plain weave.

STEP 2. Pick-up stick A (triple supplementary weft).

STEP 3. Weave 5 rows of plain weave.

STEP 4. Pick-up stick B (triple supplementary weft).

STEP 5. Repeat Steps 1–4 one time, then repeat Steps 1 and 2 once more, then end with 5 rows of plain weave.

Reverse: Alternating dots are created when 2 pick-up patterns are used.

FUZZY BOWS

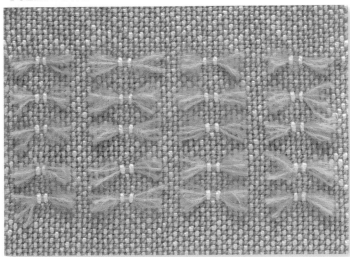

Fuzzy accents are created by weaving mohair floats and then cutting them for little fringy accents.

Weft: 3/2 pearl cotton in Pistachio (green) for the background; Louet Brushed Mohair in Sunflower (yellow), used doubled, for the supplementary pattern weft.

Pick-up stick pattern: 4 down, *2 up, 6 down; repeat from *.

STEP 1. Weave 8 rows of plain weave.

STEP 2. Pick-up stick, doubled yellow mohair.

STEP 3. Weave 8 rows of plain weave.

STEP 4. Repeat Steps 2 and 3 for pattern.

STEP 5. End with 8 rows of plain weave.

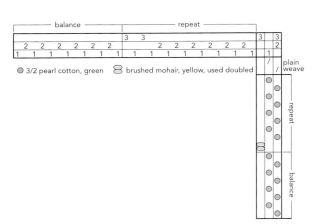

balance						repeat								
						3	3						3	3
2	2	2	2	2	2			2	2	2	2	2		2
1	1	1	1	1	1	1	1	1	1	1	1	1	1	1

● 3/2 pearl cotton, green   ⊗ brushed mohair, yellow, used doubled

ALTERNATING FUZZY ACCENTS

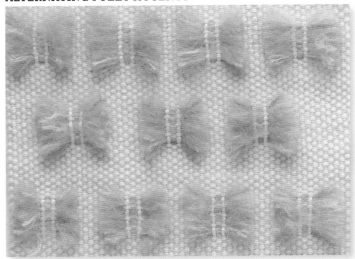

In this sample, I used Brown Sheep Nature Spun Sport Weight wool in Aran (natural) for the plain-weave background and wove alternating floats with Louet Brushed Mohair in Buttercup, Sunflower, Soft Yellow, and Lichen. I like how the colors blend together to create a soft plush look and feel.

balance				repeat								
	4	4					4	4			4	4
			3	3						3	3	
2	2			2	2		2	2			2	
1	1	1	1	1	1	1	1	1	1	1	1	

○ sportweight wool, natural
▤ brushed mohair, in three yellows and yellow green, used together

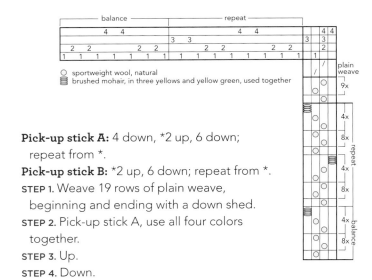

Pick-up stick A: 4 down, *2 up, 6 down; repeat from *.

Pick-up stick B: *2 up, 6 down; repeat from *.

STEP 1. Weave 19 rows of plain weave, beginning and ending with a down shed.

STEP 2. Pick-up stick A, use all four colors together.

STEP 3. Up.

STEP 4. Down.

STEP 5. Repeat Steps 2–4 three more times.

STEP 6. Weave 17 rows of plain weave, beginning and ending with an up shed.

STEP 7. Pick-up stick B, use all four colors together.

STEP 8. Down.

STEP 9. Up.

STEP 10. Repeat Steps 7–9 three more times.

STEP 11. Weave 17 rows of plain weave, beginning and ending with a down shed.

Repeat Steps 2–10 for pattern, ending with Steps 2–6 for balance.

Cut the center of the long floats.

HONEYCOMB

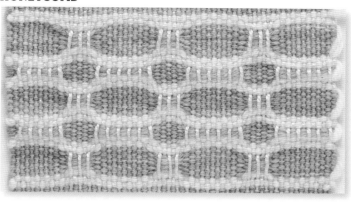

For this sample, I alternated two different sizes of cells and wove the cells with Brown Sheep Wildfoote handpainted sock yarn in Sonatino, beating it in tightly to almost completely cover the warp. The 3/2 Pearl Cotton Natural warp floats and white sportweight wool (Brown Sheep, Natural) used doubled for the outlining weft provide a stark contrast to the subtle color variations of the cell weft.

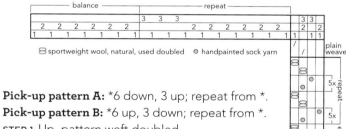

Pick-up pattern A: *6 down, 3 up; repeat from *.

Pick-up pattern B: *6 up, 3 down; repeat from *.

STEP 1. Up, pattern weft doubled.

STEP 2. Down, pattern weft doubled.

STEP 3. Up and pick-up stick A.

STEP 4. Down.

STEP 5. Repeat Steps 3 and 4 four more times.

STEP 6. Up, pattern weft doubled.

STEP 7. Down, pattern weft doubled.

STEP 8. Up and pick-up stick B.

STEP 9. Down.

STEP 10. Repeat Steps 8 and 9 four more times.

Repeat the entire sequence for desired length.

STEP 11. End with up, pattern weft doubled and down, pattern weft doubled.

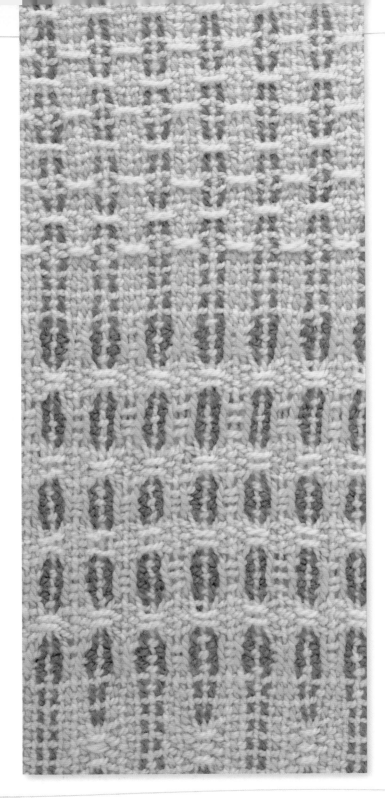

Exploring Warp Floats

When designing for warp floats you'll need to plan your warp design prior to warping your loom. On the plus side, designing floats in the warp often means you can weave with just one shuttle, speeding the weaving process. In the minus column is the fact that once you have your warp threaded, there's no changing the color order.

For this sampler, I explored simple warp float patterns and color. Notice that the same warp pattern looks quite different depending on the color of the weft. The warp is Louet Gems Fingering Wool in Goldilocks (yellow), Fern Green (dark green), and Willow (light green) sett 8½" (21.5 cm) wide at 10 epi.

For the first six samples, I used two treadling sequences, testing all three colors with both treadlings. This is often how I sample for a project, trying different combinations until I find one that I like. The only change between the two treadling sequences is an additional pick-up sequence to create slightly longer warp floats. If I were designing for a project, I would eliminate the dark green weft samples because the dark green overpowers the float structure that I want to highlight. I used yellow weft for the second two samples, which allows the dark green warp floats to predominate. However, I find the light green weft in the last sample more interesting because of the interaction between all three colors and the structure. I find the reverse of the swatches using light green and yellow weft dynamic as well.

Warp Threading Color Order

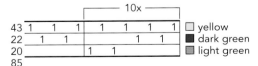

In rigid heddle, thread yellow through holes; dark and light green through slots.

SAMPLE 1, WEAVING SEQUENCE 1

Weaving sequence 1 with dark green weft.

Reverse.

Weaving sequence 1 with yellow weft.

Reverse.

Weaving sequence 1 with light green weft.

Reverse.

WEAVING SEQUENCE 1

Pick-up stick pattern: *2 up, 2 down; repeat from *
(all dark green are picked up).

STEP 1. Down.

STEP 2. Up and pick-up stick.

STEP 3. Down.

STEP 4. Up.

Repeat these 4 steps for pattern.

Treadling Sequence 1

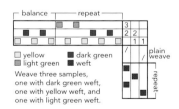

□ yellow   ■ dark green
■ light green   ■ weft

Weave three samples,
one with dark green weft,
one with yellow weft, and
one with light green weft.

SAMPLE 1, WEAVING SEQUENCE 2

Weaving sequence 2 with dark green weft.

Reverse.

Weaving sequence 2 with yellow weft.

Reverse.

Weaving sequence 2 with light green weft.

Reverse.

WEAVING SEQUENCE 2

Pick-up stick pattern: *2 up, 2 down; repeat from * (all dark green warps picked up).

STEP 1. Down.

STEP 2. Up and pick-up stick.

STEP 3. Down.

STEP 4. Up and pick-up stick.

STEP 5. Down.

STEP 6. Up.

Repeat these 6 steps for pattern.

Treadling Sequence 2

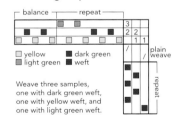

□ yellow   ■ dark green
■ light green   ■ weft

Weave three samples,
one with dark green weft,
one with yellow weft, and
one with light green weft.

SUBTLE STRIPES

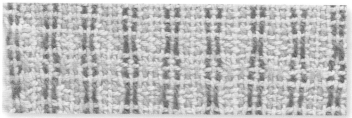

Front.

Reverse.

WAFFLE WEAVE EFFECT

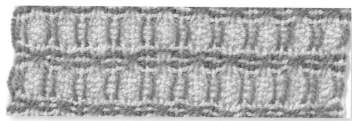

Front.

Reverse.

For this sample, two pick-up sticks are required. The first one is used to make blocks of dark green floats; the second is used for light green floats. Because the light green is closer in value to the yellow, these floats are more subtle. The weft floats on the reverse side break up the vertical lines, producing a more textural feel.

Weft: Yellow.

Pick-up stick pattern A: *2 up, 2 down; repeat from * (all dark green warps picked up).

Pick-up stick pattern B: *2 down, 2 up; repeat from * (all light green warps picked up).

STEP 1. Down.

STEP 2. Up and pick-up stick A.

STEP 3. Down.

STEP 4. Up.

STEP 5. Down.

STEP 6. Up and pick-up stick B.

STEP 7. Down.

STEP 8. Up.

Repeat these 8 steps for pattern.

While you can't achieve the deep cells of a waffle weave woven on a multi-shaft loom, you can create a waffle-weave effect. By using a contrasting color for the floats in warp and weft, you can exaggerate the look. I actually prefer the reverse of this swatch where light green warp floats contrast with vertical lines of dark green and horizontals of yellow.

Weft: Yellow (Y) for the background; dark green (DG) for the weft floats.

Pick-up stick pattern: *2 up, 2 down; repeat from * (all dark green warps are picked up).:

STEP 1. Up (Y).

STEP 2. Pick-up stick (DG).

STEP 3. Up (Y).

STEP 4. Pick-up stick (DG).

STEP 5. Up (Y).

STEP 6. Down (Y).

STEP 7. Up and pick-up stick (Y).

STEP 8. Down (Y).

STEP 9. Up and pick-up stick (Y).

STEP 10. Down (Y).

Repeat these 10 steps for pattern.

STEP 11. Balance pattern by ending with Steps 1–5.

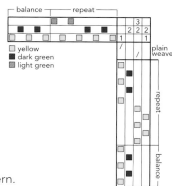

LONG FLOATS AND STRIPES

Front.

Reverse.

To gain more pattern contrast in this sample, I picked up every other pair of dark green warps. When woven, end-on-end stripes alternate with long floats. On the reverse, dark green dots are bordered by yellow weft floats and alternate with end-on-end stripes of dark green.

Weft: Yellow.

Pick-up stick pattern: 4 down, *2 up, 6 down; repeat from *, end 2 up, 4 down.

STEP 1. Down.

STEP 2. Up and pick-up stick.

STEP 3. Down.

STEP 4. Up and pick-up stick.

STEP 5. Down.

STEP 6. Up and pick-up stick.

STEP 7. Down.

STEP 8. Up.
Repeat these 8 steps for pattern.

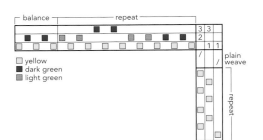

WARP FLOATS WITH ACCENT WEFTS

Front.

Reverse.

Here, I used the same pick-up pattern as in the previous sample, but just wove a single-float shed. I also inserted an end of mohair weft in each pick-up pattern row, gradating the color from dark gold to green and back to dark gold again. The result on the face is subtle weft shading and understated warp stripes. On the reverse, the weft floats of mohair are more evident. I like how they pop out of the surface.

Weft: Light green wool with four different colors of mohair: Louet Brushed Mohair in Sunflower, Buttercup, Soft Yellow, and Lichen.

Pick-up pattern: 4 down, *2 up, 6 down; repeat from *, end 2 up, 4 down.

STEP 1. Down.

STEP 2. Up and pick-up stick.

STEP 3. Down.

STEP 4. Up.
Repeat these 4 steps for pattern.

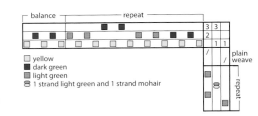

HONEYCOMB

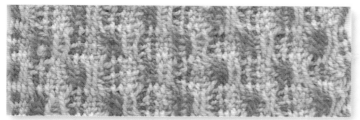

Front.

Reverse.

Allover texture results from this color-and-weave interaction. The combination of this soft wool yarn and the undulation of honeycomb weave create a fluffy fabric that would weave up into a lovely blanket.

Weft: Light green.

Pick-up stick pattern A: *4 up, 4 down; repeat from *.

Pick-up stick pattern B: *4 down, 4 up; repeat from *.

STEP 1. Down.

STEP 2. Up and pick-up stick A.

STEP 3. Down.

STEP 4. Up and pick-up stick A.

STEP 5. Down.

STEP 6. Up and pick-up stick A.

STEP 7. Down.

STEP 8. Up and pick-up stick B.

STEP 9. Down.

STEP 10. Up and pick-up stick B.

STEP 11. Down.

STEP 12. Up and pick-up stick B.

Repeat Steps 1–12 as desired, then weave 1 down for balance.

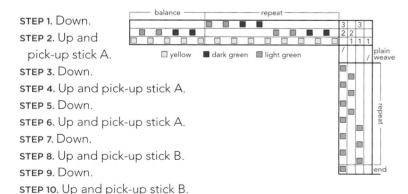

☐ yellow   ■ dark green   ▨ light green

Translating Pick-up Patterns to Drafts

Sometimes you might want to weave a pick-up pattern of your own design on a shaft loom. The best way I've found to do this is to make a line-by-line drawing on graph paper as I weave. I'll record each pick as I weave along, coloring in the warp threads that are raised. I then take this drawing to the computer and use the Sketch Pad feature in Fiberworks, a computer weave draft program. I enter this drawdown into the Sketch Pad grid and hit the "Analyze" button and . . . wowie, zowie . . . I've got a draft. The draft tells me how to thread the loom, the tie-up, as well as the treadling. If you have Fiberworks, but it doesn't have the Sketch Pad feature, you can purchase the upgrade—it's well worth it if you plan to translate a lot of pick-up patterns.

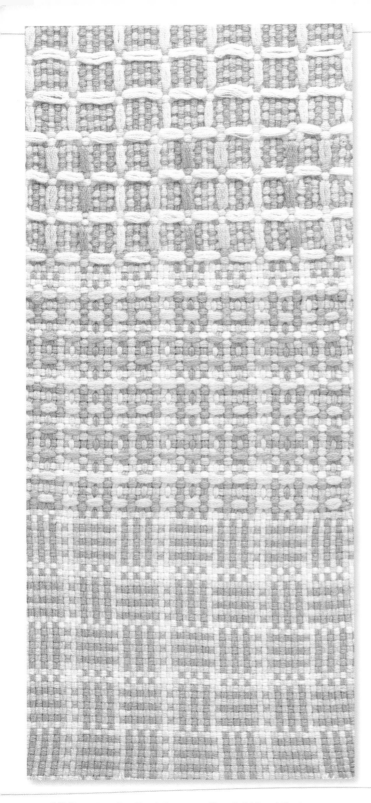

Exploring Color-and-Weave Plus Floats

For this sample, I used three colors of Cotton Clouds Bambu 7, doubled, and threaded color-and-weave blocks of Willow (green) and Blush (pink) separated by two ends of Rice (white). This sampler measured just over 5" (12.5 cm) wide on the loom. I used a 12-dent reed.

PLAIN WEAVE

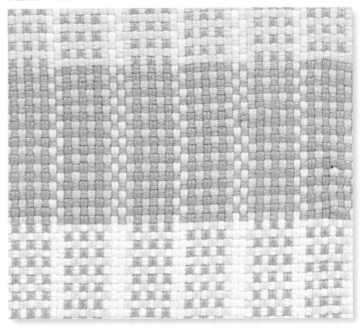

To show what can be done on just one warp, I first wove solid plain-weave areas in white, then green, then pink. I especially like the light and fresh look of the green dots against the white weft.

Warp Threading Color Order

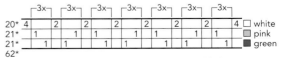

*Warp ends indicated above are doubled, i.e., 20 working ends equals 40 actual ends.

WINDOWPANE EFFECT

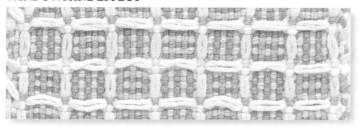

In this section, I alternated green and pink in a color-and-weave pattern for the background and wove warp and weft floats in white for a windowpane or mock waffle weave. Notice that squares of vertical and horizontal stripes alternate from block to block.

Pick-up stick pattern: 1 down, *1 up, 3 down; repeat from *, end 1 down.

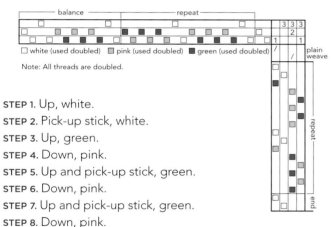

□ white (used doubled) ■ pink (used doubled) ■ green (used doubled)

Note: All threads are doubled.

STEP 1. Up, white.
STEP 2. Pick-up stick, white.
STEP 3. Up, green.
STEP 4. Down, pink.
STEP 5. Up and pick-up stick, green.
STEP 6. Down, pink.
STEP 7. Up and pick-up stick, green.
STEP 8. Down, pink.
STEP 9. Up, white.
STEP 10. Pick-up stick, white.
STEP 11. Up, pink.
STEP 12. Down, green.
STEP 13. Up and pick-up stick, pink.
STEP 14. Down, green.
STEP 15. Up and pick-up stick, pink.
STEP 16. Down, green.
Repeat these 16 steps for pattern, then end as follows.
STEP 17. Up, white.
STEP 18. Pick-up stick, white.

WINDOWPANE EFFECT, VARIATION

For this variation, I picked 1 up, 2 down all the way across the band so that all three colors were picked up. For weft, I alternated pink and green and used only white floats for a windowpane effect with a subtle look. I think this would be quite effective for a jacket pattern. Think Chanel.

Pick-up stick pattern: *1 up, 2 down; repeat from *.

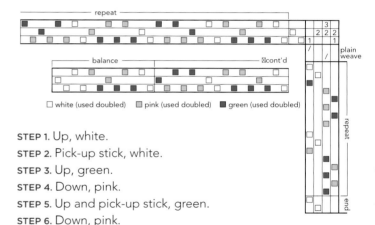

□ white (used doubled) ■ pink (used doubled) ■ green (used doubled)

STEP 1. Up, white.
STEP 2. Pick-up stick, white.
STEP 3. Up, green.
STEP 4. Down, pink.
STEP 5. Up and pick-up stick, green.
STEP 6. Down, pink.
STEP 7. Up and pick-up stick, green.
STEP 8. Down, pink.
STEP 9. Up, white.
STEP 10. Pick-up stick, white.
STEP 11. Up, pink.
STEP 12. Down, green.
STEP 13. Up and pick-up stick, pink.
STEP 14. Down, green.
STEP 15. Up and pick-up stick, pink.
STEP 16. Down, green.
Repeat these 16 steps for pattern, then end as follows.
STEP 17. Up, white.
STEP 18. Pick-up stick, white.

PLAID EFFECT

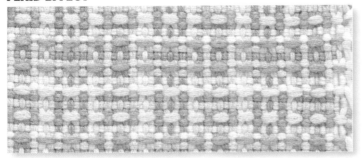

For this pattern, I wove the colors in the same order as they were threaded but added a little pick-up pattern to break up the color-and-weave pattern. This makes an energetic surface that has visual interest without shouting "Look at me." Because there is so much going on with changing shuttle colors and remembering the pick-up pattern sequence, you may find it helpful to keep a little "cheat sheet" by your side.
Pick-up stick pattern: *1 up, 1 down; repeat from *.

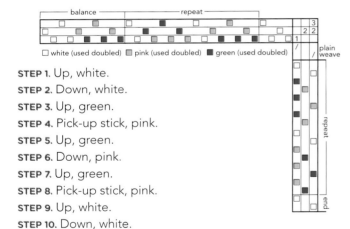

STEP 1. Up, white.

STEP 2. Down, white.

STEP 3. Up, green.

STEP 4. Pick-up stick, pink.

STEP 5. Up, green.

STEP 6. Down, pink.

STEP 7. Up, green.

STEP 8. Pick-up stick, pink.

STEP 9. Up, white.

STEP 10. Down, white.

STEP 11. Up, pink.

STEP 12. Pick-up stick, green.

STEP 13. Up, pink.

STEP 14. Down, green.

STEP 15. Up, pink.

STEP 16. Pick-up stick, green.

Repeat these 16 steps for pattern, end with balance below.

STEP 17. Up, white.

STEP 18. Down, white.

COLOR-AND-WEAVE

This sample shows what the threading would look like in plain weave, as it would be traditionally woven in color-and-weave. Weave the colors in the same sequence as they are threaded. *Note:* All yarns are used doubled.

MORE COLOR-AND-WEAVE EFFECTS

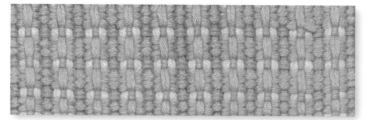

Front.

Front.

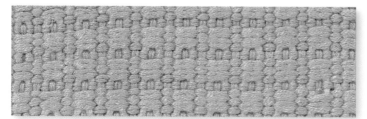

Reverse.

Reverse.

For this sample, I used the same yarns as previously, but threaded them differently in the warp. I simply alternated green and pink, placing the green in the slots. All threads are doubled in warp and weft. I wove green weft at 18 ppi.

Pick-up stick pattern: *1 down, 1 up; repeat from *.

STEP 1. Down.

STEP 2. Up and pick-up stick.

STEP 3. Down.

STEP 4. Up and pick-up stick.

STEP 5. Down.

STEP 6. Up.

Repeat these 6 steps for pattern.
Weave Steps 1–5 for balance.

Reverse: Silky weft floats dominate the reverse side. If you decide you like these better than the warp-float side, you could change the weaving sequence and weave weft-floats. I always like to see the surface I'll be using in the final project as I'm weaving it.

■ green (doubled)
☐ pink (doubled)
Weave at 18 ppi.

This is the same pick-up pattern and weaving as the previous sample, but here I wove with pink weft at 14 ppi to stretch out the long warp floats.

Reverse: Because of the interaction of the colors, and because I didn't beat it as hard as the previous sample, the pink warps are allowed a slight deflection, which in turn creates small green lozenges. This side has a lot a depth that I find quite appealing.

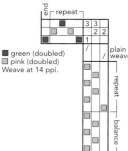

■ green (doubled)
☐ pink (doubled)
Weave at 14 ppi.

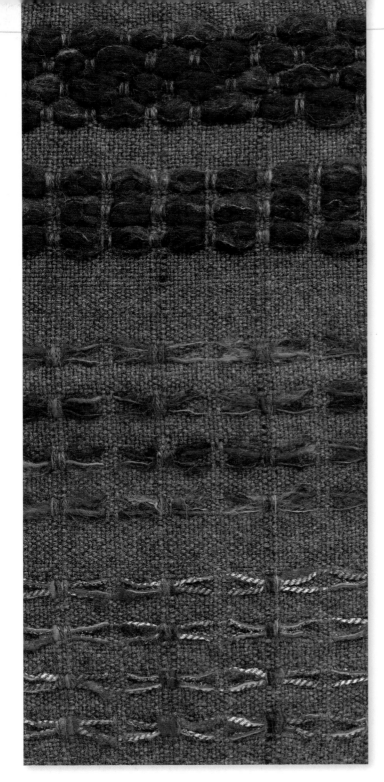

Using Yarn and Structure

For this sampler, I wanted to explore both structure and yarn to create dramatic results. The first two samples combine novelty yarns with weft deflection and the second two use a thick though lightweight novelty yarn for hefty floats.

DEFLECTED WEFT

There is one sample in Betty Davenport's *Textures and Patterns For the Rigid Heddle Loom* that has always intrigued me. It seems so complex, yet is really quite simple to weave. The main trick to this pattern is to place the supplementary tie-down warps in the correct place. If you examine what's happening, you'll see that there are pairs of long weft floats that are captured by a warp float. Because of this space, the two weft floats naturally bend together (deflect) underneath the warp float to produce a fanciful design.

For this interpretation, I wanted a fabric that was sophisticated and rich in texture and color. I chose Brown Sheep Nature Spun sportweight wool in Charcoal for the warp, sett at 10 epi. I used this same yarn for the background wefts for both samples. For the supplementary tie-down warps, I used Berroco Memoirs, a mohair/wool yarn, in color 7714. The weft for the first sample is Berroco Trilogy in color 7633; the same Memoirs is used for the supplementary weft in the second example.

This weave requires two pick-up sticks, though this is a case where both of them can stay in place during weaving because they slide past each other. The weft zigzags across the width because it is allowed extra space to do so. Remember: If a yarn is given an opportunity to escape, it will. The weaving sequence is the same for both samples.

Woven by Angela Johnson.

DEFLECTED WEFT

Berroco Trilogy supplementary weft.

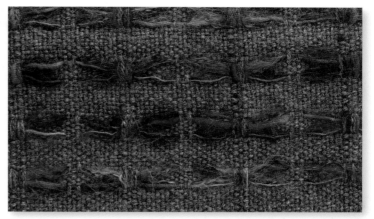

Berroco Memoirs supplementary weft.

Pattern threading: Thread 8 gray, beginning in slot, *1 novelty in slot, 1 gray in hole, 1 novelty in slot, gray for 21; repeat from *, end novelty in slot, gray in hole, novelty in slot, 8 gray.

Pick-up stick pattern A: Beginning with the novelty yarns, pick up *2 up, 10 down; repeat from *.

Pick-up stick pattern B: Beginning with the novelty yarns, pick up *2 up, 4 down, 2 up, 4 down; repeat from *.

STEP 1. Weave 8 rows of plain weave beginning in an up shed and ending in a down shed.

STEP 2. Pick-up stick B, novelty yarn.

STEP 3. Up and pick-up stick A.

STEP 4. Down.

STEP 5. Repeat Steps 3 and 4 two more times.

STEP 6. Pick-up stick B, novelty yarn.

Repeat the entire sequence for pattern.

STEP 7. Weave 8 rows of plain weave to balance.

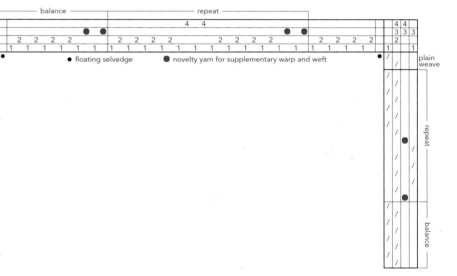

Supplementary Weft

The following two examples with soft, lofty floats are woven on the same warp as the two previous samples. Because my pattern yarn was more brown than gray, I changed the background weft to Nature Spun in Stone. The pattern weft is Lang Yarns Taiga in color 9811, a wool/nylon/acrylic blend. The mohair supplementary tie-down warps add visual and textural interest. For the first sample, the floats are stacked up one on top of the other for a restrained appeal. Just by changing how the floats are woven in the second sample creates a surface that seems more untamed, livelier. Two pick-up sticks are required for this example.

Woven by Angela Johnson.

STACKED FLOATS

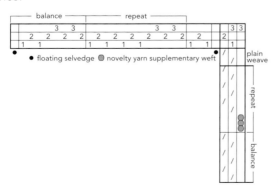

Pick-up stick pattern: 2 down, *2 up, 4 down, 2 up; repeat from *.

STEP 1. Weave 6 rows of plain weave.

STEP 2. Pick-up stick; weave 3 passes with the novelty yarn in the same shed (be sure to catch the end thread so that the novelty yarn does not slip out).

Repeat these 2 steps for pattern. Weave 6 rows of plain weave to balance.

ALTERNATING FLOATS

Pick-up stick pattern A: *3 down, 2 up, 5 down, 2 up; repeat from *.

Pick-up stick pattern B: 1 down, *2 up, 3 down, 2 up, 5 down; repeat from *.

STEP 1. Weave 6 rows of plain weave.

STEP 2. Pick-up stick A; weave 3 passes in the same shed with the novelty yarn.

STEP 3. Weave 6 rows of plain weave.

STEP 4. Pick-up stick B; weave 3 passes in the same shed with the novelty yarn.

Repeat these 4 steps for pattern. Weave 6 rows of plain weave to balance.

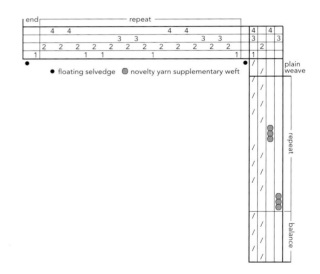

WARP AND WEFT FLOATS
WITH DIFFERENTIAL SHRINKAGE

It's fun to play around with differential shrinkage and floats. The warp and weft for this sample is Brown Sheep Nature Spun sett at 10 epi. The supplementary warps and wefts are fine 16/1 linen singles, with three ends used as one. I threaded these in the slots every other inch (2.5 cm) along with the charcoal warps. Supplementary warp colors are threaded in stripes of blue, gold, blue, red, blue. The warp floats are created during weaving by lifting them out of the way with the pick-up stick. I wove rows of solid-colored weft floats to create a bold look. Two pick-up sticks are required, one for the supplementary warp floats and the other for the supplementary weft floats. Both pick-up sticks can stay in place during weaving.

After weaving, the fabric was washed in the washing machine (on a regular cycle with detergent) until it was sufficiently fulled, and then laid flat to dry. *Note:* It is a good idea to check the fabric often to make sure it does not over felt.

Because the wool shrinks and the linen does not, the floats become longer in relationship to the ground fabric and dance around on the surface of the cloth. This idea could be pushed even further; for example, sleying the wool at 8 epi instead of 10 will cause the fabric to shrink more and accentuate the non-shrinking linen. Small, delicate floats could be made lengthwise, or very long random floats could be made for dramatic results. When weaving this type of fabric, it is important to maintain the plain-weave background. Notice that the charcoal and linen are woven together in the connecting squares.

In preparing the warp, I suggest that you measure the background and supplementary warps separately on the warping board. First sley all of the background threads, then the supplementary warp threads.

For this sample, I threaded 10 grays and then inserted the supplementary warp threads in the next 5 slots. I then skipped 4 slots and threaded the next 5 supplementary warp threads, and so on. You will have both a background and a supplementary warp in the same slot. This is as it should be.

Woven by Angela Johnson.

Above: Fabric before washing.
Below: Because the wool shrinks and the linen does not, the linen is longer in the finished fabric and creates wavy lines on the surface.

Pick-up stick pattern A: In all of the slots with supplementary warp threads, pick up the supplementary warp threads as well as the background warp threads.

Pick-up stick pattern B: Pick up all of the supplementary warp threads.

Note: You can leave both pick-up sticks in the place as you weave; they will slide past each other.

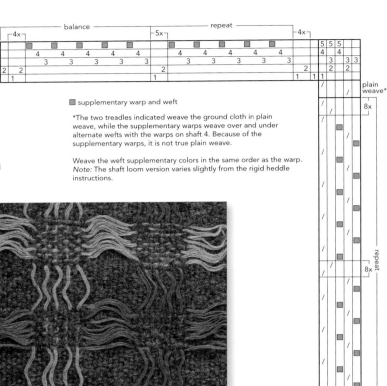

■ supplementary warp and weft

*The two treadles indicated weave the ground cloth in plain weave, while the supplementary warps weave over and under alternate wefts with the warps on shaft 4. Because of the supplementary warps, it is not true plain weave.

Weave the weft supplementary colors in the same order as the warp.
Note: The shaft loom version varies slightly from the rigid heddle instructions.

Before beginning the pattern, anchor the supplementary warp floats by weaving plain weave for an inch (2.5 cm) or so.

STEP 1. Up and pick-up stick B.

STEP 2. Down.

STEP 3. Repeat Steps 1 and 2 seven more times.

STEP 4. Up.

STEP 5. Pick-up stick A, supplementary weft.

STEP 6. Down.

STEP 7. Pick-up stick A, supplementary weft.

STEP 8. Repeat Steps 4–7 three more times.

STEP 9. Up.

STEP 10. Pick-up stick A, supplementary weft.

STEP 11. Down.

Repeat the entire sequence for pattern. To end with warp floats, finish by weaving Steps 1 and 2 eight times. End with an inch (2.5 cm) or so of plain weave.

DEFLECTED WARPS

You can achieve a dramatic bending of warp threads by threading a contrasting warp yarn and allowing it to move around by weaving floats on each side. You could think of this as sideways honeycomb because the principle is the same. But instead of weft-wise bending, there is warp-wise deflection. For this technique, the novelty or accent yarn is threaded in a hole. Weft floats are woven first on one side of this yarn and then on the other. As with anything you do in the warp, careful planning is a must prior to warping your loom.

The warp is 3/2 pearl cotton sett at 10 epi, with a novelty yarn, Roxy (Lang Yarns) in sage green threaded in the holes at intervals. I began in a slot at the right selvedge and threaded 7 ends of pearl cotton; the 8th end is a novelty yarn threaded in a hole. For the remainder of the width I repeated (11 pearl cotton, 1 novelty), always threading the novelty in a hole, for a total of 6 novelty ends. I ended at the left selvedge with 7 ends of pearl cotton.

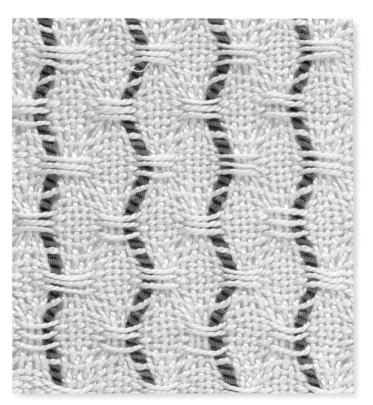

Pick-up stick pattern A: 1 up, *3 down, 3 up; repeat from *, end 2 up.

Pick-up stick pattern B: 4 up, *3 down, 3 up; repeat from *, end 2 down.

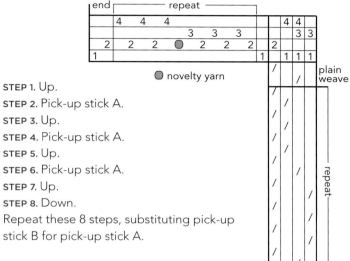

○ novelty yarn

STEP 1. Up.
STEP 2. Pick-up stick A.
STEP 3. Up.
STEP 4. Pick-up stick A.
STEP 5. Up.
STEP 6. Pick-up stick A.
STEP 7. Up.
STEP 8. Down.
Repeat these 8 steps, substituting pick-up stick B for pick-up stick A.

Repeat the entire sequence for pattern.

Conclusion

You now have three primary tools in your weaving tool box: plain weave and all its possibilities, the infinite promise of finger-controlled techniques, and the speed and design potential of pick-up-stick patterns. With these three methods of weaving, you have unlimited ways to create one-of-a kind fabric that is uniquely your own.

I find pick-up-stick patterns a blast because I can easily and quickly create patterns and change those patterns on a whim, just by picking a new sequence. Spot lace, honeycomb, and mock waffle weave are all possible on the same threading just by altering the pick-up sticks. Again, though, I must cite my disclaimer: I have not explored the entire territory of pick-up-stick patterns. This is only the beginning. My hope is that these ideas and techniques provide a sufficient foundation for you to proceed with confidence.

Felted Pin-Striped
WRAP SKIRT

Designed and woven by Jessica Knickman.

This skirt was woven 25" (63.5 cm) wide with weft-wise stripes. The woven-in belt loops were created by weft floats along one edge. After weaving, the fabric was heavily fulled in the washing machine under a careful watch so as to not felt the fabric too much—which would make this piece a mini, mini skirt. *Note:* The front flap is designed to hang below the skirt hem for an uneven hemline.

Finished Size
About 37" (94 cm) around and 16" (40.5 cm) long, when wrapped.

Weave Structure
Plain weave with weft floats.

Yarn
Warp and Weft: *Jaggerspun Zephyr* 2/18 (50% wool, 50% silk; 5,040 yd [4,608 m]/lb): Charcoal, 1,970 yd (1,801 m); Curry and Garnet, 55 yd (50 m) each (for weft only).

Equipment
Rigid heddle loom with 25" (63.5 cm) weaving width; 10-dent rigid heddle reed; one 30" (76 cm) pick-up stick; three 20" (51 cm) or longer stick shuttles; sewing machine; three ¼" (6 mm) snaps; Incredible Rope Machine (available from Schacht Spindle Co.) to make twisted cord belt.

Notions
Two beads or buttons for belt closure.

Number of Warp Ends
250.

Warp Length
4 yards (3.6 m), which allows 24" (61 cm) for take-up and loom waste.

Warp Width
25" (63.5 cm).

EPI
10.

PPI
10.

Warping

Thread a 10-dent rigid heddle reed with Charcoal for a 25" (63.5 cm) weaving width.

Weaving

Weave 6" (15 cm) plain weave with Charcoal, then weave pinstripe pattern with belt loops for 3 yd (2.7 m). Finish with 6" (15 cm) of plain weave in Charcoal. Be sure to use a gentle beat for 10 ppi. The weaving will be quite loose but it will full during the finishing process.

Pick-up stick pattern: 12 up, 11 down, 6 up, 11 down, and the remainder of the warp ends up.

STEP 1. Up, Curry or Garnet weft for pinstripe.

STEP 2. Down, Curry or Garnet weft for pinstripe.

STEP 3. Up.

STEP 4. Pick-up stick.

STEP 5. Up.

STEP 6. Pick-up stick.

STEP 7. Up.

STEP 8. Pick-up stick.

STEP 9. Up.

STEP 10. Pick-up stick.

STEP 11. Up.

STEP 12. Pick-up stick.

STEP 13. Up.

STEP 14. Down.

Repeat these 14 steps, alternating between Curry and Garnet for the pinstripes for each repeat.

Finishing

Remove the fabric from the loom. Secure the warp ends with overhand knots or machine zigzag to prevent raveling. Machine wash in warm water on the gentle cycle, checking the fabric every couple of minutes to be sure it doesn't full too much—the fabric should shrink a lot but not become too felted (or too short!). The fulled fabric should measure just over 16" (40.5 cm) wide. Handrinse in cool water and lay flat to dry. Finish the fabric with a good steam pressing.

Assembly

Turn under the ends to make a double hem and machine stitch. Fold over the top edge ¾" (2 cm), press, then sew in place. Depending on the desired final size of the skirt, add two darts, each 3" (7.5 cm) away from the center back. The darts shown are 1½" (3.8 cm) wide at the top and 3" (7.5 cm) long, but yours will vary depending on the fit.

Fold skirt in thirds and on the wrong side of the fabric, sew half of two snaps 2" (5 cm) apart and ¼" (6 mm) from the top of one end of the fabric. Sew a half of a single snap 16" (40.5 cm)—or as needed for your fit—away from the first two snaps and ¼" (6 mm) from the top. On the right side of the fabric, sew the other half of the single snap at the other end of the fabric, about 1" (2.5 cm) from the top. Sew the other half of the other two snaps at the other end of the fabric to match the first halves.

Hem

On the under layer of the overlap, fold a long triangle at the bottom edge. Fold up enough fabric so that the bottom layer does not fall below the top layer of the wrap. Sew in place.

Belt

Make two 9-strand tightly twisted ropes, one of each pinstripe color. If using the Incredible Rope Machine (see page 40), a 145" (368 cm) length of three complete rounds will yield 106" (269 m) of rope. Fold the rope in half and thread the doubled rope through the woven belt loops. Thread both cut ends through a bead or button and secure with an overhand knot. Tie a knot in the ends of the rope to prevent raveling. To secure the belt for wearing, slip the rope loop around the bead or button.

Honeycomb
PILLOW PAIR

Woven on the same warp, these pillows feature the fabulously curvy honeycomb weave. You can weave wavy lines on the loom—it's possible with the principle known as deflection, or the bending of yarns in the woven grid. Deflection is based on the phenomenon that yarns will escape if given the opportunity to do so. In other words, yarns would just as soon live free and go where they want to go, and it is only the woven structure that keeps them in place. Open the gate, so to speak, and they're off and running.

Finished Size
Yellow Pillow: about 18" (45.5 cm) square. **White Pillow:** about 18" (45.5 cm) wide and 9" (23 cm) tall.

Weave Structure
Honeycomb; the yellow pillow has a plain-weave back.

Yarn
Warp for Both Pillows: Brown Sheep Nature Spun 2-ply Sport Weight (100% wool; 1,682 yd [1,538 m]/lb): Bleached White, 550 yd (503 m).

Weft for Yellow Pillow Front: Louet Brushed Mohair Worsted Weight (70% mohair, 30% nylon; 950 yd [869 m]/lb): Sunflower,

Buttercup, and Soft Yellow, 25 yd (23 m) each. Berroco Peruvia Quick 2-ply Bulky (100% wool; 470 yd [430 m]/lb): #9100 white, 25 yd (23 m).

Weft for Yellow Pillow Back: Berroco 2-ply Cuzco (50% alpaca, 50% wool; 595 yd [544 m]/lb): #9601 white, 60 yd (55 m). Brown Sheep Nature Spun 2-ply Sport Weight (100% wool; 1,682 yd [1,538 m]/lb): Bleached White, 60 yd (55 m).

Weft for White Pillow (front and back): Berroco Peruvia Quick 2-ply Bulky (470 yd [430 m]/lb): #9100 white, 60 yd (55 m), used double. Berroco 2-ply Cuzco (50% alpaca, 50%

wool; 595 yd [544 m]/lb): #9601 white, 60 yd (55 m).

Additional Yarn: I wove 2" (5 cm) plain weave with Nature Spun between each pillow piece, requiring a total of 100 yards. The twisted rope trim requires 160 yards of Nature Spun, and the pom-poms require 30 yards of Sunflower mohair.

Equipment
Rigid heddle loom with 20" (51 cm) weaving width; 10-dent rigid heddle reed; four stick shuttles at least 16" (40.5 cm) long; two 25" (63.5 cm) pick-up sticks; sewing machine; Incredible Rope Machine (available from Schacht Spindle Co.) for making twisted cord.

Number of Warp Ends
200.

Warp Length
2²/₃ yards (2.44 m), which includes 10% take-up and 28" (71 cm) loom waste.

Warp Width
20" (51 cm).

EPI
10.

PPI
Yellow pillow front—8; Yellow pillow back—10. White pillow front and back —6 to 7.

Honeycomb is a block weave, which means there are sections, or blocks, with different interlacements. Blocks of floats alternate with blocks of plain weave, and then these exchange places for the next section to make the honeycomb cells. Using a heavy yarn to outline the cells accentuates and adds dimension.

To weave honeycomb on the rigid heddle loom, you will need two pick-up sticks, one for each block. One pick-up stick will remain in place and will weave block A; the second is used for block B and will need to be inserted and removed after each sequence. An advantage of weaving honeycomb on the rigid heddle loom is that you can weave different cell combinations on the same warp. Here, I used two different pick-up combinations. For the yellow pillow, I used equal-sized blocks; for the white pillow, I varied the size of the blocks just by changing my pick-up pattern.

Warping

Thread Nature Spun Bleached White wool in a 10-dent rigid heddle reed for a 20" (51 cm) weaving width.

Weaving

Yellow Pillow Front

Pick-up stick pattern A: *5 up, 5 down; repeat from *.
Pick-up stick pattern B: *5 down, 5 up; repeat from *.
STEP 1. Up; heavy yarn (Peruvian Quick).
STEP 2. Down, heavy yarn (Peruvian Quick).
STEP 3. Up and pick-up stick A, mohair.
STEP 4. Down, mohair.
STEP 5. Up and pick-up stick A, mohair.
STEP 6. Down, mohair.
STEP 7. Up and pick-up stick A, mohair.
STEP 8. Down, mohair.
STEP 9. Insert pick-up stick B and repeat Picks 1–8.

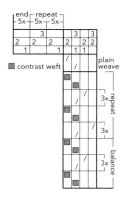

NOTES

When there are warp floats at the selvedge, the weft yarn won't catch a selvedge thread when you change sheds and weave back to the other side. To remedy this, simply go around the edge thread when you place the shuttle into the shed.

Because all of the edges will be seamed when the pillow is assembled, it is not necessary to weave in the weft ends. When ending a shuttle, simply cut off the yarn leaving a 2" (5 cm) tail. Begin the next shuttle in the same way. After washing, trim the tails flush with the selvedge.

To keep track of how long you've woven, cut a measuring cord from a non-stretchy yarn, such as pearl or crochet cotton. Measure the length you need and pin it to the beginning of your weaving with a T-pin. Use a second T-pin to secure the measuring cord to the selvedge edge as you weave. For most accurate measurements, release the tension on the warp when you move the T-pin up the measuring cord.

It is likely that you will not see the honeycomb structure when the fabric is on the loom, as it is only after the tension has been released and the fabric washed that the full effect is evident.

You can use either side of the fabric. For the yellow pillow I used the reverse side (the underside during weaving) of the fabric because I liked the mohair weft floats on this side. By comparison, I used the "right side" of the fabric for the white rectangular pillow.

To weave warp floats, place heddle in up position and slide pick-up stick forward.

The back of the yellow pillow is woven in plain weave alternating Nature Spun and Cuzco.

Front (left) and reverse (right) of white pillow fabric.

Repeat these 9 steps, rotating the mohair colors for each honeycomb cell (for example, start with Yellow and weave Steps 3–8 with Pattern A, then weave Steps 3–8 in Sunflower with Pattern B, and then weave Steps 3–8 in Buttercup with Pattern A) until 20" (51 cm) has been woven, ending with Pick 2 (down—heavy yarn).

Yellow Pillow Back

Weave plain weave for 20" (52 cm), alternating 1 pick Nature Spun and 1 pick Cuzco.

White Honeycomb Pillow

Pick-up stick pattern A: *5 up, 3 down; repeat from *.
Pick-up stick pattern B: *5 down, 3 up; repeat from *.

STEP 1. Up, heavy yarn (Cuzco).
STEP 2. Down, heavy yarn (Cuzco).
STEP 3. Up and pick-up stick A, Nature Spun.
STEP 4. Down, Nature Spun.
STEP 5. Up and pick-up stick A, Nature Spun.
STEP 6. Down, Nature Spun.
STEP 7. Up and pick-up stick A, Nature Spun.
STEP 8. Down, Nature Spun.
STEP 9. Up, heavy yarn (Cuzco).
STEP 10. Down, heavy yarn (Cuzco).
STEP 11. Up and pick-up stick B, Nature Spun.
STEP 12. Down, Nature Spun.
STEP 13. Up and pick-up stick B, Nature Spun.
STEP 14. Down, Nature Spun.

Repeat Steps 1–14 until 10" (25.5 cm) has been woven, ending with Step 1 (up—heavy yarn) and Step 2 (down—heavy yarn) to complete pillow front.

Weave 2" (5 cm) plain weave with Nature Spun.

Weave pillow back in the same way.

Finishing

Remove fabric from loom and machine stitch ends to prevent fraying. Handwash in warm water and regular detergent. Rinse well, squeeze out excess water, and lay flat to dry.

Assembly

Cut pieces apart and machine zigzag all raw edges. Decide which side of the fabric you want to be the "right" side (I used the reverse). With right sides together and using a ½" (1.3 cm) seam allowance, machine sew around three edges. Stuff pillow with purchased or custom-made pillow insert and sew seam closed by hand. For the square pillow, I used an 18" (45.5 cm) pillow form; for the rectangular pillow, I sewed a cotton pillow insert 1" (2.5 cm) larger than the finished size of the pillow and stuffed it with fiberfill. Add twisted cord trim and pom-poms, if desired.

Twisted Cord Trim

With Nature Spun yarn, use the Incredible Rope Machine (see page 40) to make a 16-strand twisted cord and stitch it around the seams, if desired.

Pom-Poms

Cut two discs from an index card, each measuring 2¼" (5.5 cm) in diameter. Cut ½" (1.3 cm) diameter holes in the center of each disk. Thread a tapestry needle with mohair and wrap it around the disk until the disk is very full. Carefully cut the yarn between the outer rims of the two disks. Insert a 12" (30.5 cm) length of mohair around the yarn, pull tight, and tie to secure the yarns in the center. Do not cut the tails; you'll use them to sew the pom-poms to the corners of the pillow. Make a vertical cut in each disk to remove the pom-pom. To reuse the disks for another pom-pom, place cellophane tape across the cuts.

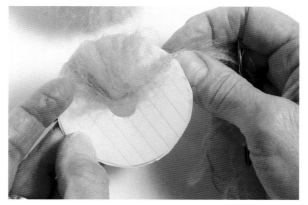

To make pom-poms, wrap yarn around two cut-out disks.

Tie a length of yarn around the center of the cut ends (between the two disks).

CHAPTER 4

Weft- and Warp-Faced
FABRICS

Now you see it, now you don't.

Thus far, the projects and fabrics in this book have mostly involved balanced weaves. That is, fabrics in which both the warp and weft appear equally in the fabric. You can, however, weave fabrics in which the warp is hidden by the weft or the weft is hidden by the warp. These fabrics are called weft-faced and warp-faced, respectively.

Generally, weft- or warp-faced fabrics are thicker, denser, and slower to weave. With weft-faced fabrics, you have the advantage of changing the wefts as you weave, whereas with warp-faced fabrics, the colors are set in the warping process. Weft-faced fabrics are ideal for household textiles and any time a pile fabric is called for; warp-faced fabrics are advantageous for bands or narrow fabrics where strength is required. As in the case of plain weave, even the simplest structure of over, under, over, under can have many different looks from a balanced plain weave, to a thick weft-faced one, to a densely woven warp-faced one.

Weft-Faced Fabrics

To create a weft-faced fabric, you need to spread the warp far enough apart so that when you beat in the weft it will pack in densely enough to obscure the warp completely. Generally, you will choose a warp yarn that is smoother and stronger and of a smaller size than the weft yarn. Most likely, your weft will be of a larger size than the warp, as well as softer and squishier so it will pack in well and cover the warp.

Design-wise, the warp, because it is hidden by the weft, is not a factor in the finished design. I particularly like weft-faced fabrics because the pattern is developed solely from the colors used in the weft. Generally, a weft-faced fabric is denser and heavier than a balanced weave and will not have the same drape. You would not choose this structure, for example, for a shawl, but you might choose it to weave a warm vest.

When I think of designing for a weft-faced fabric, I look to color patterning for the action. Because the warp is hidden, other than holding the fabric together structurally, it doesn't enter into the design. If you have ever examined ethnic rugs, you'll see just how very far weft-faced patterns can go. You can weave different color sequences selvedge to selvedge, create pictures by using tapestry techniques where many wefts travel across the weaving to make a design, or create a fuzzy pile surface, to name a few of the possibilities. Some of the techniques explored here, specifically ghiordes knots, picked-up loops, and soumak, could also be included in finger-controlled techniques (Chapter 2). I've included them in this chapter because their primary use is as a weft-faced technique.

Even though you can weave rug techniques on a rigid heddle loom, I am of the opinion that you cannot weave a dense, sturdy rug on a rigid heddle loom. A rug of any size demands much of a loom—a lot of tension to create a dense and strong fabric and a heavy beater to beat the weft into place. Do not be discouraged, however, because there are wonderful weft-faced fabrics that can be created on a rigid heddle loom.

Weft-Faced Plain-Weave Sampler

Woven by Angela Johnson.

Wool rug warp (Navaho Warp from Davidson) forms the base of this weft-faced sampler. I used a worsted-weight wool/mohair singles for the weft (Lamb's Pride from Brown Sheep in Tiger Lily, Winter Blue, Pistachio, and Aran). The warp sett is 10 epi; the weft is packed in at about 18 ppi.

When multiple rows of a color are repeated, horizontal stripes result. Here, 8 rows of each color are woven.

A checkerboard effect is created when the colors swap places. Four repeats of alternating picks of green and orange are followed by 4 repeats of alternating picks of orange and green, followed by 4 repeats of alternating green and orange, and so on.

Vertical stripes are created when two colors are alternated, called "pick-and-pick." One pick each of white and blue are alternated, then green and orange, then blue and white. Each band of pick-and-pick stripes is separated by 8 rows of solid blue.

Even though the weaving is very similar to the previous example, here the blue is repeated on each side of the orange-and-blue pick-and-pick rows so that the pattern seems to float on a ground of blue.

For this example, 5 rows of white, 5 rows of orange, and 5 rows of white each alternate with 1 row of blue. Because blue is always woven in the same shed, solid blue vertical lines are created across the width of the cloth.

Alternating 2 rows of green and 2 rows of orange produces narrow wavy stripes.

A lively striped design is formed when 2 rows each of several colors are alternated.

Stacks of spots result when 3 rows of white are followed by a single pick of orange.

Here, 3 rows of white are followed by single picks of different colors to produce a light and airy look.

A little border motif can be made by framing pick-and-pick rows of alternating blue and white with "daisy chains" made by weaving 2 rows of white, a single row of green, followed by 2 more rows of white.

In this example, green-and-white sections are offset by blue and red "daisy chains." The predominately green stripes are similar, but different.

Blue-and-white pick-and-pick stripes form vertical lines that contrast with horizontal rows of solid colors. This is a fun way to use just two colors to make an interesting border.

Weft-Faced Coasters

Try out new weft-faced techniques by weaving a set of coasters. Although I wove different patterns for each coaster, the four have a unified look because they all have the same colors. Here, 8/4 cotton carpet warp is sett at 8 epi and a worsted-weight knitting yarn weft is packed in to completely cover the warp at 28 ppi.

Ghiordes Knot or Cut Pile

When you enter into the tradition of knot tying to create cut pile, you join with others who created thick, substantial textiles of sophisticated design long before 500 B.C. We know this from a rug discovered in a tomb in the Altai Mountains of Siberia, preserved there by ice for centuries. The ghiordes knot, which I present here, was used to make this rug. So, as you create something knot by knot, be reminded of the weavers who created textiles both for warmth and beauty many centuries ago. (I'd also like to mention that this book just barely touches the world of knotting. To learn more about knotted textiles, search out a copy of Peter Collingwood's *The Techniques of Rug Weaving*. It is the definitive resource and worth every penny.)

The ghiordes knot is probably the most-used knot for pile rugs because it is highly secure—it doesn't ravel or come undone. It is also quite versatile in that it can be tied from either a continuous strand or from cut pieces. Because every knot can be a different color, ghiordes knots offer absolute design freedom. There are many variations to this knot; instructions for a basic knot are given on page 143.

In general, there are two elements to a cut-pile fabric: the ground and the pile. A row of knots is followed by 2 or more rows of plain weave, depending on the use and length of pile. The warp should be set for a weft-faced fabric so that the background weave completely covers the warp. The ghiordes knot is tied over two warp ends.

CUT-PILE NOTES

Choose a warp yarn that is strong and smooth and proportionally the correct size for the weft. The warp yarn for weft-faced weaving should be able to withstand high tension as well as the abrasion of beating with a beater. Cotton carpet warp or wool rug warp at 900 yd (823 m)/lb are both good choices. I generally set either of these at 8 epi for a worsted-weight weft yarn.

In general, wool yarns (singles or plied) are used for pile weft. But I encourage you to try all kinds of yarns. I've experimented with a variety of materials, such as variegated ribbon yarn, shiny metallics, pearl cotton, and cotton-mohair worsted weight. For a lively surface, I like to use two yarns together, sometimes juxtaposing shiny yarn with a matt one, or two of the same yarns in slightly different colors. When blending different yarns together, try to make the yarn bundles about the same size so that the knots are all about the same size, thus preventing unevenness in the pile surface.

To weave cut pile using ghiordes knots, weave a header, packing it in to cover the warp. This is a good time to stop and hemstitch the edge. If you prefer a knotted edge, be sure to allow enough warp length for tying after the piece is removed from the loom.

I like to use a belt shuttle for weft-faced pile weaves because it allows me to use the beveled edge to beat in the weft. Sometimes the reed is just not able to pack in the weft sufficiently.

I find it helpful to use a hand beater to press in the weft. If additional heft is needed, a weighted hand beater works wonders and can handle a lot of the beating chore for you.

Use a pair of cuticle scissors for cutting knots. I keep them handy over my fingers as I work the knots, cutting as I go.

For subtle color changes and detail patterning, try using pre-cut yarn lengths. They allow you to combine different colors for gradual color variations.

Generally, the longer the pile, the more rows of plain weave are needed between knot rows.

Leaving the two selvedge warps free of knots is traditional in rug making because it prevents the textile from curling. To accomplish this, do not tie knots at these edge warps, but rather, when beginning the next row of plain weave, weave two rows back and forth at the selvedge to fill in the space as shown on page 149. Weave across to the other selvedge and weave two filler rows of plain weave at this selvedge as well.

Note that these ideas are presented for use in making pillows or bags or a trim on a garment, which don't have the same constraints as weaving rugs.

Making a Ghiordes Knot with a Continuous Length of Yarn

I used ghiordes knots for the pattern in the Blue Star sample shown on page 144. For the warp, I used Davidson's Navaho Wool Warp at 900 yd (823 m)/lb sett at 8 epi and Brown Sheep Lamb's Pride Worsted (a worsted-weight singles wool/mohair at 760 yd/lb [695 m]/lb) for the weft. For the knots, wind a small butterfly of the weft yarn or use the yarn right out of the ball.

STEP 1. Weave a background base of plain weave, pressing the weft in firmly so that it completely covers the warp.

STEP 2. Bring the working end of weft yarn down through a pair of warps. The working end shown is under the right warp (Figure **1**).

STEP 3. Bring the working end over the top of the pair, from right to left (Figure **2**).

STEP 4. Finish by bringing the working end (from left to right) up through the center (Figure **3**).

STEP 5. Pull the ends down to the woven web and snug up the knot (Figure **4**).

STEP 6. Cut off the working end.

STEP 7. Repeat Steps 2–6 across the warp.

STEP 8. After you've completed a row of knots, use a hand beater to push the knots evenly and firmly against the fabric (Figure **5**), then weave at least 2 rows of background weft. The number of background rows will depend on the look, as well as the stability, you're after.

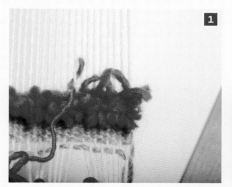

Front.

Reverse.

Blue Star Ghiordes Knot or Cut-Pile Sample

For this project, I first drew my design on graph paper, each square representing one knot or 2 warp ends. In this design, there are 32 squares across. Because each knot requires 2 warp ends, this design needs a total of 64 warp ends. For warp, I used Davidson's Navaho Wool Warp sett at 8 epi. For weft—both the background plain weave and the knots—I used Brown Sheep Lamb's Pride Worsted. I wove 1"(2.5 cm) plain weave before beginning the first row of knots. I wove the beginning and ending borders with single rows of knots and doubled the rows, weaving 2 rows of knots for every square on my graph paper, for the star. I used a heavy, weighted hand beater to pack in the knots and background weft very densely.

I finished this sample with a Philippine edge (shown at right) as a weft protector and edge finish after taking the sample off the loom. This edge is certainly slower than tying overhand knots, but well worth the extra time.

Chart of Blue Star pattern.

Philippine Edge

A Philippine edge makes a handsome finish for a weft-faced fabric. I like to work two rows for a braid-like effect. I begin on the wrong side and work a row left to right, then turn the fabric over to the right side and repeat as for the first row, again working left to right.

STEP 1. Beginning at the left selvedge, take up 3 warp ends. Hold the 2 leftmost ends in your left hand and place the third end over the top of these 2 (Figure **1**).

STEP 2. Encircle these 2 warp ends, drawing the end up through the loop (Figure **2**).

STEP 3. Pull up on the working end to tighten (Figure **3**).

STEP 4. Drop the leftmost end (Figure **4**).

STEP 5. Take up the next warp end (the fourth warp end) and repeat Steps 1–4, moving over one warp end for each group (Figure **5**).

STEP 6. Repeat Step 5 across the entire width.

STEP 7. To finish, use a rotary cutter to trim the fringe to an even length (Figure **6**).

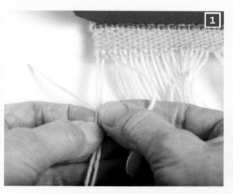

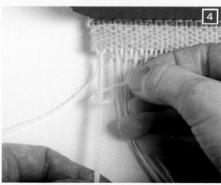

DESERT CACTI

To highlight certain areas of a design, you can trim the pile to different lengths. Here, I left the cacti pile in the foreground longer and cut the background very short. I find it easiest to trim the pile as I weave, stopping every 1" (2. 5 cm) or so and trimming with cuticle scissors. Then I do a final trimming after I've removed the piece from the loom.

To create this design, I first drew it on proportional graph paper, coloring in the design with colored pencils. I then tried to match my colors with yarns from my stash. I went for color rather than yarn, meaning if I didn't have the blue I wanted in a worsted weight, I felt free to substitute two sportweight yarns. I like the effect of wool and pearl cotton together, so I used one wool and one 3/2 pearl cotton in each bundle.

Cut the pile every 1" (2.5 cm) or so.

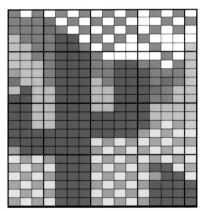

Graph for Desert Cacti.

What's Rya?

Rya is a traditional Scandinavian rug made with ghiordes knots with pile as long as 6" (15 cm). *Flossa*, another term you may have heard, is also a Scandinavian rug made with the same ghiordes knot, but generally with a shorter pile. Since rya is a weft-faced fabric, space the warp as described above.

CONFETTI PILE WITH BORDER

Here, the blending of yarn and color creates a pointillist effect. I made two different bundles of yarn with four yarns in each. To soften the line between the border and the center, I used the same off-white yarn in both color bundles. I cut the pile to just under ½" (1.3 cm) for a short, thick pile. Think of this as an idea for a soft, squishy throw pillow.

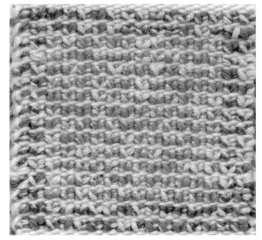

Back of finished sample.

Using Graph Paper

In weaving, just as in knitting or stitching, it is handy to plot a design on graph paper. This is especially useful in cut-pile and loop-pile work because you can plot the design to fit exactly in the available spaces. In graphing loop pile, count the number of spaces between the raised warps and plan your design in the same shed, i.e., always in the up or down position. Each pair of warp threads will represent one knot or one space on the graph paper.

In weaving, just as in knitting and stitching, seldom are the knots the same size horizontally and vertically. For example, ten knots may yield 2" (5 cm) horizontally but 3" (7.5 cm) vertically. This difference becomes a problem if you want to create a square design.

For years, I plotted my design on regular squared graph paper and modified my design as I wove so that it would end up square, which is what I did for the Blue Star sample on page 144. To prevent surprises, it is best to first weave a 4" (10 cm) square sample with the yarns you intend to use for your project. Count the number of knots warp-wise and weft-wise in 2" (5 cm) and divide each by two to determine the number of warp-wise and weft-wise knots. From these numbers, you can choose just the right proportioned graph paper to draw out your design. This takes the guess work out of weaving your design and helps you create just the right weave plan.

This is how I planned the Desert Cacti. Having woven several ghiordes knot pieces prior to this sample, I knew that based on my yarn, sett, and beat, my knot yield was 4.5 × 6. My 4" (10 cm) warp, sleyed at 8 epi, gave me 32 warp ends or 16 warp pairs. On my graph paper, I marked off 16 horizontal spaces, took this measurement and then measured the same height to produce a square. I then plotted my design to fit within these confines.

I have a book of many different proportional graph papers that I copy on my desk printer. You'll likely find, though, that if you weave the same yarns and sett from project to project, once you know your proportions, you won't need to make additional samples.

RYA WITH PLAIN-WEAVE BACKGROUND

Sometimes, you might want to isolate a pile design in the center of a weft-faced background, as I've done for this butterfly. When weaving such designs, the background does not build up as fast as the knot areas and the weaving will bulge around the knots. The solution to this problem is in a traditional rug technique called "fill-in." Simply weave back and forth in just the background areas to build them up to the same point as the pile design. At each selvedge or anywhere there is background, you'll weave back and forth in that section before continuing to the next.

Rya Butterfly on Blue.

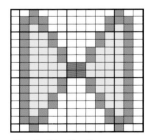

Chart of butterfly.

Weaving Fill-In

STEP 1. To weave the fill-in after a row of knots, open the shed and weave over to the first knot, exiting just before the knot (Figure **1**).

STEP 2. Change shed, place the shuttle into the shed on the warp adjacent to the knot, and return to the selvedge (Figure **2**).

STEP 3. Change sheds and weave across the section just woven, the first section of knots, and the next area of plain weave (Figure **3**).

STEP 4. Change sheds and weave back across the background to the knots (Figure **4**), change sheds and weave across to the next section (Figure **5**). Repeat as before for the third area of background (Figures **6** and **7**).

STEP 5. Change the shed one more time and return the shuttle to the other side of the weaving (Figure **8**), thus creating 2 rows of plain weave after each row of knots as well as the filled-in areas around the pile design. Use a hand beater to pack in the weft (Figure **9**).

Note: If you see an exposed warp thread alongside a section of knots, you did not go around the adjacent warp when you were weaving the fill weft. This will show in the final piece, and it's best to go back and correct the error.

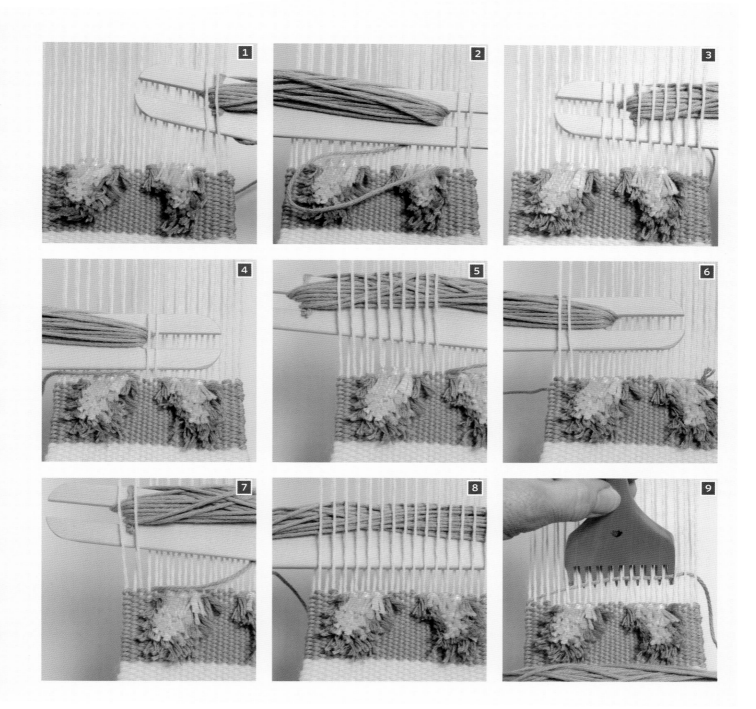

Pile Ideas
CONFETTI PILE

This super cheerful patch is made with many different bundles of yarns. I used two to three different yarns for each bundle and inserted the colors randomly in the knots across the warp. I wove 2 rows of plain weave between each row of knots, trimming the knots as I made them to about ½" (1.3 cm).

CONFETTI PILE, VARIATION

For this sample, I used the same yarns as the previous sample, but I bundled all ten yarns together for each knot. Because the bundles were so thick, I spaced the knots in every other warp pair. I wove 4 rows of plain weave between rows of knots, and I shifted the placement of the knots 2 warp ends to stack them brick fashion. I trimmed the knots to about 1" (2.5 cm) for a showy explosion of yarn.

Loops

In Chapter 2, I used loops as an embellishment on a balanced fabric, one in which both the warp and weft showed somewhat equally. However, loops are more traditionally used for weft-pile, completely or partially covering the warp. The technique for making the loops is the same as described on page 44. Loop pile is a favorite technique of mine because it is so easy and quick to do.

Loop Sampler

When I start a new project, I like to try out ideas to see where I can take my initial inspiration. I usually do this on a very narrow warp, perhaps just 4" to 5" (10 to 12.5 cm) wide. In the sampler shown on pages 151 and 152, I wanted to explore using a novelty yarn for the loops. This thick-and-thin yarn in shades of blue seemed like a good candidate. I tried it both as a single strand and doubled for more impact. For the background weft, I used worsted-weight wool in white. For the warp, I used Davidson's Navaho wool warp yarn sett at 8 epi; the weft is woven to cover the warp at about 22 ppi. For the background weft, I used worsted-weight Cascade in white. For the loops, I used Crystal Palace Musique in Faded Jeans.

SOLID LOOPS

I doubled the loop weft for this sample and picked up loops over a size U.S. 15 (10 mm) knitting needle in every space, resulting in a very dense pile. If you look at the back of the sample, you'll see loops in alternating sheds.

STEP 1. Pick up a loop in every space.
STEP 2. Weave 2 rows of plain weave with background weft. Repeat these 2 steps for pattern.

SOLID LOOPS, VARIATION 1

I wove this sample just like the previous one (doubled loop weft; size 15 [10 mm] knitting needle), but instead of 2 rows of background between each row of loops, I wove 3 rows. This put the loops always in the same shed and causes them to align vertically. Again, a very dense pile is created, with little difference in feel or look from the first sample.

STEP 1. Pick up a loop in every space.
STEP 2. Weave 3 rows of plain weave with background weft. Repeat these 2 steps for pattern.

SOLID LOOPS, VARIATION 2

For a more pliable and less dense fabric, I wove 5 rows of background between each row of loops. Again, the loop weft is doubled and the loops are made on a size 15 (10 mm) knitting needle.

STEP 1. Pick up a loop in every space.

STEP 2. Weave 5 rows of plain weave with background weft. Repeat these 2 steps for pattern.

SOLID LOOPS, VARIATION 3

For an even softer feel, I picked up loops in every other space and wove 4 rows of plain weave in between each loop row. Again, the loop weft is doubled and the loops are made on a size 15 (10 mm) knitting needle. I might choose this sample for a border on the bottom of a skirt because it is more flexible than, and not as heavy as, the first three variations.

STEP 1. Pick up a loop in every other space.

STEP 2. Weave 4 rows of plain weave with background weft. Repeat these 2 steps for pattern.

CHECKERBOARD LOOPS

By picking up loops in certain areas and skipping others, you can create a checkerboard effect that could be a blast of a pillow design. Keep in mind that because the loop yarn continues in the shed between groups of loops, it'll show on the surface, but this is only a problem if you see it as one. Loop pile in this fashion has it hands down over ghiordes knots because it is much, much faster to weave. Again, the loop weft is doubled and the loops are made on a size 15 (10 mm) knitting needle.

STEP 1. *Pick up a loop every 3 spaces, skip 3 spaces; repeat from *.

STEP 2. Weave 5 rows of plain weave with background weft.

STEP 3. Repeat Steps 1 and 2 once more.

STEP 4. Pick up a loop in the opposite spaces as in Pick 1: skip 3 spaces, pick up loops in next 3 spaces, and so on.

STEP 5. Weave 5 rows of plain weave with background weft.

STEP 6. Repeat Steps 4 and 5 once more. Repeat these 6 steps for pattern.

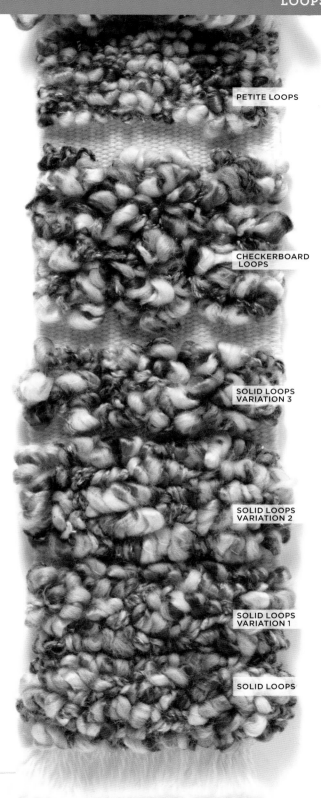

PETITE LOOPS

CHECKERBOARD LOOPS

SOLID LOOPS VARIATION 3

SOLID LOOPS VARIATION 2

SOLID LOOPS VARIATION 1

SOLID LOOPS

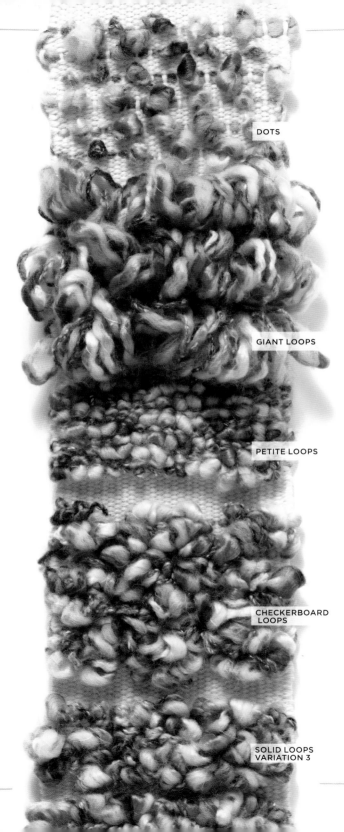

DOTS

GIANT LOOPS

PETITE LOOPS

CHECKERBOARD LOOPS

SOLID LOOPS VARIATION 3

PETITE LOOPS

I used a single weft to make tiny loops over a size 9 (5.5 mm) knitting needle. The thick-and-thin nature of this yarn is evident in this sample.

STEP 1. Pick up a loop in every space.

STEP 2. Weave 3 rows of plain weave with background weft.
Repeat these 2 steps for pattern.

GIANT LOOPS

Working in the other extreme, I doubled the loop weft and made gigantic loops over a 1½" (3.8 cm) wide stick shuttle. Doubling the weft averages out the thick-and-thin nature of this yarn.

STEP 1. Pick up a loop in every space.

STEP 2. Weave 5 rows of plain weave with background weft.

STEP 3. Weave plain weave with loop weft.

STEP 4. Weave 3 rows of plain weave with background weft.

STEP 5. Repeat Steps 3 and 4 two more times.
Repeat these 5 steps for pattern.

DOTS

By picking up loops every so often, you can create little puffs of yarn. The loop weft is doubled and the loops are made on a size 10 (6 mm) knitting needle.

STEP 1. *Pick up loops in the first space, skip 2 spaces; repeat from *.

STEP 2. Weave 7 rows of plain weave with background weft.

STEP 3. Step over 1 space at the beginning (this will be the second space), then *pick up a loop in the next space, skip 2 spaces; repeat from *.

STEP 4. Weave 7 rows of plain weave with background weft.

STEP 5. Step over a space (this will be the third space), then *pick up a loop in the next space, skip 2 spaces; rep from *.

STEP 6. Weave 7 rows of plain weave with background weft.
Repeat these 6 steps for pattern.

CUT LOOPS

Just for fun, make giant loops, then cut them for a long and wild pile. The plus: it's quick to do; the minus: it's not nearly as stable as ghiordes knots. If I had a pillow woven in this fabric in my 1970s dorm room, I would have thought myself super cool! I used doubled thick-and-thin yarn for the loop weft and worsted-weight wool singles for the background weft. I picked up loops every other space and wove 3 rows of plain weave between each row of loops.

CLOUD PUFFS

In this sample, small clusters of loops dance cloud-like on a deep blue worsted-weight background. I doubled the white worsted-weight loop weft for greater impact. I made loops in the first 2 spaces, skipped the next 2 spaces, picked up 2, skipped 2, and so on. I wove 1 row of plain weave with blue weft, then repeated the first loop row. I then wove ½" (1.3 cm) of blue background weft and repeated the loop pattern as before, but began the loops in the second space so as to shift the position of the loops. I began the next loop row in the third space, and the next row in the fourth space. On the fifth repeat, I began again at the first space.

Because there is so much space between the loops, the supplementary loop weft forms distinct white horizontal lines between the loop clusters. I cut the loop yarn after each repeat so I didn't have to carry it along the selvedge. By beginning with the selvedge thread down, you can neatly tuck the end over the first 2 down warps, then leave the end hanging off the back to be sewed in or clipped flush later.

FUZZY WUZZY LOOPS

There's nothing shy about this weft-faced hot-pink background accented with an explosion of loops. Two yellow eyelash, and an end each of 3/2 pearl cotton in pistachio, 10/2 pearl cotton in fuchsia, and golden mohair combine for a textural extravaganza of loops. To give my loops plenty of space to show off, I picked up loops every third space (beginning in the second space from the edge) and wove ¾" (2 cm) of background in hot pink worsted-weight yarn between each row of loops. This sample makes me smile.

ALL TOGETHER NOW

Blocks of loops alternate on changing fields of color for this riotous sample suitable for a bag or wall hanging. I've used dark gray, yellow, lime green, and olive 3/2 pearl cotton and completely covered the warp for a smooth weft-faced fabric. The soft ribbon yarn (Deco-Ribbon #123 from Crystal Palace), looped around a size 11 (8 mm) knitting needle, is a puffy, fun detail against the colorful background. Think of the loop areas as blocks and alternate the blocks with each repeat of the pattern. Part of the charm of this piece is the shifting background colors.

Soumak

Soumak is another rug technique that I use to add a textural accent to both weft-faced and balanced weaves. Soumak, a wrapping technique, is a cousin to Brook's bouquet (see page 59) in that warp ends are encircled with the weft yarn. In the case of soumak, the warp is completely covered instead of creating the lacy, or open, effect of Brook's bouquet. Another difference between the two is that soumak is always worked on a closed shed while Brook's bouquet is most often (though not always) worked on an open shed.

As with many of the rug techniques I've presented in this book, consider this just an introduction. There is so much to soumak that whole books could—and have!—been devoted to it. The soumak I present here is just another tool to use in designing your own unique pieces.

Traditionally, soumak is used to create pattern in rugs. Because it does not provide structural integrity to the textile, it is used in conjunction with a plain-weave ground. Work soumak on a closed shed and weave at least 2 rows of plain weave between each soumak row. Though there are numerous ways to work soumak, I present the two most common: soumak and locked soumak.

You'll notice that soumak has a directional angle. When you work from right to left in regular soumak, the wraps lean to the right. On the return trip, the wraps lean to the left. When these 2 rows are beaten close together, they give the appearance of a knitted fabric. But what if you want every row of soumak to lean to the right? That's where locked soumak comes in. By just varying how you encircle the warps, you can change the angle of the soumak.

Although I present soumak as a weft-faced technique here, I often employ it as an accent on a balanced weave. In this application, soumak gives a contrasting raised surface and creates a solid line of color that is a perfect accent along a border of a mat or at the edge of a cuff.

HOW TO WORK SOUMAK

Sett the warp for a weft-faced weave and choose a ground weft that covers the warp completely. For the soumak, or pattern weft, choose a yarn that is at least equal in size or larger than the background weft. Also consider the way that the yarn is constructed. For example, when I've used a singles worsted yarn and made wraps slanting in the same direction by alternating rows of regular and locking soumak, the wrappings are crisp and even. But, when I make every row in regular soumak to create a chevron pattern, the motion of the wrappings on the return trip untwists the yarn, making it fluffier and less crisp. Plied yarns are a good option for soumak, but they too are affected by the wrapping motion, both adding and subtracting twist, depending on which

direction you wrap. I've found that the tighter the twist, the more even and uniform the soumak. Should you find that the yarn has become too untwisted, you can add twist back into the yarn as you go just by giving your butterfly a turn or two after you've made a wrap. Likewise, you can untwist the yarn in the same way, should it become overly kinked.

Besides deciding on the direction of the slant of the soumak, you also need to decide how many warp ends to include in each grouping. Generally, notations are written as ratios—3:1, 2:2, 4:2, for example. The first number refers to the number of warp ends that the weft travels over and the second number refers to the number of warp ends that the weft encircles. The groupings are determined by the sett, yarn size, and desired effect.

Regular Versus Locking Soumak

The only difference between regular and locking soumak is how the warp is encircled. In regular soumak, the working end is toward the reed, above or to the heddle side of the wrap, as it wraps around the warp. In locking soumak, the wrap is made between the working end and the fell of the cloth, or below the wrap. To make soumak that creates a chevron, use regular soumak when you work the first row to the right and return from the left. To create rows that slant in the same direction, work regular soumak from right to left and locking soumak left to right.

Regular soumak worked to the left.

Locking soumak worked to the left.

Weaving 3:1 Soumak

To begin, wind a butterfly of the pattern yarn (see page 159).

STEP 1. Weave 1" (2.5 cm) or so of plain weave with the background yarn before beginning the soumak.

STEP 2. Insert the tail of the pattern weft under the selvedge thread and then over, under, over the next 3 warps, then pull the tail to the back of the weaving (Figure **1**).

STEP 3. On a closed shed and working from right to left, bring the pattern yarn over 3 warps.

STEP 4. Wrap the pattern yarn around the leftmost of these 3 warps (Figures **2** and **3**).

STEP 5. Bring the pattern weft over 3 warps, back around 1 warp, and so on to the other selvedge (Figure **4**).

STEP 6. Weave 2 rows of plain weave with ground weft (Figure **5**).

STEP 7. To begin the next row, insert the butterfly between the last 2 warps and bring it out at the side, then over the first 3 warps, and around the rightmost of these 3 warps (Figure **6**).

STEP 8. Weave back to the other selvedge in the same manner, traveling over 3 and back around 1 (Figure **7**).

STEP 9. Weave at least 2 rows of plain weave with ground weft.

Repeat Steps 3–9 as desired for pattern.

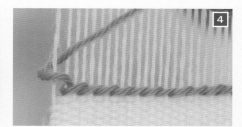

Two-Color Soumak with Locking Soumak

You can use two colors in the same soumak row to create a barber-pole effect. This is just one of any number of ways to work with two colors. Play around with color combinations to see what you can create.

STEP 1. Beginning at the selvedge, weave both tails into the first 4 warps by going under, over, under, and over.

STEP 2. Begin with the color farthest away from you (yellow shown here), travel over 2 warps and wind around the second-most left warp using locking soumak. You'll travel over just 2 warps with this first wrapping, which will offset the two colors by 1 warp end (Figure **1**). Thereafter travel over 3.

STEP 3. Bring the other color (green shown here) over 3 warps, then wind it around the third warp using locking soumak (Figure **2**).

STEP 4. Repeat Steps 2 and 3 all the way across the web, leapfrogging the 2 colors one after the other (Figure **3**) and snugging up the yarns as you go for even tension.

STEP 5. Weave 2 rows of plain weave.

STEP 6. Carry the two weft butterflies up to the next row in between the first and second warp threads.

STEP 7. Beginning with the color you started with on the other side, travel over 2 warp ends, then wrap around the second using locking soumak.

STEP 8. As on the opposite side, take up the second color and travel over 3 warps, then travel over 3 warps with the first color, and so on all the way to the other selvedge.

TWO-COLOR SOUMAK, VARIATION

For this sample, I worked this soumak just like the previous example, but I did not twist the yarns around each other. I began as before by going over 2 warps at the beginning with one color, and then following with the second color by traveling over 3 warps and around the last of these 3 (3:1 soumak). Because I didn't wrap the yarns around each other, each color works independently to create a straight line. On the return trip, I started with the color I didn't start with on the first trip, framing two lines of one color by the second one.

SOUMAK BLOCK

For this sample, I made soumak just in the center of the background. To do this, I wove about a third of the way across, then closed the shed and worked soumak for several wraps, then I opened the shed and wove across to the other edge. I changed sheds, wove across to the soumak area, made locking soumak in the center, and then resumed plain weave across to the edge. Like in ghiordes knots (see page 143), the soumak area will build up more than the plain weave so you'll need to weave some plain weave fill on each side of the soumak. Accomplish this in the same way as working fill-in for ghiordes knots (see page 149).

Winding a Butterfly

You'll find it handy to use small packages of yarn for finger-controlled weaves such as soumak in which the weft yarn needs to wrap around warp or go in and out of the shed. You can make small hand hanks, or butterflies, quite quickly, and you'll find them to be a low-tech convenience.

Step 1. With the palm of your hand turned upward and fingers spread wide, wind between your little finger and thumb, holding the tail between your thumb and palm (Figure 1).

FIGURE 1

Step 2. Wind back and forth between your little finger and thumb in a figure-eight path (Figure 2), winding enough yarn to make a comfortable butterfly. Too small and you have to change wefts too often; too large, the butterfly becomes unwieldy.

FIGURE 2

Step 3. Remove the butterfly from your hand and snugly wrap the working tail a couple of times around the center, tucking the end under the last wrap to secure it (Figure 3).

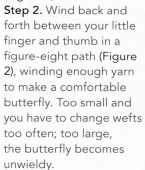
FIGURE 3

Feed the yarn from the butterfly from the other end; it will easily pull out of the center of the butterfly.

CHANGING BLOCKS

For this example, I worked 4 repeats of 3:1 regular soumak.
I then switched to locking soumak for the next 4 wraps,
and changed again to regular soumak, ending with locking
soumak. I wove 2 rows of plain weave before beginning the
next row of soumak, where I again alternated between 4 wraps
of regular soumak and 4 wraps of locking soumak.

SOUMAK TIPS

When starting and stopping the pattern weft, you can
split the plies or singles yarn to reduce bulk. To begin the
pattern weft, weave the tail under the selvedge thread, and
then over, under, over, the next 3 warps, then poke the tail to
the back of the weaving.

To travel from one row of soumak to the next, carry the weft
yarn up to the next row and down in between the selvedge
thread and the next thread, bringing it to the outside and
then over the top to make the first wrap.

Snug up the wraps as you work. If you notice that one wrap
is too loose or too tight, go back and adjust the tension so
that the surface of the soumak is smooth and even.

Krokbragd

Krokbragd is a twill-based weave (the name means "crooked path") that comes to us from Norway. This thick weft-faced weave is characterized by spirited patterning. I imagine it providing a bright spot in an otherwise cold room where it was used over doorways and windows to keep out the bitter winter cold.

If you examine krokbragd on the loom, you'll notice that every third pick is actually a plain-weave row, adding stability and keeping the fabric from excessive curling, which is apt to happen when there are long floats on one side of the fabric. Even though this is a twill structure, the characteristic twill diagonal isn't evident due to the nature in which krokbragd is woven.

In krokbragd, 3 weft rows equal 1 row of pattern. Think of columns, rather than rows, of colors. Also, keep in mind that the weaving sequence never changes—only the colors change. For example, it takes 3 weft picks to create a solid line of red. If you weave 2 picks of red and 1 of green, spots of green will appear in that row.

In designing a krokbragd pattern, it is helpful to remember that the weft color shows over the warp threads that are not raised and that the weaving sequence (treadling) never changes (again, only the colors change). It's fun to watch patterns develop while weaving krokbragd, although it is slow to weave.

Here, I've woven krokbragd with one rigid heddle reed and two pick-up sticks. Begin by placing the heddle in the down shed, insert pick-up stick A and pick up every other raised thread. Next, insert pick-up stick B and pick up all of the threads not picked up on pick-up stick A. To avoid re-picking every 3rd row, install string heddles and a heddle rod as described on page 98.

Sampler designed and woven by Angela Johnson.

KROKBRAGD NOTES

To keep straight selvedges, you may sometimes need to go over or under the selvedge thread separately, depending on your color sequence. When weaving with three colors, there are three separate ends to deal with, which can get messy. I try not to wind the colors together at the selvedge because it creates bulk. Rather, I like to see what is happening each time with my sequence and determine what needs to be done with each pass, as shown in the photos below. (To weave krokbragd on a shaft loom, you can use floating selvedges to take care of the problem.)

Because the weft does not catch the selvedge thread on this pass, I manually placed my shuttle over the edge thread and into the shed.

Here, the new weft passes over the last thread and into the shed, with no wrapping around the previous weft required.

Weft-faced weaves, such as krokbragd, have a tendency to draw in. To counter this, be sure to allow at least a 45-degree angle in the shed when you insert the weft.

Because you cannot beat as hard on a rigid heddle loom as you might on a floor loom, you may find it necessary to use a hand beater to press the weft into place. You want to beat enough to cover the warp but not so densely that the pattern becomes squished. It's helpful to practice at the beginning of a piece.

TO WEAVE KROKBRAGD

Pick-up stick pattern A: *1 up, 1 down; repeat from *.
Pick-up stick pattern B: *1 down, 1 up; repeat from *.
STEP 1. Up and pick-up stick A.
STEP 2. Up and pick-up stick B.
STEP 3. Down.
Repeat these 3 steps for each "row" of pattern.

Remember: One row of pattern requires three passes with the shuttle.
W = white; B = blue; P = pink; G = green.

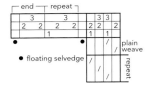

FLAME POINT 1

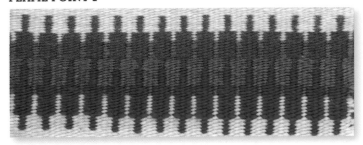

This pattern seems to be a cousin to Scandinavian knitted sweater design.
STEP 1. Weave [BWW] 4 times.
STEP 2. Weave [BWB] 7 times.
STEP 3. Weave [BGB] 3 times.
STEP 4. Weave [BGG] 7 times.
STEP 5. Weave [PGG] 3 times.
STEP 6. Weave [PGP] 7 times.
STEP 7. Weave [PWP] 3 times.
STEP 8. Weave [PWW] 7 times.

ZIGZAG BORDER

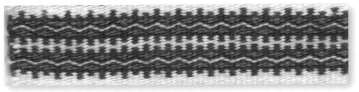

Because this sample has so many color order changes for each line of the design, you may find it helpful to label your shuttles 1, 2, 3 to help you keep track of the sequences.

GROUP 1:
STEP 1. Weave WWW.
STEP 2. Weave PWW.
STEP 3. Weave PPW.
STEP 4. Weave PPP.
STEP 5. Weave PGG.
STEP 6. Weave PGP.
STEP 7. Weave WPW.
STEP 8. Weave PWP.
GROUP 2:
STEP 9. Weave GPG.
STEP 10. Weave GPP.
STEP 11. Weave PPW.
STEP 12. Weave PPW.
STEP 13. Weave PWW.
GROUP 3:
STEP 14. Weave WPW.
STEP 15. Weave PPW.
STEP 16. Weave PPP.
STEP 17. Weave PGG.
STEP 18. Weave PGP.
STEP 19. Weave WPW.
STEP 20. Weave PWP.
STEP 21. Weave GPG.
STEP 22. Weave GPP.
STEP 23. Weave PPW.
STEP 24. Weave PPW.
STEP 25. Weave WPW.
END:
STEP 26. Weave WWW.

DOTS

By surrounding green and pink with white, individual dots of color appear on a background of white.

STEP 1. Weave [WWW] 2 times.
STEP 2. Weave [GPW] 3 times.
STEP 3. Weave WWW.
STEP 4. Weave [PGW] 3 times.
STEP 5. Weave WWW.
STEP 6. Weave [GPW] 3 times.
STEP 7. Weave [WWW] 2 times.

FLAME POINT 2

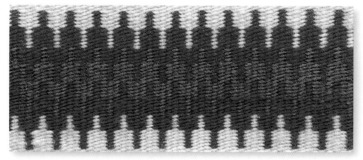

This is a typical treadling for krokbragd.

STEP 1. Weave [BWW] 5 times.
STEP 2. Weave [BWB] 5 times.
STEP 3. Weave [GBB] 5 times.
STEP 4. Weave [GBG] 5 times.
STEP 5. Weave [PGG] 5 times.
STEP 6. Weave [PGP] 5 times.
STEP 7. Weave [WPP] 5 times.
STEP 8. Weave [WPW] 5 times.

FLOWER GARDEN

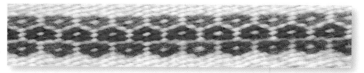

Where the last sample is bold in nature, this example is light and delicate.

STEP 1. Weave WWW.
STEP 2. Weave PWP.
STEP 3. Weave WWP.
STEP 4. Weave PWW.
STEP 5. Weave WBB.
STEP 6. Weave WWB.
STEP 7. Weave WBW.
STEP 8. Weave GWG.
STEP 9. Weave WWG.
STEP 10. Weave GWW.

SQUARES

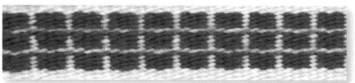

Wavy lines divide 3 rows of blue squares.

STEP 1. Weave WWW.
STEP 2. Weave [WBB] 4 times.
STEP 3. Weave GWW.
STEP 4. Weave [WBB] 4 times.
STEP 5. Weave GWW.
STEP 6. Weave [WBB] 4 times.
STEP 7. Weave GWW.

GUITARS

With color and pattern, you can suggest motifs.

STEP 1. Weave PWP.

STEP 2. Weave [WWP] 4 times.

STEP 3. Weave [PWP] 4 times.

STEP 4. Weave [WWP] 4 times.

STEP 5. Weave [PWW] 5 times.

STEP 6. Weave PWB.

STEP 7. Weave PWW.

STEP 8. Repeat Steps 6 and 7 three times.

STEP 9. Weave WPP.

STEP 10. Weave [WWP] 4 times.

STEP 11. Weave [WPP] 4 times.

STEP 12. Weave [WWP] 4 times.

STEP 13. Weave [WPW] 5 times.

STEP 14. Weave WPG.

STEP 15. Weave WPW.

STEP 16. Repeat Steps 14 and 15 three times.

Clasped Weft

Clasped-weft technique, also known as "meet and separate," is a way to create a tapestry-like effect with a single shuttle, but is much, much quicker. Generally, clasped weft technique is used in a weft-faced or weft-emphasis fabric, one in which a bit of the warp shows but where the weft dominates.

In clasped weft there are two wefts, one on a shuttle and one from a ball of yarn. The shuttle weaves across from one side to the other, encircles, or interlocks the weft from the ball of yarn and draws it into the shed as far as you want the new color to go. The shuttle then returns to the side from which it began. There are therefore doubled wefts in the shed. The shed is changed after each row.

A clasped-weft design is determined by how far the loop from the ball of yarn is drawn into the shed. For example, if you want your colors to meet in the center, you'll draw the loop of yarn from the ball to the center and return the shuttle to the selvedge from which it came. You'll change sheds and repeat. That's all there is to it!

CLASPED-WEFT NOTES

When choosing yarn, remember that it will be woven double in the shed.

When you draw the loop from the ball of yarn into the shed, keep a watchful eye on the selvedge to make sure that it doesn't pull in too much. It is helpful to keep the yarn loose in the shed so that it can be easily pulled into position.

To maintain straight lines, align the joins between warp ends. Adjust the joins as necessary.

To pack in the weft, beat on a closed shed.

Clasped Weft, Step by Step

STEP 1. Place the ball of yarn on the left, open the shed, and insert the shuttle from right to left (Figure **1**). *Note:* I have placed the yarn on the table for photographic purposes; you'll just set your ball on the floor by the side of your loom.

STEP 2. Encircle the yarn from the ball of yarn with the shuttle and re-enter the shuttle into the shed without changing the shed (Figure **2**). The weft will be doubled in this shed.

STEP 3. Draw the yarn loop from the ball of yarn into the shed and adjust the position between 2 warp threads according to your pattern (Figure **3**).

STEP 4. Beat this weft row into place (Figure **4**), then change sheds.

Repeat these 4 steps as desired for pattern.

This technique is used for the Summertime Coasters on page 174.

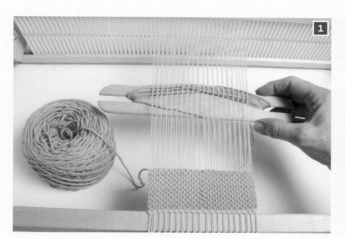

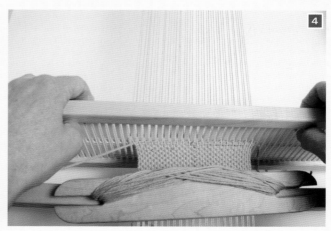

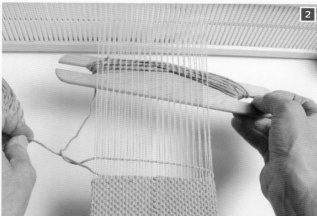

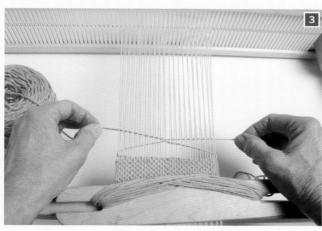

Weft-Faced Fabrics and Pick-Up Patterns

Weft-faced or weft-emphasis fabrics can be combined with pick-up patterns for intriguing textures. This sampler is warped at 10 epi with 3/2 pearl cotton in natural and accented every sixth thread with a heaver cotton warp thread (Brown Sheep Cotton Fleece in Charcoal). It is woven at about 18 ppi.

Woven by Melissa Ludden Hankens.

Front.   Reverse.

WEFT-EMPHASIS WITH FLOATS

Both warp floats and weft floats work together to create a dense textured surface where weft floats predominate. The same pattern is woven with three different background colors, off-white, medium gray, and dark gray. The heavier pattern weft, a dark charcoal, is the same for all three samples.

Pick-up stick pattern: *1 up, 2 down; repeat from *.

STEP 1. Up.

STEP 2. Pick-up stick, pattern weft.

STEP 3. Up.

STEP 4. Down.

STEP 5. Up and pick-up stick.

STEP 6. Down.

STEP 7. Up and pick-up stick.

STEP 8. Down.

The reverse side of the fabric reveals vertical paired spots of weft floats. Because this fabric is very dense and the floats are quite short, it is ideally suited for a table mat or runner.

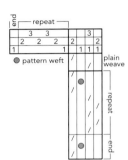

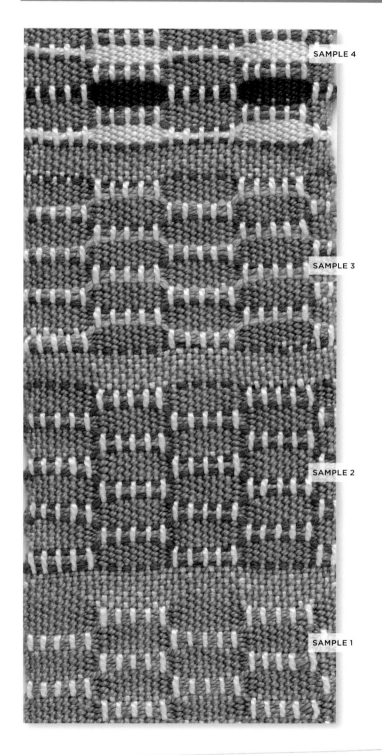

SAMPLE 4

SAMPLE 3

SAMPLE 2

SAMPLE 1

HONEYCOMB STUDIES

This is a sturdy fabric of densely packed weft with warp- and pattern-weft accents. For the bottom sample, no contrasting weft is used. The fabric has a quilted feel with the warp floats predominating, but without the characteristic curvy lines of honeycomb. This is evident in the next three examples where a single supplementary weft is used at the exchange of the blocks, first in dark charcoal for Sample 2, then alternating charcoal and blue for Sample 3, and dark charcoal for Sample 4. In this final sample, medium gray is alternated with first white and then dark gray for cells of different colors.

Pick-up stick pattern A: *5 up, 5 down; repeat from *.
Pick-up stick pattern B: *5 down, 5 up; repeat from *.

STEP 1. Up and pick-up stick A.

STEP 2. Down.

STEP 3. Up and pick-up stick A.

STEP 4. Down.

STEP 5. Up and pick-up stick A.

STEP 6. Down.

STEP 7. Up and pick-up stick A.

STEP 8. Down.

STEP 9. Up and pick-up stick B.

STEP 10. Down.

STEP 11. Up and pick-up stick B.

STEP 12. Down.

STEP 13. Up and pick-up stick B.

STEP 14. Down.

STEP 15. Up and pick-up stick B.

STEP 16. Down.

Repeat these 16 steps for pattern.

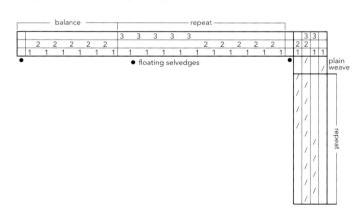

HONEYCOMB VARIATION

This sample is woven honeycomb fashion as well, but the warp floats are not as long because they have been tied down with another row of plain weave between blocks, which creates a subtle, undulating blue line.

Pick-up stick pattern A: *5 up, 5 down; repeat from *.
Pick-up stick pattern B: *5 down, 5 up; repeat from *.

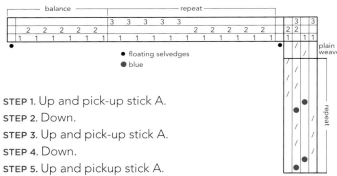

STEP 1. Up and pick-up stick A.
STEP 2. Down.
STEP 3. Up and pick-up stick A.
STEP 4. Down.
STEP 5. Up and pickup stick A.
STEP 6. Up, blue weft.
STEP 7. Down, blue weft.
STEP 8. Up and pick-up stick B.
STEP 9. Down.
STEP 10. Up and pick-up stick B.
STEP 11. Down.
STEP 12. Up and pick-up stick B.
STEP 13. Up, blue weft.
STEP 14. Down, blue weft.
Repeat these 14 steps for pattern.

WEFT FLOATS—HONEYCOMB FASHION

The same pick-up stick pattern is used to create these dynamic weft floats. Two strands of worsted-weight cotton in pink and dark pink float on top of a background woven in 3/2 pearl cotton.

Pick-up stick pattern A: (dark pink) *5 up, 5 down; repeat from *.
Pick-up stick pattern B: (light pink) *5 down, 5 up; repeat from *.

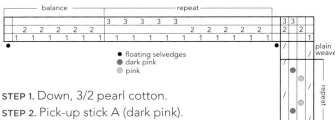

STEP 1. Down, 3/2 pearl cotton.
STEP 2. Pick-up stick A (dark pink).
STEP 3. Pick-up stick B (light pink).
STEP 4. Up, 3/2 pearl cotton.
STEP 5. Down, 3/2 pearl cotton.
STEP 6. Pick-up stick B (light pink).
STEP 7. Pick-up stick A (dark pink).
STEP 8. Up, 3/2 pearl cotton.
Repeat these 8 steps for pattern.

Warp-Faced Fabrics

Just as you can create fabrics where only the weft shows, you can also create fabrics where just the warp is seen. Like weft-faced fabrics, warp-faced fabrics are denser and less flexible than a corresponding balanced weave. Warp-faced fabrics are super for handles and belts, where density and strength are required.

In a warp-faced fabric, the warps are so close together that no weft yarn shows on the surface of the fabric. Generally, a warp-faced fabric should be made from smooth yarn. Because the warp yarns are close together, they need to be able to slide past each other easily when the sheds are changed. Fuzzy yarns will tend to grab onto each other and frustrate the weaving process. Because the warp threads are lined up closer together than a rigid heddle reed can accommodate, the heddle is often used just for making the sheds, not beating. A belt shuttle, a special shuttle with a beveled edge, is indispensable for pressing the weft into place and for carrying the weft to and fro.

Weaving a true warp-faced fabric, one in which none of the weft shows at all, except at the edge where it wraps around a selvedge thread, takes some practice and patience. The angle of the threads coming from the reed makes the weaving want to splay out. Your job is to be constantly vigilant in controlling the width as you weave. I keep a ruler at my side and check the width often. I also weave as close to the front of the loom as possible, advance the warp every 2" (5 cm), and place the heddle as far back on my loom as possible, even using the cross brace at the back of the loom when it's in the up position. For the best result, crank up the tension on your loom as much as physically possible.

In warp-faced weaving, all the action is in the warp. The fun and challenge come from playing around with the warp colors to create patterns. For example, two colors threaded together will create a wavy line. A single warp end surrounded by another color will create a dot. Alternating two colors, one in the hole and the other in a slot, will create horizontal bars. Once you start playing around, you'll see just how many possibilities there are. If you add pick-up patterns, you can increase the options exponentially.

Rigid Heddle Versus Inkle Loom for Band Weaving

I would say that the rigid heddle loom is not ideal for band weaving because of the angle of the warp from the heddle. I include it here because I want you to know that you can weave a warp-faced band on your rigid heddle loom, with some adjustments. However, it is not my loom of choice should I want to weave bands and nothing else. For band weaving, I prefer an inkle loom.

If you become keen about weaving warp-faced bands, I recommend you invest in an inkle loom—a simple loom designed specifically for warp-faced band weaving. Like a rigid heddle loom, warps on an inkle loom are threaded alternately fixed and open. But instead of a reed, string heddles are used. The warp ends are threaded alternately in string heddles (like the holes in a rigid heddle loom) and open (like the slots in the rigid heddle loom). Refer to the pick-up techniques in Chapter 3 to see how to apply this technique to the inkle loom where patterns are made by picking up the open (slot) threads.

Starting and Stopping Wefts

At the beginning of the band, leave a tail of weft hanging at the edge. Weave across, change sheds, and return the shuttle to the side you began from. Now, place the tail into this same shed all the way across (Figure 1). Beat well. Trim this tail off after you have removed the band from the loom.

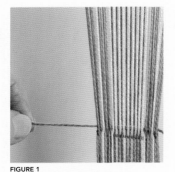

FIGURE 1

At the end of the band you'll use a tapestry needle that has an eye large enough to thread the weft yarn. On the next-to-the-last pick, working right to left, open the shed and weave across, then insert the tapestry needle (with the eye on the right) into this same shed (Figure 2). Change sheds and weave back to the right, cut off the yarn from the shuttle, leaving a tail that you'll thread through the needle (Figure 3). Draw this end through the shed with the tapestry needle, and your end is secure.

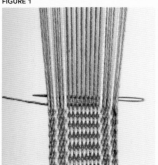

FIGURE 2

FIGURE 3

Weaving Warp-Faced Fabrics

STEP 1. Tie the warp onto the front apron bar as close together as you possibly can (Figure 1).

STEP 2. Place heddle in the up position. Pass the shuttle from one side of the shed to the other (Figure 2).

STEP 3. Pull the weft tight, place the heddle in the down position, and press the weft into place with the shuttle. Check the width of the weaving and pull on the weft to further draw in the weaving as necessary.

Repeat Steps 2 and 3 as desired. *Note:* The weft will stay put and pack in better if you beat after changing the shed. I find that I weave most evenly if I use both hands on the shuttle and pull straight down to pack the weft.

FIGURE 1

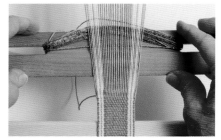

FIGURE 2

Pick-Up on Warp-Faced Fabrics

Just as for balanced fabrics, you can create warp-faced pick-up patterns on your rigid heddle loom. Instead of a pick-up stick, you can use your fingers.

Step 1. Place the heddle in the down position (slot threads are raised).
Step 2. Weave across with the shuttle.
Step 3. Beat.
Step 4. With the heddle still in the down position, pick-up the desired warp threads near the fell of your cloth.
Step 5. Hold the threads up with one hand and change the shed with the other hand.
Step 6. Insert the shuttle and weave across, beat, change sheds, and beat again.
Repeat these 6 steps as desired.

If you struggle to hold the threads up with one hand while changing the shed with the other, place the threads on a small pick-up stick. When you insert the shuttle in the shed, be sure that you are in front of where the picked-up threads exchange layers.

You'll find this a bit slow at first, but after you have the steps firmly in mind, the pick-up process will be almost automatic.

Exploring Warp-Faced Pick-Up

The following bookmarks are little mini warp-faced samplers. They show warp floats worked in pairs and singly. Long floats are created by picking up the same warp threads for several passes. The first sample is woven in plain weave, the next one has a picked-up field of paired warp floats and the final two illustrate single warp floats. Yarns are 10/2 pearl cotton, sleyed in a 12-dent reed and drawn in to about 40 epi.

Warp Color Order:

Gray	4				4	1		4			4
White		4		4					4	4	
Pink			2				1			2	
						12×					

Note: Begin threading in a slot and be sure to sley the gray threads in the central field (alternating gray and pink threads) in the slots so that they can be picked up for the pattern.

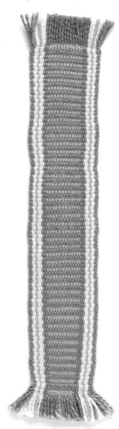

BAND WITH PAIRED WARP PATTERN

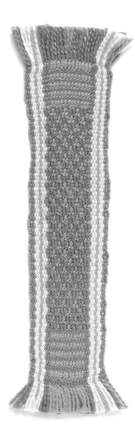

Pick-up pattern A (in central field only): *2 up, 2 down; repeat from *.

Pick-up pattern B (in central field only): *2 down, 2 up; repeat from *.

STEP 1. Weave up, down, up as long as desired for end of band, ending with the up shed.

STEP 2. Down; pick up threads and hold on fingers or pick-up stick.

STEP 3. Up with pick-up pattern A (or held by fingers).

STEP 4. Down; pick up threads and hold on fingers or pick-up stick.

STEP 5. Up with pick-up pattern B (or held by fingers).

STEP 6. Repeat Steps 2–5 for pattern.

STEP 7. Weave down, up, down, up as long as desired for end of band.

BAND WITH SINGLE WARP FLOATS

Pick-up pattern: *1 down, 1 up; repeat from *.

STEP 1. Up.

STEP 2. Down.

STEP 3. Up and pick-up pattern.

STEP 4. Down.

Repeat these 4 steps for pattern.

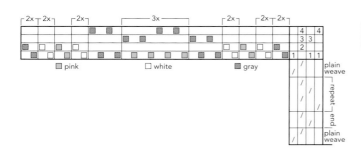

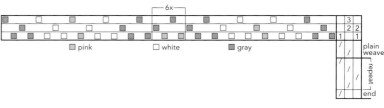

BAND WITH LONG SINGLE WARP FLOATS

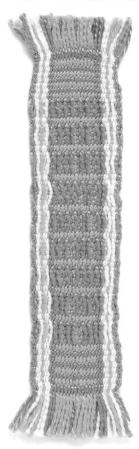

Pick-up pattern: *1 down, 1 up; repeat from *.

STEP 1. Down.

STEP 2. Up and pick-up pattern.

STEP 3. Down.

STEP 4. Up and pick-up pattern.

STEP 5. Down.

STEP 6. Up.

Repeat these 6 steps for pattern.

Conclusion

In this chapter, I've touched on warp- and weft-faced fabrics. While I've introduced the concept of warp-faced weaving, the bulk of the material focuses on weft-faced weaving. This is because I have a penchant for weft-faced fabrics—I like the freedom of working weft-wise and I don't find the rigid heddle loom ideal for band weaving (I prefer an inkle loom designed specifically for this purpose).

In weft-faced fabrics, you can change the color order at any time and create color patterns, add highlights of pile or texture, or use ghiordes knots to create a picture. I like the sturdiness of weft-faced fabrics—they are ideal for any use requiring a hefty material.

Because all of the design happens warp-wise in warp-faced fabrics, you need to make all of the design decisions prior to warping the loom. Generally, you'll want to use smooth yarns that can pack in closely for the warp. Because the yarns need to be pressed tightly together, I suggest you limit warp-faced rigid heddle weaving to narrow bands. Pick-up patterns, using your fingers or a pick-up stick, are easily accomplished and create delightful designs.

You may find these techniques slower than weaving balanced plain-weave fabric, but I urge you not to let this deter you from trying techniques in this chapter. The important thing is to choose the right technique, weave, and accent to produce the result you want—it's a thrill to solve a little design problem with just the right weave technique.

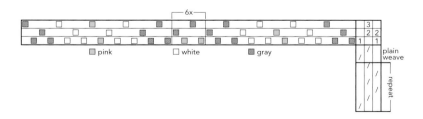

Summertime
COASTERS

Designed and woven by Judy Steinkoenig.

These coasters in clasped-weft technique are a fun way to try out patterns and create something useful in the process. Once you get started weaving these, you'll just keep coming up with more pattern ideas. See page 165 for instructions on weaving clasped weft. I like using hemstitching for a coaster or table mat because it lies completely flat on the table, unlike a knotted fringe that creates bumps on the ends.

Finished Size
Four coasters, each about 4" (10 cm) wide and 4¼" (11 cm) long, excluding fringe.

Weave Structure
Plain weave with clasped weft.

Yarn
Warp: *Great Northern 8/4 Cotton Carpet Warp* (100% cotton; 1,680 yd [1,536 m]/lb): Pear, 60 yd (55 m), or about ⅗ oz.
Weft: *Brown Sheep Cotton Fleece* (80% cotton, 20% merino wool; 975 yd [891 m]/lb; 215 yd [196 m]/100 g skein): #CW255 Coral Sunset, #CW145 Robin Egg Blue, and #CW355 Dark Khaki Green, about 20 yd (18 m) each for set of four coasters.

Equipment
Rigid heddle loom with at least a 5" (12.5 cm) weaving width; 8-dent rigid heddle reed; one shuttle; tapestry needle for hemstitching.

Number of Warp Ends
40.

Warp Length
2 yards (1.8 m), which includes 28" (71 cm) of take-up and loom waste and 2" (5 cm) of fringe between each of the four coasters.

Warp Width
5" (12.5 cm).

EPI
8.

PPI
11.

Warping

Thread an 8-dent rigid heddle reed with cotton carpet warp for a 5" (12.5 cm) weaving width.

Weaving

Leaving a long tail (about 20" [51 cm] or four times the weaving width) for hemstitching, weave 2 picks of cotton carpet warp for a border, hemstitch the first edge (see page 69), follow the pattern diagram for the center of the coaster, weave 2 picks of cotton carpet warp, then hemstitch the other end. Each coaster should measure 4½" (11.5 cm) under tension on the loom. Advance the warp, allowing 2" (5 cm) fringe between coasters, and begin the next coaster.

Finishing

Remove fabric from loom and cut the coasters apart. Handwash in warm water and lay flat to dry. Steam-press, then trim off tails.

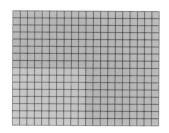
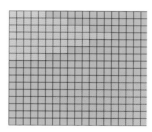
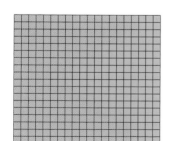
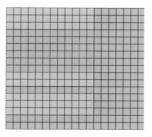

NOTES

To avoid bulk at the edges when changing colors, split the plies of the yarn when beginning and ending a color.

For even selvedges, snug up both sides of the yarn against the selvedges, bring the clasped yarns up to a 45-degree angle, then beat. The shuttle side may tend to draw in more; adjust the two yarns as necessary to keep the selvedges even.

For nice, even joins, always loop the shuttle around the second yarn (from the ball) in the same direction.

CHAPTER 5

More is More with

TWO HEDDLES

By using two rigid heddles, you can expand the capabilities of your rigid heddle loom. You can double your warp sett to weave finer fabrics, thread different warp densities, create simple patterns, weave 1/3 twills with ease, as well as tackle doubleweave. To double the number of warp ends per inch, you'll need two identical rigid heddles (i.e., two 10-dent rigid heddles). You'll also need a rigid heddle loom that can accommodate two heddles. I use the Flip folding rigid heddle loom, which has slots for two heddles built into the frame. An additional block can be secured to many other rigid heddle looms to accommodate a second heddle.

Besides the patterning you can create with different combinations of the heddles, you can weave any of the pick-up patterns presented in Chapter 3, as well as any of the finger techniques described in Chapter 2. To warp for two heddles, you can either use the direct warping peg method or the indirect method of measuring the warp first, then threading the first, or front, heddle (we'll call this Heddle I), then the second, or back, heddle (we'll call this Heddle II), winding the warp onto the back beam, and finally, tying onto the front beam. Though not as quick as the direct warping peg method (which I use most often), the indirect method eliminates twisted warp threads behind the heddles that can cause frustrations during weaving, especially when weaving very fine threads.

To understand the two-heddle technique, imagine that the fingers on your hands are the threads in your heddles. Place the fingers of one hand in the spaces between the fingers of the other and you essentially have what's happening when you take the threads from Heddle I and thread them in Heddle II.

Using Two Heddles for Fine Fabrics

For fabrics woven with fine threads, you can use two 10-dent reeds to weave 20 ends per inch. Likewise, with two 12-dent reeds you can weave as fine as 24 ends per inch. Why use two heddles for fine fabrics? Wouldn't it be easier to use a finer reed? Theoretically, yes, but practically, no. This is because rigid heddles are molded out of plastic with alternating slots and holes. While it might be possible to make a rigid heddle reed with a finer sett, it isn't physically feasible to make a reed finer than 12 dents per inch and still have enough space for the threading hook to pass through the holes and slots, nor to provide sufficient space for the yarn to move freely. Using two rigid heddles together to produce a finer sett solves this problem. It's easier than you might at first suspect.

Indirect Warping For Two Heddles

Threading the Front Heddle (Heddle I)

Working from the back of the loom and from right to left, begin by threading 1 end in a hole (**Figure 1**). Thread the next 3 ends in the next slot (**Figure 2**), then 1 end in the next hole, then 3 ends in the next slot, and so on across the warp.

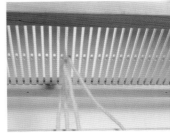

FIGURE 1   FIGURE 2

Threading the Back Heddle (Heddle II)

In threading from Heddle I to Heddle II, think in terms of four-end groupings. Working right to left, select the ends from the first hole and slot (4 ends total) in Heddle I. Find the corresponding hole in Heddle II (the back heddle). Place the hole thread and one of the slot threads from Heddle I into the slot to the right of the corresponding hole in Heddle II. Two threads will remain in the slot in Heddle I. Thread one of these in the hole to the left and the other in the next slot to the left. Move onto the next 4-end grouping and thread these in the same way. Heddle I will have 3 threads in the slots and 1 thread in a hole. Heddle II will also have 3 threads in the slots and 1 thread in the hole (except at the selvedges), but the threads have shifted—and this is the key to two-heddle weaving. This may be confusing at first, but rest assured that it's easy to find a rhythm in the threading.

Let me stress that it is important to begin in the correct spot. I check to make sure by counting all of the slots from the end of the heddle to the edge of the threads in Heddle I, and then do the same for Heddle II. I begin threading Heddle II at this point.

To begin, place Heddle II behind (closest to the back of the loom) Heddle I.

STEP 1. Taking care to begin at the same point on both heddles, thread the first hole thread from Heddle I into the slot to the right of the corresponding hole in Heddle II (**Figure 1**).

STEP 2. Move onto the first slot in Heddle I, which contains 3 warp ends, and thread the first of these ends in the same slot that contains the end from the hole in Heddle I (**Figure 2**)—there will be 2 warp ends in the selvedge slot in Heddle II.

STEP 3. Thread the second warp end from the slot in Heddle I into the next hole to the left in Heddle II (**Figure 3**).

STEP 4. Thread the third warp end from the slot in Heddle I into the next slot to the left in Heddle II (**Figure 4**).

Repeat these 4 steps across the warp. There will be 3 threads in every slot and 1 thread in every hole (selvedges excepted), but the threads will have shifted from their position in Heddle I.

Tying onto the Apron Rod and Winding onto the Back Beam

Once both heddles are threaded, tie the warp ends into 1" (2.5 cm) bundles with overhand knots. Loop each knotted bundle around the apron rod and tuck the knotted end under the wrap to secure it in place (**Figure 1**). Wind the warp onto the back beam, placing stiff paper between wraps to ensure an even warp tension (**Figure 2**).

Both heddles are threaded and the ends are ready to be tied onto the apron rod and wound onto the back beam.

FIGURE 1

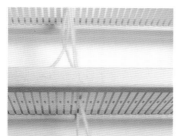

FIGURE 2

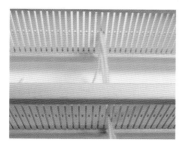

FIGURE 3

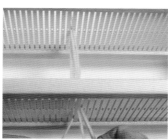

FIGURE 4

FIGURE 1

FIGURE 2

Weaving with Two Heddles

Weaving plain weave is easy as pie: just hold the two heddles together and place them together in the up position for the first pick, then together in the down position for the next pick. Before you realize it, you won't even know that you're using two together instead of one. For looms that do not have a two-heddle block, you will need to raise and lower the heddles individually.

It should come as no surprise that I suggest you begin by weaving a sample to explore the possibilities of two-heddle weaving. If you don't want to thread an entire warp for a sample, at least allow 12" (30.5 cm) of extra warp on your first two-heddle project so that you can play around before you begin the project.

Notice that when Heddle I is in the up position, the hole threads are raised. To see what is happening, look at the fell of the cloth: 1 thread is raised and 3 are down. When Heddle I is in the down position, the slot threads are raised, which means that 3 slot threads are raised to every 1 hole thread that is lowered. Therefore, you could weave a stable cloth by moving just Heddle 1. I call this structure a 3/1 modified basket weave.

What if you wanted to weave with Heddle II only—up, down, up, down? You'd essentially have the same interlacement as you did with Heddle I, only the threads would have

FIGURE 1

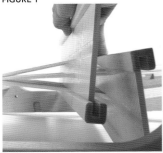

FIGURE 2

shifted. But you'll soon notice that the front heddle (Heddle I) gets in the way when you try to place Heddle II in the down position. To counteract this physical limitation, bring both heddles forward and leave them hanging free in front of the heddle block. Then, with one hand, push down on the back heddle and pull up on the front heddle (**Figure 1**). This creates a split shed; viewed from the side there are two openings (**Figure 2**). Be sure to use the lower shed for the Heddle II down shed. Although this is awkward at first, you'll get the hang of it after a very short time. But this does take more time than moving just Heddle I up and down. Therefore, I prefer patterns that don't require Heddle II in the down shed very often.

Measuring the Warp

When measuring warp for two-heddle weaving, I like to measure each color separately, unless I'm alternating warp colors, in which case I measure the two together on the warping board (Figure **1**).

STEP 1. When winding the warp, be sure to make a cross by winding in a figure-eight configuration at the end of the warp (Figures **2** and **3**).

STEP 2. Secure the cross by tying a piece of waste yarn of a different color around the center of it, then tie a piece of waste yarn around each leg of the cross (Figure **4**).

STEP 3. For long warps, tie an additional tie halfway along the length of the warp to keep the warps together. I use a bow tie, which is easy to remove (Figure **5**).

STEP 4. Remove the warp from the warping board and cut the loops at the end opposite the cross (Figure **6**), then tie this end in a loose overhand knot to prevent tangles.

STEP 5. Wrap the warp chain around the front brace or beam of the loom (Figure **7**).

STEP 6. Secure the cross in your hand with the loop end between your thumb and first finger and the chain side between your little finger and your open hand, then cut off the five cross ties (Figure **8**).

STEP 7. Cut the loops at the end of the cross.

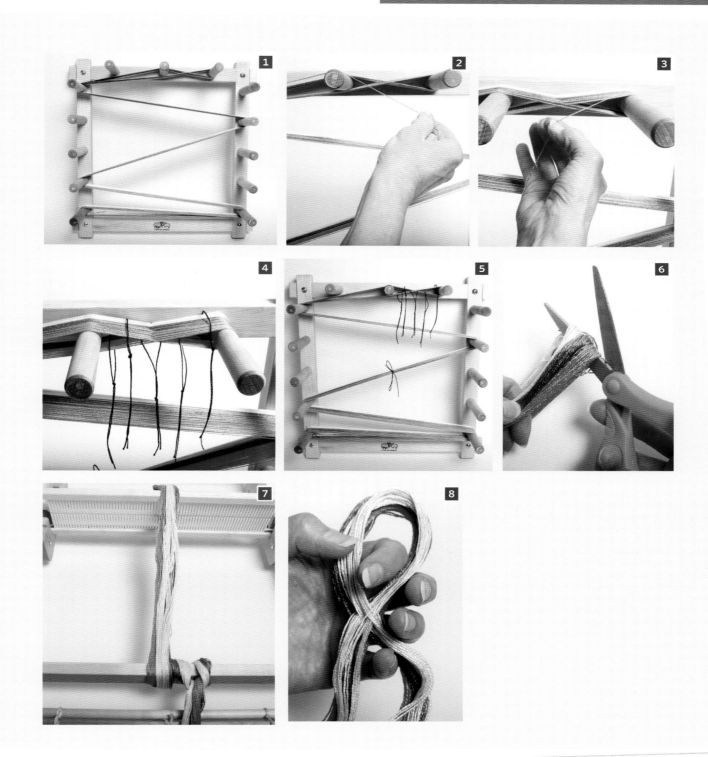

Threading a Striped Warp

For the warp shown opposite, I threaded solid stripes of white, pink, and sage 5/2 pearl cotton, and separated these solid warp stripes with stripes of alternating white and sage and sage and pink (this is a good exercise to try when threading two heddles!), following the threading diagram below. Thread Heddle I as follows:

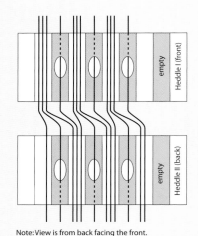

Note: View is from back facing the front.

Threading path between Heddle I and Heddle II (as viewed from the back of the loom).

Step 1. Beginning with all white threads and beginning in a hole, thread 1½" (3.8 cm) of 1 white in each hole and 3 whites in each slot, then thread 1 white thread in each hole and slot for 1½" (3.8 cm; Figure 1).

Step 2. Thread 2 ends of sage in every slot that has a single white thread for 1½" (3.8 cm), then 1 end of sage in each hole and 3 ends of sage in each slot (Figure 2) for 1½" (3.8 cm) for a solid sage stripe.

Step 3. For the next 1½" (3.8 cm), thread 1 end of sage in every slot and hole, and finally, finish with pink, threading 2 ends with each individual sage slot thread. Finish by threading 3 pink ends in the slots and 1 pink end in the holes for the remaining 1½" (3.8 cm).

Be sure to check your work—especially the first color—as you go along. It's a pain to start over (I know!). Next, insert Heddle II behind Heddle I (when working from the back of the loom, Heddle II will be closest to the back of the loom), and follow the directions for threading Heddle II. You'll see

FIGURE 1

FIGURE 2

when you begin threading the blended color stripes that you have a choice of whether to place a color in a slot or hole in Heddle II. For this sampler, in the white and sage stripes, I placed sage in the holes; in the pink and sage stripes, I placed the pink in the holes in Heddle II.

Textures with Two Heddles

A bonus of two-heddle weaving is the ability to make some simple textured fabrics. For this sampler, I wove as many combinations as I could think of. In addition to plain weave (both heddles up followed by both heddles down), you can have Heddle I up, Heddle I down, Heddle II up, and Heddle II down. If you add a pick-up stick or two, the pattern possibilities increase dramatically. In truth, I was surprised at just how many options I had. If you add color and texture, the potential patterns increase exponentially.

Patterns and Textures Sampler

For this sampler, I used two 10-dent rigid heddles to yield 20 epi. Both warp and weft are 5/2 pearl cotton in three colors—white, pink, and sage. For pattern weft, I used a heavier-weight yarn (Brown Sheep's Cotton Fleece) in cream and pink.

Threading sequence:
1½" (3.8 cm): White.
1½" (3.8 cm): Alternate white and sage.
1½" (3.8 cm): Sage.
1½" (3.8 cm): Alternate sage and pink.
1½" (3.8 cm): Pink.

Key:
Heddle I = front heddle
Heddle II = back heddle
Pick-up stick = both heddles in neutral, pick-up stick turned on edge.
Up and pick-up stick = both heddles in the up position with the pick-up stick slid flat up behind the heddles.

PLAIN WEAVE

STEP 1. Heddles I and II up.
STEP 2. Heddles I and II down.
Repeat these 2 steps for pattern.

3/1 MODIFIED BASKET WEAVE

STEP 1. Heddle I up.
STEP 2. Heddle I down.
Repeat these 2 steps for pattern.

3/1 MODIFIED BASKET WEAVE, VARIATION

This is essentially the same as the previous sample, but the 3/1 interlacement is just the opposite, which illustrates that each heddle used by itself weaves the same structure. The previous sample is easier to weave, though.
STEP 1. Heddle II up.
STEP 2. Heddle II down.
Repeat these 2 steps for pattern.

WARP FLOATS

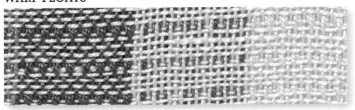

STEP 1. Heddle I up.
STEP 2. Heddle II up.
STEP 3. Heddle I up.
STEP 4. Heddle II up.
STEP 5. Heddle I down.
Repeat these 5 steps for pattern.

WARP AND WEFT TEXTURE

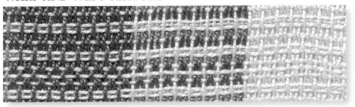

STEP 1. Heddle I up.
STEP 2. Heddles I and II down.
STEP 3. Heddle I up.
STEP 4. Heddles I and II up.
Repeat these 4 steps for pattern.

WARP AND WEFT FLOATS

STEP 1. Heddle I up.
STEP 2. Heddle I down.
STEP 3. Heddle II up.
STEP 4. Heddle II down.
Repeat these 4 steps for pattern.

LONG WARP FLOATS

STEP 1. Heddle I down.
STEP 2. Heddle II down.
STEP 3. Heddle I down.
STEP 4. Heddle II down.
STEP 5. Heddles I and II up.
STEP 6. Heddles I and II down.
STEP 7. Heddles I and II up.
Repeat these 7 steps for pattern.

ZIGZAGS

STEP 1. Heddle I up.
STEP 2. Heddle II up.
STEP 3. Heddle I down.
STEP 4. Heddle II down.
Repeat these 4 steps for pattern.

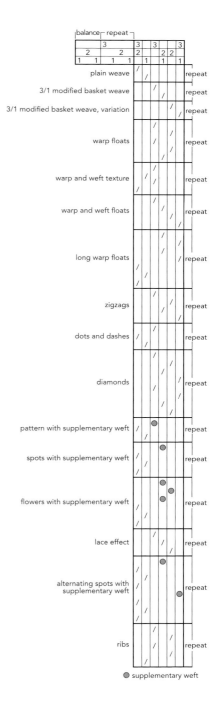

The diagram lists the following patterns, each ending with "repeat":

- plain weave
- 3/1 modified basket weave
- 3/1 modified basket weave, variation
- warp floats
- warp and weft texture
- warp and weft floats
- long warp floats
- zigzags
- dots and dashes
- diamonds
- pattern with supplementary weft
- spots with supplementary weft
- flowers with supplementary weft
- lace effect
- alternating spots with supplementary weft
- ribs

● supplementary weft

DOTS AND DASHES

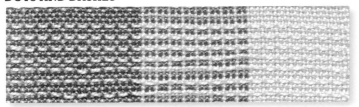

STEP 1. Heddle I up.
STEP 2. Heddles I and II up.
STEP 3. Heddles I and II down.
Repeat these 3 steps for pattern.

DIAMONDS

STEP 1. Heddle I up.
STEP 2. Heddle II up.
STEP 3. Heddle I down.
STEP 4. Heddle II down.
STEP 5. Heddle I up.
STEP 6. Heddle II down.
STEP 7. Heddle I down.
STEP 8. Heddle II up.
Repeat these 8 steps for pattern.

PATTERN WITH SUPPLEMENTARY WEFT

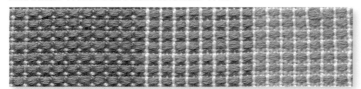

STEP 1. Heddle I up, supplementary weft.
STEP 2. Heddles I and II up.
STEP 3. Heddles I and II down.
Repeat these 3 steps for pattern.

SPOTS WITH SUPPLEMENTARY WEFT

STEP 1. Heddle I down, supplementary weft.
STEP 2. Heddles I and II up.
STEP 3. Heddles I and II down.
STEP 4. Heddles I and II up.
Repeat these 4 steps for pattern.

FLOWERS WITH SUPPLEMENTARY WEFT

STEP 1. Heddle I down, supplementary weft.
STEP 2. Heddle II up, supplementary weft.
STEP 3. Heddle I down, supplementary weft.
STEP 4. Heddles I and II up.
STEP 5. Heddles I and II down.
STEP 6. Heddles I and II up.
Repeat these 6 steps for pattern.

LACE EFFECT

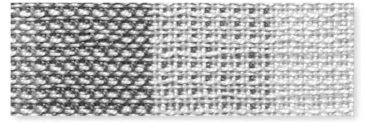

STEP 1. Heddle I up.
STEP 2. Heddle I down.
STEP 3. Heddle II up.
Repeat these 3 steps for pattern.

ALTERNATING SPOTS WITH SUPPLEMENTARY WEFT

STEP 1. Heddle I down, supplementary weft.
STEP 2. Heddles I and II up.
STEP 3. Heddles I and II down.
STEP 4. Heddles I and II up.
STEP 5. Heddle II down, supplementary weft.
STEP 6. Heddles I and II up.
STEP 7. Heddles I and II down.
STEP 8. Heddles I and II up.
Repeat these 8 steps for pattern.

Using a Pick-Up Stick on Fine Two-Heddle Warps

If the warp ends are fine and close together, it is easiest to see which threads to pick up at the fell of the cloth. Place the heddle in the down position as you pick up. Notice that the threads form pairs, which can also help guide you. After completing the pick-up, place the heddle in neutral, make a shed with this pick-up stick, and transfer it to behind the heddles with a second pick-up stick.

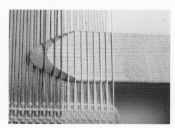

Fine threads are easiest to see at the fell of the cloth.

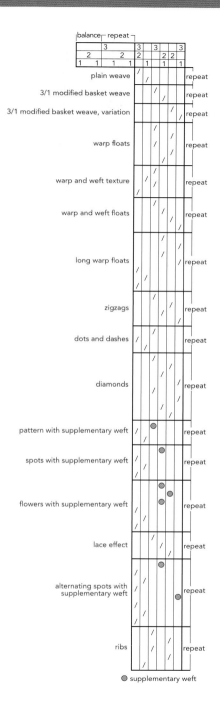

plain weave
3/1 modified basket weave
3/1 modified basket weave, variation
warp floats
warp and weft texture
warp and weft floats
long warp floats
zigzags
dots and dashes
diamonds
pattern with supplementary weft
spots with supplementary weft
flowers with supplementary weft
lace effect
alternating spots with supplementary weft
ribs

● supplementary weft

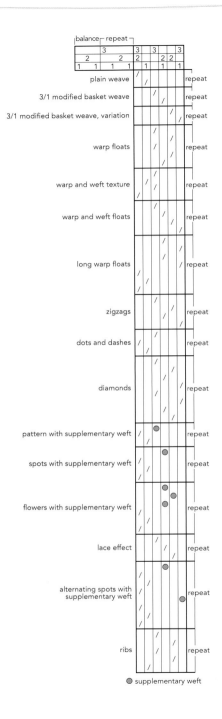

RIBS

STEP 1. Heddle I up.
STEP 2. Heddle II up.
STEP 3. Heddle I up.
STEP 4. Heddle II up.
STEP 5. Heddles I and II down.
Repeat these 5 steps for pattern.

TEXTURE WITH PICK-UP STICK

Pick-up stick pattern: Heddles I and II down, *1 up, 1 down; repeat from *.
STEP 1. Heddles I and II up with pick-up stick.
STEP 2. Heddle I up.
STEP 3. Heddles I and II down.
Repeat these 3 steps for pattern.

PLAIN WEAVE WITH DIFFERENT WEFT COLORS

Here, I've woven plain weave with different weft colors to create color-and-weave patterning. Swatches top to bottom: all white weft, all sage weft, alternating pink and sage weft.

STEP 1. Heddles I and II up.

STEP 2. Heddles I and II down.

Repeat these 2 steps for pattern.

TEXTURE WITH HEAVY WEFT

STEP 1. Heddle I up.

STEP 2. Heddle I down.

STEP 3. Heddle I up.

STEP 4. Heddle I down.

STEP 5. Heddle II up.

STEP 6. Heddle II down.

STEP 7. Heddle II up.

STEP 8. Heddle II down.

Repeat these 8 steps for pattern.

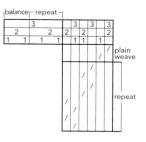

STRAIGHT 1/3 TWILL WITH HEAVY WEFT

Pick-up stick pattern A: Both heddles down, *1 down, 1 up; repeat from *.

Pick-up stick pattern B: Both heddles down, *1 up, 1 down (to save the pattern, you could place the threads on a heddle rod; see page 98); repeat from *.

STEP 1. Heddle I up.

STEP 2. Pick-up stick pattern A.

STEP 3. Heddle II up.

STEP 4. Pick-up stick pattern B.

Repeat these 4 steps for pattern.

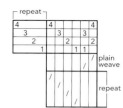

RETURN 1/3 TWILL

WEFT PATTERN FLOATS WITH PICK-UP STICK

Pick-up stick pattern A: Both heddles down, *1 down, 1 up; repeat from *

Pick-up stick pattern B: Both heddles down, *1 up, 1 down; repeat from *.

STEP 1. Heddle I up.

STEP 2. Pick-up stick pattern A.

STEP 3. Heddle II up.

STEP 4. Pick-up stick pattern B.

STEP 5. Repeat Steps 1–4.

STEP 6. Heddle II up.

STEP 7. Pick-up stick pattern A.

STEP 8. Heddle I up.

STEP 9. Pick-up stick pattern B.

STEP 10. Heddle II up.

STEP 11. Pick-up stick pattern A.

Repeat these 11 steps for pattern.

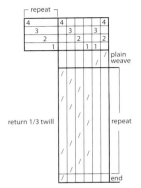

Pick-up stick pattern: Both heddles down, *2 up, 2 down; repeat from *.

STEP 1. Pick-up stick.

STEP 2. Heddles I and II up.

STEP 3. Heddles I and II down.

Repeat these 3 steps for pattern.

LONG WEFT FLOATS WITH PICK-UP STICK

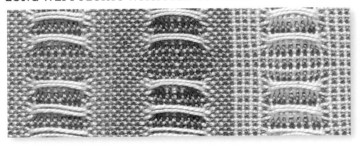

Pick-up stick pattern: Both heddles down, 4 up, *8 down, 8 up; repeat from *.

STEP 1. Pick-up stick.

STEP 2. Heddles I and II up.

STEP 3. Pick-up stick.

STEP 4. Heddles I and II up.

STEP 5. Heddles I and II down.

STEP 6. Heddles I and II up.

Repeat these 6 steps for pattern.

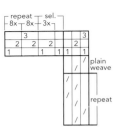

Exploring Twill

Simply put, twills are diagonal lines in weaving—like the fabric in jeans. Twills are a wonderful addition to a weaver's repertoire because they make a fabric that has better drape than plain weave, which is a handy thing for blankets or shawls. Although it will drape better, the fabric will be denser than a corresponding plain-weave fabric.

Plain weave, you'll remember, has the most stable interlacement of over, under, over, under. In a twill structure, the warp and weft float over 2 or more threads. For example, in a 1/3 twill the weft goes over 3 warp threads and under 1 warp thread. Then, on the next pass, the weft steps 1 one warp, then weaves over 3, under 1. Because the pattern steps over 1 thread each row, a diagonal line is created. If you turn your 1/3 twill fabric over, you'll see 3/1 twill on the reverse side—the weft travels over 1 warp and under 3. The top side—the one you see while weaving—features weft floats and the reverse side features warp floats. Check out the two sides of the twill samples on pages 192 and 193 to see what I mean.

It is true that you don't have as many twill threading options with two heddles on the rigid heddle loom (there are more options if more heddles are used, but this is not within the scope of this book) as you do with a shaft loom. You are pretty much limited to straight twill threadings, but you can, however, weave zigzags in the weft by weaving awhile in one sequence and then reversing direction.

Thread 1/3 twill just like you would for plain weave. The structure is created by a series of 4 weft picks that involve both heddles and a couple of pick-up sticks.

Pick-up stick pattern A: Place both heddles in the down position; the warp threads will be grouped in pairs at the fell line. Pick up the leftmost thread of each pair (i.e., every other thread).

Pick-up stick pattern B: Pick up every other thread not picked up on pick-up stick A (i.e., the rightmost thread of each pair), checking your work as you go. To speed weaving, install these threads on a heddle rod (see page 98).

STEP 1. Heddle I up.

STEP 2. Pick-up stick pattern A.

STEP 3. Heddle II up.

STEP 4. Pick-up stick pattern B.

Repeat these 4 steps for a straight twill pattern. Work these

4 steps in the opposite order to reverse the direction of the twill, i.e., pick-up stick pattern B, Heddle II up, pick-up stick pattern A, Heddle I up.

You can also weave a 1/3 twill for a fabric in which you want to use the heddles to create a structure but don't necessarily want to double your ends per inch. For the twill examples that follow, I used two 8-dent heddles to weave an 8-ends-per-inch sett. By skipping dents in the heddles, I maintained the 8 epi sett, but expanded my patterning potential by spreading the threads out between the two heddles.

Twill Samples

The swatches on pages 192 and 193 are woven on the same warp. For the warp, I alternated a wool loop and a 2-ply sportweight wool, threading the wool loop in the slots.

Heddle I threading: (right to left) *Three threads in a slot, 1 thread in the hole to the left, skip a slot, skip a hole; repeat from *.

Heddle II threading: *One thread in the slot to the right of the corresponding hole in Heddle I, 1 thread in the next hole, 2 threads in the next slot, skip a hole; repeat from *. The 3 slot threads from Heddle I will be distributed one each in a slot, hole, and slot in Heddle II; the hole thread from Heddle I will be in the same slot as the previous thread in Heddle II.

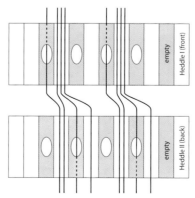

Threading two heddles for 1/3 twill without doubling the sett, i.e., two 8-dent heddles are threaded for an 8 epi sett.

Note: View is from back facing the front

STRAIGHT 1/3 TWILL

Here, I used a dark heather-gray wool 2-ply and wove at 8 ppi using the straight twill pattern. On the front, gray weft floats dominate; on the reverse, white warp floats dominate. I like how the wool loops are shown off by the longer warp floats.

Pick-up stick pattern A: Both heddles down, 1 down, 1 up.

Pick-up stick pattern B: Both heddles down, 1 up, 1 down.

STEP 1. Heddle I up.

STEP 2. Pick-up stick pattern A.

STEP 3. Heddle II up.

STEP 4. Pick-up stick pattern B.

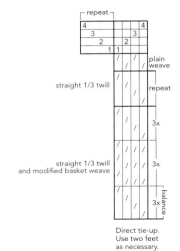

Direct tie-up.
Use two feet
as necessary.

Front.

Reverse.

STRAIGHT 1/3 TWILL AND MODIFIED BASKET WEAVE

For this sample, I sandwiched modified basket weave (by weaving up and down with Heddle I only) between straight twill borders. The weft is wool singles (Lanaloft from Brown Sheep in Maple Praline) in variegated shades of brown. The subtle variation in the yarn adds depth to this fabric.

Pick-up stick pattern A: Both heddles down, 1 down, 1 up.

Pick-up stick pattern B: Both heddles down, 1 up, 1 down.

STEP 1. Heddle I up.

STEP 2. Pick-up stick pattern A.

STEP 3. Heddle II up.

STEP 4. Pick-up stick pattern B.

STEP 5. Repeat these 4 steps 2 more times.

STEP 6. Heddle I up.

STEP 7. Heddle I down.

STEP 8. Repeat Steps 6 and 7 nine times.

STEP 9. Finish by weaving Steps 1–5.

Front.

Reverse.

Two Heddles, Two Densities, and Two Structures

I discovered another option for using two heddles by watching backstrap weaving in Oaxaca, Mexico. The weavers attached sections of heddles made from fishing line to the backs of their rigid heddles. They used these additional heddles to double the epi at each edge so that they could weave a fabric that was twice as dense at the selvedges as in the center. You can do the same thing with two heddles, the second heddle taking the place of the set of fishing-line heddles.

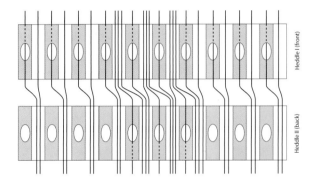

Threading two heddles for two densities.

Two Heddles, Two Densities Sampler

For this sampler, I used two 10-dent rigid heddles. I alternately threaded 10 ends of 3/2 pearl cotton at 10 epi and 20 ends of 5/2 pearl cotton at 20 epi, ending with 10 ends of 3/2 pearl cotton. I used the indirect warping method (measuring the warp first).

10 epi threading: *Thread slot, hole, slot, hole in Heddle I, then sley a slot and hole thread together into the corresponding slot in Heddle II, skipping all of the holes.

20 epi threading: *Thread the two heddles as usual for two-heddle weaving (see page 182).

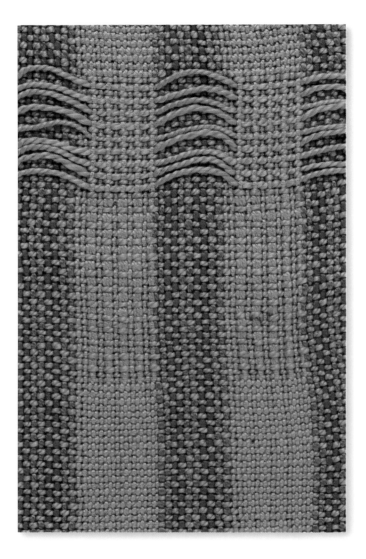

PLAIN WEAVE AND MODIFIED BASKET WEAVE

The weft for this sample is 5/2 pearl cotton in green. The 10-epi areas result in plain weave; the 20-epi areas result in modified basket weave.

STEP 1. Heddles I and II up.

STEP 2. Heddles I and II down. Repeat these 2 steps for pattern.

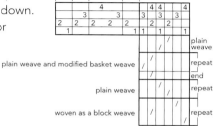

PLAIN WEAVE

The weft in this sample is 3/2 pearl cotton in blue. The entire width is woven in plain weave.

STEP 1. Heddle I up.

STEP 2. Heddle I down.

Repeat these 2 steps for pattern.

WOVEN AS BLOCK WEAVE

Here, I treated the different densities as a block weave, where Block A (the 3/2 stripes) is a plain-weave ground with weft floats and Block B (the 5/2 stripes) is a 3/1 modified basket weave. This produces a very stable fabric with floats that can be left to drape or could be cut for pile.

STEP 1. Heddle II up.

STEP 2. Heddle I down.

STEP 3. Heddle I up.

Repeat these 3 steps for pattern.

DOUBLED WARP ENDS

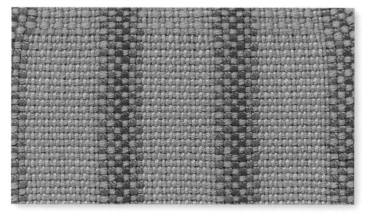

This sample is the same as the previous three, but I doubled the warp threads in the 10 epi stripes to make them narrower and denser. I think this idea could be expanded even further with the wider-sett stripes threaded with even heavier yarns for a raised contrast to the finer-sett stripes. Woven as plain weave.

Two Heddles to Achieve the Proper Sett

You can use two heddles as a way to achieve the proper sett for the yarns you want to weave with. In some cases, you'll want to use a thin yarn that would be too loosely sett in a 12-dent heddle. If you use two 8-dent heddles, however, you can achieve a sett of 16 epi. In such cases, the extra heddle is just used to establish the proper sett, otherwise, everything progresses as for single-heddle weaving. You'll pick-up the threads just as you would for single-heddle weaving and you'll raise and lower both heddles together—something that you hardly notice during weaving.

Patterns on Two Heddles Sampler

Designed and woven by Sara Goldenberg White.
Yarns in a variety of fibers and colors provide sparkle and texture to create a rich and luxurious cloth. Two 8-dent heddles are used to yield 16 epi. The pick-up honeycomb and windowpane patterns require two pick-up sticks. This is a good example of the value of two heddles to produce the sett you desire. The 16 epi sett produced just the results we were after. These yarns sett at 12 epi would have produced a too-loosely sett fabric.

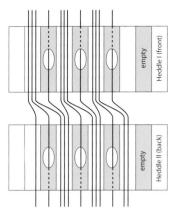

Thread the heddles as usual for two-heddle weaving. Thread the colors according to the Threading Guide.

Note: View is from back facing the front.

Threading Guide

Block A ALTERNATE PURPLE AND BROWN	X						X
Block B ALTERNATE PURPLE AND GREEN		X			X		
Block A ALTERNATE PURPLE AND GOLD			X		X		
Block B ALTERNATE PURPLE AND BLUE				X			

Each block is 16 threads (1"; 2.5 cm) wide, 8 of each color. All purple yarns are threaded in the slots in both heddles.

Warp Yarns: Purple = Louet Gems Sport Weight wool in Grape

Brown = Berroco Yarn Seduce in color 4436, Rye

Green = Berroco Lumina in color 1618, Space Ship

Gold = Berroco Lumina in color 1620, Gold Coast

Blue = Dusty blue hand-dyed cashmere from Redfish Dyeworks

Weft Yarns: Purple = Louet Gems Sport Weight wool in Grape

Outline weft is doubled strands of Berroco Lustra in either Haricot Vert or Champagne.

This sampler illustrates once again the importance of sampling and how it can help you get to where you want to go. I've provided the drafts for all of these variations, but the weaving is pretty much the same—just the weft yarn and the number of repeats within each block are changed. If I were using this sample to plan a project, I'd assess it as I went along, always asking what if I tried . . . and considering whether or not it's what I had in mind . . . or, it needs a little contrast . . . or, the repeat is too small . . . or, I really like what is happening, what can I do to make it better . . . and so on.

For the five variations of honeycomb, I tried different wefts and repeats. The last two samples (page 199) are woven windowpane fashion; a bit more quiet, but pleasing all the same.

HONEYCOMB

Pick-up stick pattern A: Both heddles down, *9 up, 7 down; repeat from *, end 9 up.

Pick-up stick pattern B: Both heddles down, *9 down, 7 up; repeat from *, end 9 up.

Wefts: Purple background weft and doubled Lustra Champagne for outlining weft.

STEP 1. Up, heavy weft.

STEP 2. Down.

STEP 3. Up and pick-up stick A.

STEP 4. Down.

STEP 5. Up and pick-up stick A.

STEP 6. Down.

STEP 7. Up and pick-up stick A.

STEP 8. Down.

STEP 9. Repeat Steps 1–8 with pick-up stick B.

Repeat these 9 steps for pattern.

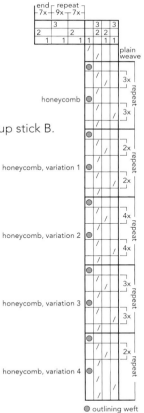

HONEYCOMB, VARIATION 1

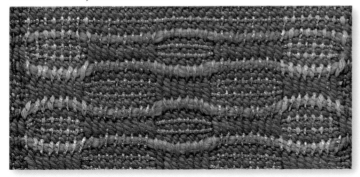

This pattern is the same as the one above except that there is 1 fewer repeat of up and pick-up stick A, down. The wefts are doubled Haricot Vert for the outline and Lumina Gold Coast for the background.

HONEYCOMB, VARIATION 2

Pick-up stick pattern A: Both heddles down, *7 up, 9 down; repeat from *, end 7 up.

Pick-up stick pattern B: Both heddles down, *7 down, 9 up; repeat from *, end 7 down.

Wefts: Lumina in Space Ship for background and doubled Lustra Champagne for outline weft.

STEP 1. Up, heavy weft.

STEP 2. Down.

STEP 3. Up and pick-up stick A.

STEP 4. Repeat Steps 2 and 3 three more times.

STEP 5. Repeat Steps 1–4 with pick-up stick B.

Repeat these 5 steps for pattern.

HONEYCOMB, VARIATION 3

The pick-up pattern sequence is the same as the above sample. The only difference is that only 3 repeats are made of the pattern for pattern stick B. The outline weft is the same throughout—doubled Lustra in Haricot Vert. The background weft changes with each block change, creating a lively movement from block to block. Weave in this order: brown, green, gold, blue, gold, green, brown.

HONEYCOMB, VARIATION 4

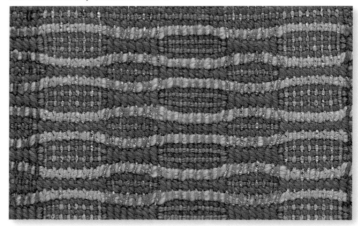

This is the same pick-up sequence as the above. The wefts are blue cashmere for background and doubled Lustra in Champagne for the outline weft. Because only 2 repeats (up and pick-up stick, down) of Block A and one of Block B, the honeycomb outline is a shallow, subdued wavy line.

WINDOWPANE FASHION

On the same warp, by just changing the pick-up pattern and weaving sequence, you can create a whole other look and feel. Here, purple weft yarn was used throughout.

Pick-up stick pattern: Both heddles down, *2 up, 4 down; repeat from *, end 2 up.

STEP 1. Up.

STEP 2. Pick-up stick.

STEP 3. Up.

STEP 4. Pick-up stick.

STEP 5. Up.

STEP 6. Down.

STEP 7. Up and pick-up stick.

STEP 8. Down.

STEP 9. Up and pick-up stick.

STEP 10. Down.

Repeat these 10 steps for pattern, ending with Steps 1–5 to balance.

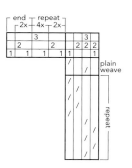

WINDOWPANE VARIATION

This sample is like the last one, except that only 1 repeat of the pattern rows is made.

Pick-up stick pattern: *2 up, 4 down; repeat from *, end 2 up.

STEP 1. Up.

STEP 2. Pick-up stick.

STEP 3. Up.

STEP 4. Down.

STEP 5. Up and pick-up stick.

STEP 6. Down.

Repeat these 6 steps for pattern, ending with Steps 1–3 to balance.

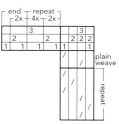

A Note about Threading Colors

When designing a warp color order, begin by thinking about plain weave where threads alternate between slots and holes. When both heddles are in the up position, all of the hole threads are up—every other warp thread is lifted. Likewise, when both heddles are in the down position, all of the slot threads are raised—the alternate warp threads are lifted. This is important to remember when threading two heddles. Let's say, for example, that Heddle I is threaded with white in the holes and one white and two blacks in the slots. If you want alternating white and black in the finished piece, when you thread Heddle II, you'll need to be sure to place the white thread from the slot in Heddle I into the hole in Heddle II. That way, when both heddles are raised all of the white threads (hole threads) will be raised and all of the black threads (slot threads) will be lowered. Sometimes I make a drawing of the threads in the heddles to help me think about how to thread colors.

Embroidery on the Loom

If you're someone who's inclined to stitch as well as weave, here's a way to combine the two techniques. Even if you aren't already an embroiderer, you may find this just the way to add a special detail. Although you can create accents with a pick-up pattern, embroidery will appear more on the surface of the fabric. With stitched accents, you can create curvy lines as well as a layer-on-layer effect. You can also apply stitching to an allover woven pattern, such as a lace weave. Think of the woven fabric as a grid—which it is, of course. Use weft or warp floats as the base for your embroidery.

Because these embroidery techniques lend themselves to finer fabrics, I included them here in the two heddle chapter. You could also weave them on heavier setts, but you will need to be mindful of the length of the stitches.

SIMPLE ZIGZAG

Pick-up stick pattern: Both heddles down, *1 up, 1 down; repeat from *.

STEP 1. Pick-up stick, dark gray.

STEP 2. Weave 5 rows of plain weave.

STEP 3. Repeat Steps 1–2 for pattern.

STEP 4. End pick-up stick, dark gray.

Embroidery: Thread a contrasting color (blue) on a tapestry needle. Beginning at the selvedge, lace up and down along each line of weft pattern floats to create a zigzag pattern. The looser the lacing, the more pronounced the design.

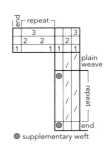

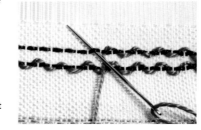

Embroider the accent color in and out of weft floats.

LOZENGES

ZIGZAG ON STRIPES

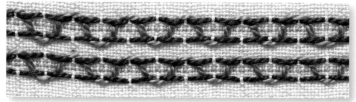

Pick-up stick pattern: Both heddles down, *2 up, 4 down; repeat from *.

STEP 1. Pick-up stick, gray weft.

STEP 2. Weave 4 rows of plain weave.

STEP 3. Pick-up stick, gray weft.

STEP 4. Weave 4 rows of plain weave. Weave ½" (1.3 cm) of plain weave and repeat Steps 1–4 for pattern.

Embroidery: Thread a contrasting color (blue) on a tapestry needle. Beginning at the selvedge, lace up and down between 2 rows of gray pattern weft, going up through one set of floats and back down through the next set and pulling the thread taut to create curves. Return to the edge where you began, lacing in the opposite direction to form lozenge shapes.

● supplementary weft

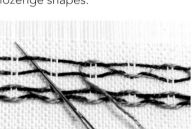

Embroider the accent color up and down between pairs of weft floats.

This sample introduces a third color as a single plain-weave pick. By now you should have the idea that the variations are endless. For more on this technique, seek out Penelope Drooker's long-out-of-print book, *Embroidering With the Loom.*

Pick-up stick pattern: Both heddles down, 1 down, *1 up, 3 down; repeat from *.

STEP 1. Pick-up stick, gray weft.

STEP 2. Heddles I and II up.

STEP 3. Heddles I and II down.

STEP 4. Heddles I and II up, pink weft.

STEP 5. Heddles I and II down.

STEP 6. Heddles I and II up.

STEP 7. Pick-up stick, gray weft. Weave ½" (1.3 cm) of plain weave and repeat these 7 steps for pattern.

Embroidery: Thread a contrasting color (blue) on a tapestry needle. Beginning at the selvedge, lace back and forth between 2 pattern rows, going up through a pair of floats, down through the next pair of floats, and so on.

● supplementary weft
○ accent weft

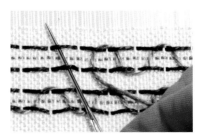

Embroider the accent color up and down between pairs of weft floats.

EMBROIDERY ON LACE

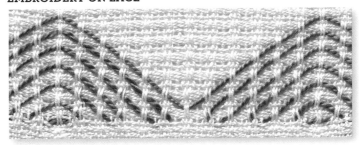

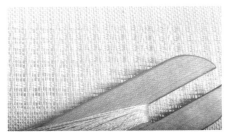

Lace pattern under tension on the loom.

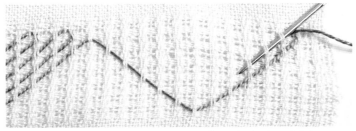

Embroider the accent color through warp floats in the lace fabric.

For this sample, I wove a lace weave and then stitched a pattern through the warp floats to create a chevron design. I first drew the pattern on graph paper where each square represented a pair of warp floats on the fabric. In general, embroidery is easiest to do while the fabric is still taut on the loom, but for this fabric, the weave structure wasn't pronounced enough while under tension. Therefore, after weaving, I removed the fabric from the loom, washed and pressed it, and then worked the embroidery.

Pick-up stick pattern: Both heddles down, *2 up, 1 down; repeat from *.

STEP 1. Heddles I and II down.

STEP 2. Heddles I and II up and pick-up stick.

STEP 3. Heddles I and II down.

STEP 4. Heddles I and II up and pick-up stick.

STEP 5. Heddles I and II down.

STEP 6. Heddles I and II up.

Repeat these 6 steps for pattern.

Embroidery: For embroidery, I threaded a tapestry needle with blue yarn and stitched a diagonal line through the warp floats. I carried the yarn across on the back to begin the next row, then stitched a chevron pattern out again. This is a very fluid technique with endless possibilities.

NOTES ON LACE AND EMBROIDERY

The samples shown here are woven at 20 epi with two 10-dent heddles. I like these delicate samples, but you could create embroidered patterns using a single heddle at a wider sett. You'll just need to adjust your yarns accordingly.

For a bold look, use a supplementary yarn that is two to three times heavier than the background fabric. But be aware that if the pattern yarn is too thick, the stitching may not show up. Adjust the proportions to achieve the look you're after.

While weaving, I left the pattern wefts hanging at the edges. After washing and pressing the fabric, I stitched the weft ends under the pattern weft on the back of the fabric. The stitching is visible on the back, so for a reversible fabric, consider securing the pattern wefts with a row of machine stitching along the edge of the fabric and then cutting the pattern wefts off flush with the selvedge.

Doubleweave

It is possible to weave two layers at once with a technique known as doubleweave. Doubleweave, for example, allows you to weave one layer on the top of another or to connect the layers at one edge for a doublewidth fabric or to weave tubes or pockets that can be stuffed. Besides these practical reasons, you can use doubleweave to create designs by exchanging layers or create pick-up patterns where parts of the bottom layer are brought to the top layer. Weaving two layers in doubleweave also makes a denser fabric for a placemat that stays put on the table, a heavier-weight jacket fabric of lightweight yarns, or a gossamer curtain fabric filled with Mylar strips or found objects.

Though I don't recommend weaving doubleweave for your first project, it's really easier than you think. The best way to learn doubleweave is to weave a sampler (there goes my mantra again). It's far better to learn the technique on a sampler than on your first project.

For doubleweave, you'll need two heddles of the same dent and two pick-up sticks (four if you want to exchange layers). Thread each layer at the sett you would use for a single layer of that particular yarn. For example, 3/2 pearl cotton sett at 10 epi for a single layer would be sett at 20 epi for doubleweave (10 epi per layer). Thread the heddles just as for doubling the sett (see page 196), but be mindful of the position of the two colors if you plan to weave the two layers in different colors (such as light and dark), which I suggest you do for your first sampler.

Here's a way to think about weaving doubleweave: If it takes 2 warp threads to weave plain weave, 4 separate warp threads are then needed to weave two layers of plain weave, 2 for the top and 2 for the bottom. Let's say that the top layer is dark and the bottom is light. To weave the bottom layer, you have to hold the top layer up out of the way. You'll leave the 1 light warp of the bottom layer down and lift the other light thread of the bottom layer with the 2 dark threads of the top layer up out of the way. To weave the second light warp thread of the lower layer, lift the other light and 2 darks. To weave the top layer, first lift 1 of the dark threads and leave the other dark thread and the 2 light threads of the bottom layer down. Finally, lift the other dark thread, leaving the first dark thread and the 2 bottom light threads down. In other words, it takes 2 weft picks on the bottom layer and 2 picks on the top layer to complete one sequence.

Threading for Two Layers

For this example, we'll use two different colors—one color for the top layer and another for the bottom layer. Use the indirect method of warping, measuring the warp first on a warping board (see page 181).

STEP 1. Working at the back of the loom from right to left and beginning with a hole, thread Heddle I (front heddle) with 1 light thread per hole and 3 threads per slot—2 dark and 1 light (**Figure 1**).

STEP 2. Insert Heddle II and working from right to left, sley the light hole thread from Heddle I into the slot to the right of the corresponding hole in Heddle II (**Figure 2**).

STEP 3. Sley the light slot thread from Heddle I into the same slot in Heddle II as the previous thread (**Figure 3**).

STEP 4. Sley 1 of the dark slot threads from Heddle I in the next hole to the left in Heddle II (**Figure 4**).

STEP 5. Sley the other dark slot thread from Heddle I into the next slot to the left in Heddle II (**Figure 5**).

Repeat these 5 steps for the remaining warp threads.

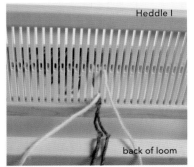

FIGURE 1

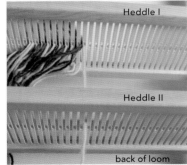

FIGURE 2

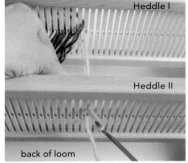

FIGURE 3

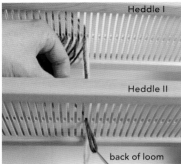

FIGURE 4

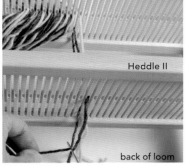

FIGURE 5

TWO LAYER TIPS

When weaving two separate layers, it is easier to see what's going on if you weave the bottom layer first and then the top layer.

It is important to weave the two layers evenly. That is, always follow 2 picks of the bottom layer with 2 picks of the top layer.

To determine sett for doubleweave, multiply the sett for a single layer of plain weave by two. For our sampler, for example, each layer is 8 ends per inch, yielding 16 ends per inch for both layers.

Preparing Pick-Up Sticks for Dark Layer on Top

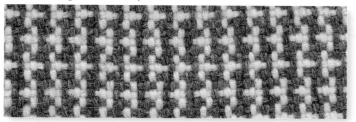

Before starting to pick up the threads, weave a plain-weave base by weaving up and down with both heddles. Here, I alternated 2 picks of dark with 1 pick of light.

In preparation to weave two layers, first weave about 2" (5 cm) in a single layer of plain weave (move the two heddles up and down together) to align the warp ends. Because it can be difficult to see which threads to pick up, I like to pick up the threads in front of the heddle along the fell line of the cloth. To transfer the threads to behind the heddles, place the heddles in neutral, turn the pick-up stick on edge to make a shed, and slide another pick-up stick into the shed behind the heddles. Remove the first pick-up stick.

Pick-up stick pattern A: Both heddles down. Working from right to left along the fell of the cloth, pick up every other thread starting with the second dark thread (**Figure 1**). Put the heddles in neutral, then turn this stick on edge. Insert a second pick-up stick in the same shed behind the heddles. Slide this pick-up stick (A) to the back of the loom (**Figure 2**) where it will be used to weave the top layer. Remove the first pick-up stick.

Pick-up stick pattern B: With both heddles up, slide pick-up stick A forward to just behind the heddles, then slide a pick-up stick (B) into the narrow bottom shed (**Figure 3**) behind the heddles (it will go between the light threads and under all the dark threads). This pick-up stick will be used for the lower layer.

Both pick-up sticks will remain in place as you weave.

Figure 1. Pick up the dark threads (the left one of the paired warps).

Figure 2. Slide pick-up stick A to the back of the loom.

Figure 3. Slide pick-up stick B into the narrow bottom shed.

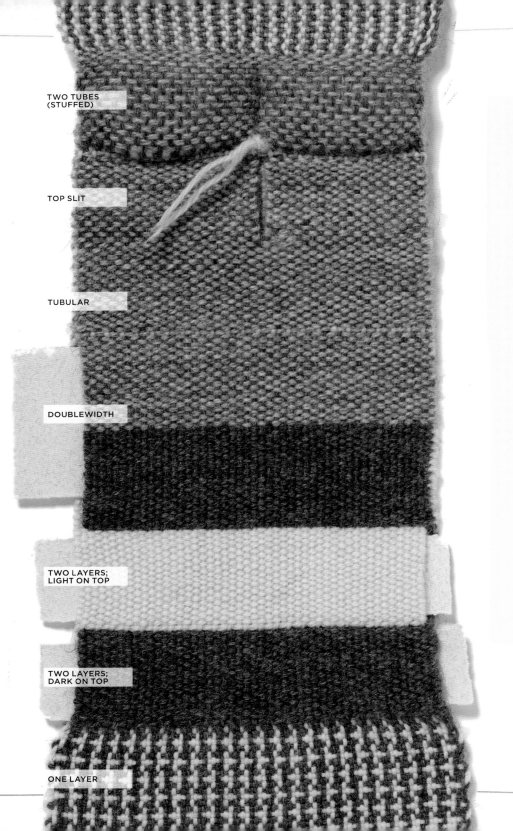

TWO TUBES (STUFFED)

TOP SLIT

TUBULAR

DOUBLEWIDTH

TWO LAYERS; LIGHT ON TOP

TWO LAYERS; DARK ON TOP

ONE LAYER

Doubleweave on a Shaft Loom

If you are going to weave this sampler on your floor loom, I suggest you use a direct tie-up. That is, just tie one shaft to each treadle, i.e., shaft 1 to treadle 1, shaft 2 to treadle 2, shaft 3 to treadle 3, and shaft 4 to treadle 4. Weave the layers accordingly, using two feet as necessary to raise the appropriate shafts for each row.

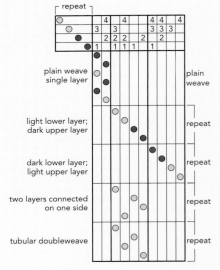

● dark thread ○ light thread

Note: You could also tie each treadle to one shaft and weave the treadling direct-tie-up fashion, using two feet to lift the necessary shafts.

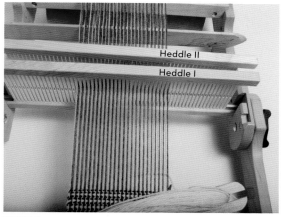

Heddle II

Heddle I

FIGURE 1

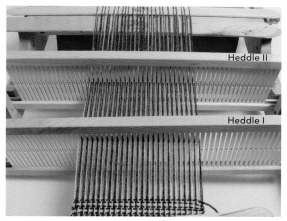

FIGURE 2

Doubleweave Sampler

TWO SEPARATE LAYERS; DARK ON TOP

LOWER LAYER (LIGHT):

STEP 1. Pick-up stick B, light weft (**Figure 1**).

STEP 2. Heddle I down, light weft (**Figure 2**).

UPPER LAYER (DARK):

STEP 3. Heddle II up, dark weft (**Figure 3**).

STEP 4. Pick-up stick A, dark weft (**Figure 4**).

Repeat these 4 steps for pattern.

Note: You will use two shuttles, one with white yarn that weaves the lower layer and one with dark gray yarn that will weave the upper layer.

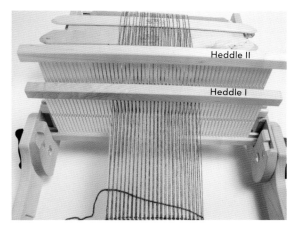

Heddle II

Heddle I

FIGURE 3

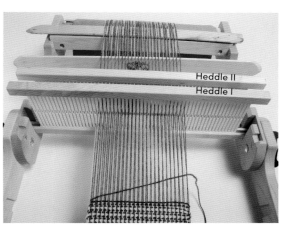

Heddle II

Heddle I

FIGURE 4

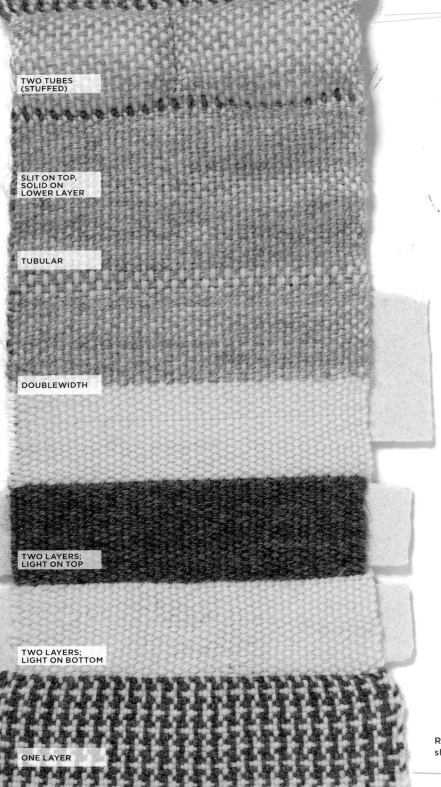

TWO TUBES (STUFFED)

SLIT ON TOP, SOLID ON LOWER LAYER

TUBULAR

DOUBLEWIDTH

TWO LAYERS; LIGHT ON TOP

TWO LAYERS; LIGHT ON BOTTOM

ONE LAYER

Weaving with Heddle II in the Down Position

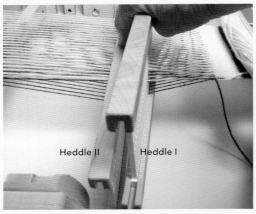

Heddle II   Heddle I

With one hand, pull up on Heddle I as you push down on Heddle II.

Note: To weave with Heddle II in the down position, bring both heddles in front of the heddle block, pull up on the front heddle (Heddle I) and simultaneously push down on the back heddle (Heddle II) with one hand and use the other hand to insert the shuttle. There will be a split shed, slide this pick-up stick into the bottom opening.

Reverse side of sampler shown on page 206.

TWO SEPARATE LAYERS; LIGHT ON TOP

To change the layers so that the light threads are on top and the dark threads are on the bottom, you'll need two more pick-up sticks. (The first two can stay in place at the back of the loom until needed again.)

Pick-up stick pattern C: Both heddles down. Pick up the first light thread to the right of the dark threads (**Figure 1**). Transfer these threads onto another pick-up stick behind the heddles (**Figure 2**). Place the pick-up stick on edge to create a shed, and insert a second pick-up stick into the shed behind the heddles. Remove the first pick-up stick.

Pick-up stick pattern D: Both heddles up. Slide pick-up stick C forward to behind the heddles, then slide pick-up stick D into the resulting lower shed (**Figure 3**). Slide both pick-up sticks to the back of the loom.

LOWER LAYER (DARK):

STEP 1. Pick-up stick D, dark weft.

STEP 2. Heddle II down (see box on page 208), dark weft.

UPPER LAYER (LIGHT):

STEP 3. Heddle I up, light weft.

STEP 4. Pick-up stick C, light weft.

Repeat these 4 steps for pattern.

FIGURE 1

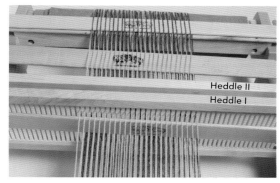

FIGURE 2

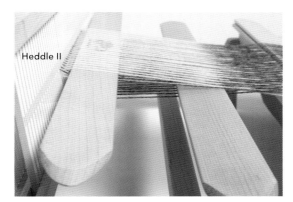

FIGURE 3

JOIN LAYERS ON ONE SIDE

To join the top and bottom layers along one selvedge, the weaving is the same as for two single layers, but the wefts are interlocked at one selvedge edge. For this example, the dark layer is on top, the light layer is on the bottom, and they are joined along the right selvedge. Be sure to interlock the wefts at the right selvedge only; interlocking them at both selvedges will create a tube.

Weave the bottom layer first, weaving left to right with the light weft (pick-up stick B). When you bring the shuttle out of the shed on the right, pass it under the dark weft thread, place the shuttle over the dark weft thread, change sheds (Heddle I down), place the shuttle over the dark weft thread to interlock it, and weave the light weft back to the left.

Next, weave the top layer with the dark weft, weaving right to left (Heddle II up). Change sheds and weave back to the right with the dark weft (Pick-up stick A). Here's the weaving sequence:

Lower layer (light):

STEP 1. Pick-up stick B, light weft; weave left to right. When the shuttle comes out of the shed, pass it under the dark weft.

STEP 2. Heddle I down, light weft; weave right to left, bringing the light shuttle over the dark weft to interlock the two.

Upper layer (dark):

STEP 3. Heddle II up, dark weft.

STEP 4. Pick-up stick A, dark weft.

Repeat these 4 steps for pattern.

DOUBLEWIDTH

To weave a doublewidth fabric, use just one shuttle. The join between the layers is on the opposite side that you start on, i.e., if you start from the left, the join will be at the right. For this sample, I started at the left selvedge with medium-gray weft.

STEP 1. Pick-up stick B (lower layer).

STEP 2. Heddle II up (upper layer).

STEP 3. Pick-up stick A (upper layer).

STEP 4. Heddle I down (lower layer).

Repeat these 4 steps for pattern. After a few repeats, you'll see that the layers are connected at the right. Examine the interlacement at the selvedge, if a double warp thread appears, remove it by cutting out one end. The interlacement should be over, under, over, under on each layer and at the connecting point.

TUBULAR DOUBLEWEAVE

To weave two layers closed on both sides to form a tube, you will use one shuttle and alternately weave 1 pick each of the top and bottom layers. An odd number of warp ends are required to avoid a doubled warp thread (two threads at the selvedge in the same shed).

STEP 1. Pick-up stick B (lower layer).

STEP 2. Heddle II up (upper layer).

STEP 3. Heddle I down (lower layer).

STEP 4. Pick-up stick A (upper layer).

Repeat these 4 steps for pattern.

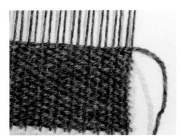

Bring the light weft under the dark weft at the joining edge.

Change sheds, then bring the light weft over the dark weft to weave the next pick.

TOP SLIT

To weave a tube with a slit in the center of the top layer, use a single shuttle and start in the center of the top layer, instead of at the selvedge. Weaving is a 6-step sequence, always worked over, under, over, under on each layer, weave from left to right from the center of the top layer to the selvedge, then from right to left across the

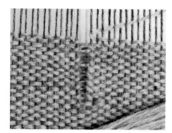

Weaving a slit in the center of the top layer.

bottom layer, then from left to right (in the same shed as first half of the top layer) across the other half of the top layer, ending at the center. Change sheds and weave from right to left across the half of the top layer just worked, across the bottom from left to right, and across the other half of the top from right to left.

STEP 1. Heddle II up (upper layer; begin in center, weave out to selvedge).

STEP 2. Pick-up stick B (lower layer).

STEP 3. Heddle II up (upper layer; weave to center).

STEP 4. Pick-up stick A (upper layer; weave back to selvedge).

STEP 5. Heddle I down (lower layer).

STEP 6. Pick-up stick A (upper layer; weave to center).

Repeat these 6 steps for pattern.

TWO TUBES

Now, if you really want a challenge, try this! By exchanging layers (i.e., changing sheds) at the center of the piece, you can weave two vertical tubes at the same time. The only hard part of weaving two tubes is to keep track of where you are—you may want to have a "cheat sheet" that lists the sequence of steps. It helps if you always complete a sequence before leaving the loom. I tie a piece of contrasting yarn around the center warp thread to mark where to take my

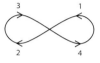
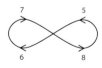

To weave two tubes side by side, the shuttle travels in a series of two figure-eight paths.

shuttle out of the shed before changing sheds. You may find a hand beater helpful in beating the layers. After weaving, I stuffed the tubes with polyester fiberfill.

STEP 1. Heddle II up (upper layer; begin at right selvedge and weave to center).

STEP 2. Pick-up stick B (lower layer; center to left selvedge).

STEP 3. Heddle II up (upper layer; weave from left selvedge to center).

STEP 4. Pick-up stick B (lower layer; weave from center to right selvedge).

STEP 5. Pick-up stick A (upper layer; weave from right selvedge to center).

STEP 6. Heddle I down (lower layer; weave from center to left selvedge).

STEP 7. Pick-up stick A (upper layer; weave from left selvedge to center).

STEP 8. Heddle I down (lower layer; weave from center to right selvedge).

Repeat these 8 steps for pattern.

PATTERNED
UPPER LAYER

PICK-UP FOR
SOLID BLOCKS

PICK-UP FOR
COLOR-AND-WEAVE

BROOK'S BOUQUET
ON UPPER LAYER

LENO ON UPPER
LAYER

FINGER-CONTROLLED UPPER LAYER

Leno on the upper layer.

Working leno on the upper layer.

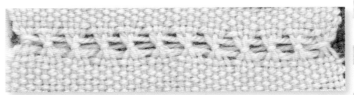

Brook's bouquet on the upper layer.

You can weave a solid background and accent it with a finger-controlled weave on the upper layer—leno and Brook's bouquet are shown here. Weave the lower layer only, leaving the upper layer unwoven for an inch or so, then work leno or Brook's bouquet on the threads of the upper layer as described in Chapter 2.

PICK-UP FOR "STITCHED" DOUBLEWEAVE

Front.

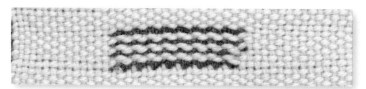

Reverse.

Pick-up on double weave allows you to stitch the two layers together in areas, as well as add design elements to the cloth. I've shown two different methods here. The first is fairly quick to do and produces a color-and-weave design in the pick-up area when two or more colors are used. The second method is slow to weave but solid areas are created. For this sample, I used the dark weft for the upper layer and the light weft for the lower layer. A color-and-weave design is created where the light lower layer is picked up and brought up to the upper layer. A row with a single pick-up "stitched" design requires three steps.

ROW 1: UPPER LAYER; DARK WEFT

STEP 1. Heddle II up, weave from selvedge to pick-up area, remove shuttle.

STEP 2. Heddle I up (change sheds), weave across pick-up area, remove shuttle.

STEP 3. Heddle II up (change sheds), weave from pick-up area to selvedge.

ROW 2: UPPER LAYER; DARK WEFT

STEP 1. Pick-up stick A, weave from selvedge to pick-up area, remove shuttle.

STEP 2. Place both heddles in down position, use a small pick-up stick to pick up light warps, turn this stick on edge to make a shed and weave across. Remove shuttle from shed and take out the pick-up stick.

STEP 3. Pick-up stick A (change sheds), weave from pick-up area to selvedge.

ROW 3: LOWER LAYER; LIGHT WEFT

Pick-up stick B; weave selvedge to selvedge.

ROW 4: LOWER LAYER; LIGHT WEFT

Heddle I down; weave selvedge to selvedge.

Repeat these 4 rows for pattern; stripes appear on the reverse side.

PICK-UP FOR SOLID BLOCKS

Front.

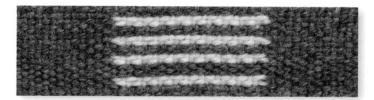

Reverse.

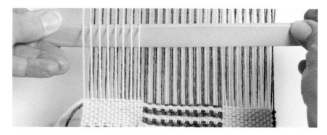

Mark the sides of the pick-up blocks with red threads secured to the fabric with T-pins and weighted off the back of the loom.

Sometimes you might want to pick up solid-colored blocks such as narrow blocks of the dark lower layer picked up to the light upper layer. This is possible on a rigid heddle loom, but it's not a speedy process—it takes 12 steps to weave a single block; many more if more blocks are woven.

Pick-up works like this: Insert shuttle into the shed, weave over to where you want your block to be, remove the shuttle from the shed, change sheds and weave across the block area, and then finish in the same shed you began the row with. If you look, for example, at row 1, weaving right to left, you begin by weaving dark weft across the bottom layer, then you bring the shuttle up to the surface, change sheds to bring the bottom dark layer to the top, insert the shuttle into this shed and weave to the other side of this block. Change sheds to the same shed you started with, finishing by weaving the dark lower layer.

ROW 1: DARK WEFT

STEP 1. Pick-up stick D. Weave from selvedge to block area (take out the shuttle).

STEP 2. Heddle II up. Weave across block (pick-up) area (take out the shuttle).

STEP 3. Pick-up stick D. Weave to selvedge.

ROW 2: LIGHT WEFT

STEP 1. Heddle I up. Weave from selvedge to block area (take out the shuttle).

STEP 2. Pick-up stick B. Weave across block (pick-up) area (take the shuttle out).

STEP 3. Heddle I up. Weave to selvedge.

ROW 3: DARK WEFT

STEP 1. Heddle II down. Weave from selvedge to block area.

STEP 2. Pattern stick A. Weave across block (pick-up) area.

STEP 3. Heddle II down. Weave to selvedge.

ROW 4: LIGHT WEFT

STEP 1. Pick-up stick C. Weave from selvedge to block area.

STEP 2. Heddle I down. Weave across block (pick-up) area.

STEP 3. Pick-up stick C. Weave to selvedge.

PATTERNED UPPER LAYER

Here, I wove a light lower layer and a dark upper layer with supplementary weft.

Pick-up stick pattern C: Pick up every other warp thread from pick up stick A.

Weave as for two separate layers, with an added supplementary weft pick.

LOWER LAYER (LIGHT):

STEP 1. Pick-up stick B; light weft.

STEP 2. Heddle I down; light weft.

UPPER LAYER (DARK):

STEP 3. Heddle II up; dark weft.

STEP 4. Pick-up stick A; dark weft.

STEP 5. Pick-up stick C: supplementary weft.

Repeat these 5 steps for pattern.

Checked Doubleweave

By warping different stripe sequences in the upper and lower layers and exchanging the layers as you weave, you can mix colors and textures in inviting ways. For the following five swatches, I alternated wool and cotton in two color sequences for two blocks. For block A, yellow wool alternates with yellow cotton so that each weaves a different layer. For block B, green wool alternates with blue cotton, again so that each weaves a different layer. Depending on the weaving sequence, wool and cotton can appear on the upper or lower layer for each block.

The warp is Louet Gems Fingering Wool in Willow (light green) and Goldilocks (yellow) and 3/2 Pearl cotton in Poplin (blue) and Flaxon (pale yellow). The warp is threaded in 1" (2.5 cm) stripes of yellow wool and pale yellow cotton (block A) that alternate with 1" (2.5 cm) stripes of light green wool and blue cotton (block B), for a total of seven blocks.

SAMPLE 1

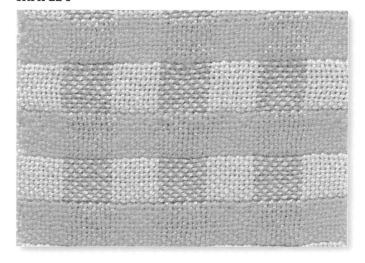

Weaving sequence A: Pale yellow cotton on the upper layer; yellow wool on the lower layer.

Weaving sequence B: Yellow wool on the upper layer; pale yellow cotton on the lower layer.

STEP 1. Weave Sequence A for 1" (2.5 cm) with 3/2 pale yellow cotton weft on the upper layer and yellow wool weft on the lower layer.

STEP 2. Exchange layers and weave Sequence B for 1" (2.5 cm) with yellow wool weft on the upper layer and pale yellow cotton weft on the lower layer.

Repeat these 2 steps for pattern.

Note: The front and reverse are similar except that color blocks change places with each layer exchange.

WEAVING TWO SEPARATE LAYERS:

Weaving sequence A:

LOWER LAYER (YELLOW WOOL AND BLUE PEARL COTTON):

STEP 1. Pick-up stick B, yellow wool.

STEP 2. Heddle I in down shed, yellow wool.

UPPER LAYER (YELLOW PEARL COTTON AND GREEN WOOL):

STEP 1. Heddle II up, yellow pearl cotton.

STEP 2. Pick-up stick A, yellow pearl cotton.

Weaving sequence B:

Exchange layers.

LOWER LAYER (YELLOW PEARL COTTON AND GREEN WOOL):

STEP 1. Pick-up stick D, yellow pearl cotton.

STEP 2. Heddle II down, yellow pearl cotton.

UPPER LAYER (YELLOW WOOL AND BLUE PEARL COTTON):

STEP 1. Heddle I up, yellow wool.

STEP 2. Pick-up stick C, yellow wool.

SAMPLE 2

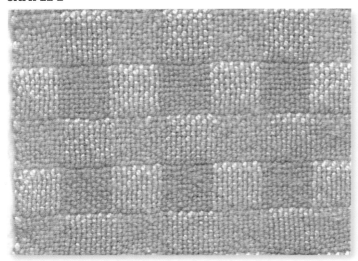

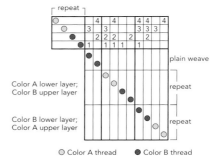

repeat

plain weave

Color A lower layer;
Color B upper layer
repeat

Color B lower layer;
Color A upper layer
repeat

○ Color A thread   ● Color B thread

Note: Follow the color sequences used for the rigid heddle weaving instructions.

I wove this sample the same as Sample 1, but I used light green wool weft for both the upper and lower layers.

SAMPLE 3

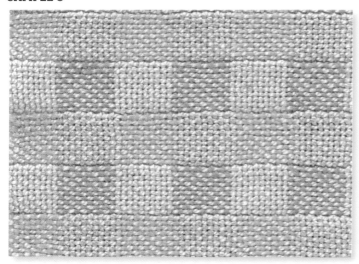

Here, I used blue cotton weft for both layers and wove the same as Sample 1.

SAMPLE 4

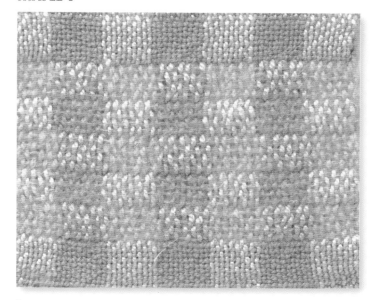

Front.

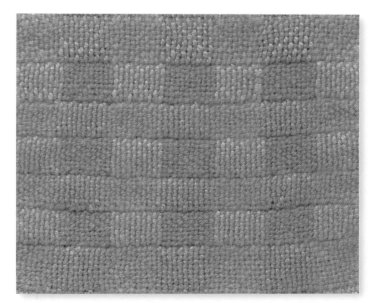

Reverse.

For this two-faced fabric, I wove the lower layer with light green wool in willow and the top layer with brushed mohair—Louet Brushed Mohair in Buttercup (gold). Because the mohair is quite a lot thicker than the wool, I wove 4 picks of wool on the lower layer for every 2 picks of mohair on the upper layer.

STEP 1. For the border, weave Sequence A (see page 215) for 1" (2.5 cm) with light green wool for the upper and lower layers.

STEP 2. Exchange layers and use Sequence B (see page 215) to weave 4 picks of light green wool on the lower layer, then 2 picks of gold mohair on the upper layer. Repeat 1 more time.

STEP 3. Exchange layers, weave Sequence A in the same manner as in Step 2 (4 picks of light green wool for every 2 picks of gold mohair).

Repeat these 3 steps for pattern, ending with the border (Step 1).

Fixing Errors

Unless you turn your loom over and look at the underside of your weaving, you can't see the bottom layer while you're weaving, and it's difficult to know if there are any warp or weft skips on the bottom layer. Therefore, it is important to inspect the cloth when you remove it from the loom. The time to fix errors is before washing, but sometimes, if the weaving is somewhat loose, you may find that an error doesn't present itself until after the fabric has been washed. If this is the case, go ahead and fix the error, then give the cloth a good steam pressing.

To repair errors in doubleweave cloth, thread a length of the same yarn onto a tapestry needle. Insert the needle between the two layers of the fabric for 1" (2.5 cm) or so before the error. Use the needle to re-weave the correct path across the error, ending 1" (2.5 cm) or so on each side of the error. Because only one side of each layer is visible in doubleweave, you don't need to cut the errant thread—it will be hidden on the inside. After washing, cut the repair tails flush with the surface of the fabric.

Doubleweave Layers at a Glance

Equipment
Two rigid heddles with the same epi, two or four pick-up sticks, two shuttles.

Preparation
Pick-up pattern for color A on top:
1. Place both heddles in the down position.
2. For pick-up stick A: Pick up all of the color A threads to the left of the Color B threads (working along the fell of the cloth makes it easy to see which threads to pick up). Transfer threads to another pick-up stick behind the heddles and slide it to the back of the loom.
3. For pick-up stick B: place both heddles in the up position, slide pick-up stick A forward to behind the heddle and slide pick-up stick B into the narrow bottom shed.

Weaving
LOWER LAYER (COLOR B)
STEP 1. Pick-up stick B, color B.
STEP 2. Heddle I down, color B.
UPPER LAYER (COLOR A)
STEP 1. Heddle II up, color A.
STEP 2. Pick-up stick A, color A.

Preparation
Pick-up pattern for color B layer on top:
If you want to exchange the layers so that the color B threads are on top and the color A threads are on the bottom, you'll need an additional two pick-up sticks. The first two can stay in place at the back of the loom until needed again.
1. For pick-up stick C: Place both heddles in the down position and pick-up all of the color B threads to the right of the color A threads.
2. For pick-up stick D: Place both heddles in the up position and slide pick-up stick C forward to behind the heddles and slide pick-up stick D into the resulting lower shed. Slide both pick-up sticks to the back of the loom.

Weaving
LOWER LAYER (COLOR A)
STEP 1. Pick-up stick D, color A.
STEP 2. Heddle II down*, color A.
UPPER LAYER (COLOR B)
STEP 1. Heddle I up, color B.
STEP 2. Pick-up stick C, color B.

*Note: In order to be able to weave with Heddle II in the down position, bring both heddles in front of the heddle block, pull up on the front heddle and push down on the back heddle. This is a little awkward, but I can do it with one hand and then use my other hand to insert the shuttle.

Window Screen

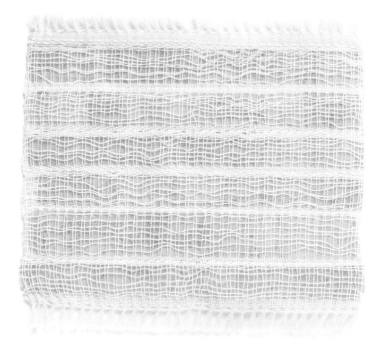

For this stuffed doubleweave fabric for a window screen, I wove "pockets" that I filled with ¾" (2 cm) strips of papyrus paper. For the warp, I alternated one end each of natural 10/2 unmercerized cotton and natural 10/2 pearl cotton. The two yarns aren't distinguishable in the finished fabric, but the slight differences in sheen make it easier to thread the warp ends in the proper order, as well as pick up the necessary ends for each layer.

Because the tubes are very loosely woven, the subtle color variations in the papyrus are visible when the screen is back lit. Also, the loose weave allows the weft to meander, adding character to the fabric.

I measured the pearl cotton and unmercerized cotton together, then threaded them in two 10-dent heddles. I threaded the pearl cotton in the holes in Heddle I (the front heddle) and the unmercerized cotton in the holes in Heddle II (the back heddle).

Using unmercerized cotton for the weft, I wove a tube (see page 210) for 1" (2.5 cm) using a very light beat. To stuff the tube, I lifted Heddle II and then slid pick-up stick B on its side up to behind the heddle to lift one layer up. I inserted a ¾" (2 cm) strip of papyrus cut to just less than the weaving width, then I closed the tube by weaving plain weave (both heddles up and down together) for 6 picks. I wove 4 picks of plain weave on each layer before beginning the next tube. To prevent the brittle papyrus from cracking, I cushioned it by winding it around thin corrugated cardboard board on the front beam. I did not finish the fabric in any way.

Reversible Jacket or Vest Fabric

Doubleweave is a great choice for jackets or vests because you can weave a dense fabric without bulk. By weaving two layers with finer yarns, you are rewarded with a very wearable thick fabric that isn't too stiff.

The sample shown on page 220 was woven on the same warp as the window-screen fabric shown at left, but the results are quite different. For weft, I used 5/2 pearl cotton in bright pink for the lower layer and a fine 20/2 pearl cotton in gold for the upper layer. For a completely solid background, I wove the lower layer as a weft-faced fabric. I used a fine yarn and a light beat for the upper layer to create a delicate fabric that allows the ribbon and pink background to peek through.

I wove this fabric as two separate layers (instead of a tube) that I joined every 1" (2.5 cm) with shiny metallic Lurex yarn woven in plain weave with both heddles. I inserted a diaphanous ribbon in between the layers as I wove. Closing the layers with plain weave instead of exchanging layers is fast to do; it doesn't require a second set of pick-up sticks (which would be necessary if the layers were exchanged). Additionally, because you are weaving the layers together, the fabric will be thinner and will contrast with the thicker dimension of the doubleweave areas.

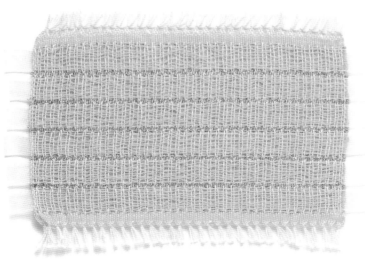

Front.

Imagine this perky fabric constructed into a short cropped evening jacket or vest. Trim it with a bias knitted trim in pink to create a fully reversible garment.

To weave this fabric, weave 4 picks of pink on the lower layer, followed by 2 picks of yellow on the upper layer. Repeat this sequence 5 times for a total of about ¾" (2 cm). Raise the top layer and insert the ribbon, allowing it to hang out the edges. Join the two layers with 6 picks of plain weave using the Lurex yarn. The resulting fabric is solid pink on the reverse with thin strips of gold; the front has a lacy quality.

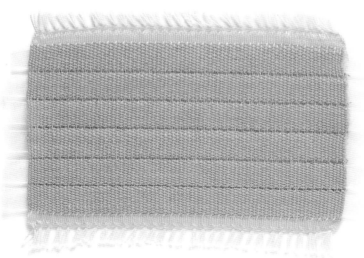

Reverse.

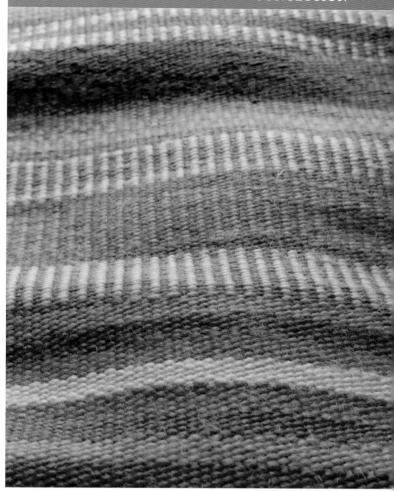

Conclusion

My mission in writing this book has been to explore the potential of the rigid heddle loom through samples, samplers, and projects. While plain weave is always an option—and never "plain" as I like to say—finger-control techniques, pick-up patterns, and two heddles expand what's possible with this simple loom. I think I could weave forever on my rigid heddle loom and never tire of it, though I may, from time to time, find that I'll prefer to use my floor loom for finer fabrics and doubleweave—just because it's faster. I know for sure, though, that I'll often choose my rigid heddle loom for sampling—it's so easy to take my pick-up stick in and out to try something different, it's a snap to warp up, and I can put on relatively short warps to sample a color or structure. I hope you've grown to appreciate through these discoveries not just techniques and ideas, but a deep understanding of the vast possibilities weaving offers for creating unique and exciting cloth.

Country Girl/City Girl
APRON

Designed and woven by Jane Patrick;
sewn by Gail Matthews.

Growing up, my sisters and I would reach for our aprons
where they hung in the kitchen just above the dryer. If
the dryer happened to be running, we were rewarded
with a slightly warm apron, especially welcome if we'd
just walked home on an icy Nebraska afternoon. Our
aprons were full-coverage with healthy bibs and ample
skirts. Wearing aprons was just something we did, like
saying grace before the meal.

Finished Size
About 18" (45.5 cm) wide at
the waist and 24" (61 cm) long.

Weave Structure
Plain weave with picked-up
loops.

Yarn
Warp: *10/2 unmercerized
cotton* (100% cotton; 4,200 yd
[3,840 m]/lb): Natural, 585 yd
(535 m). *10/2 pearl cotton* (100%
cotton; 4,200 yd [3,840 m]/lb):
Natural, 585 yd (535 m).

Weft: *Cottolin* (50% cotton, 50%
linen; 3,172 yd [2,900 m]/lb):
Natural, 150 yd (137 m); Bleached,
80 yd (73 m). *16/2 linen* (100%
linen; 3,000 yd [2,743 m]/lb):
Unbleached, 35 yd (32 m).
10/2 pearl cotton (100% cotton;
4,200 yd [3,840 m]/lb): Natural,
250 yd (229 m). *Textura Trading
2/16 Hemp* (100% hemp; 3,960 yd
[3,621 m]/lb): Natural, 25 yd
(23 m).

Pick-up loops: *Habu Shosenshi
Viscose Item A-60* (100% linen
paper; 4,300 yd [3,932 m]/lb):
#117 Brown, 250 yd (229 m).

Equipment
Rigid heddle loom with 25"
(63.5 cm) weaving width and
two-heddle capability; two
10-dent rigid heddle reeds, four
stick shuttles (one for each weft
yarn), and three double-point
size 10 (6 mm) knitting needles.

Number of Warp Ends
500.

Warp Length
2⅓ yards (2.1 m), which includes
44" (112 cm) for the project and
28" (71 cm) for take-up and
loom waste.

Warp Width
25" (63.5 cm).

EPI
20.

PPI
18–20.

I've maintained a fondness for aprons and always don one upon entering the kitchen. Lately, I've noticed aprons in catalogs, fashion magazines, and even in the *New York Times*. This apron is not for cooking Sunday dinner, but it would be a nice hostess apron (something you'd understand if you lived in the 1950s) or an unusual accessory to a simple linen skirt or long straight pants.

For this apron, I wove 2½" (6.5 cm) bands that I accented with two rows of picked-up loops (see page 44). Each band is woven in a different stripe pattern. Weave each band the same or play around with color gradation, blending from dark at the hem to light at the waist—you can't go wrong with any of these yarns or combinations.

Warping

Alternate one strand each of 10/2 unmercerized cotton and 10/2 pearl cotton for a 25" (63.5 cm) weaving width.

Weaving

Stripe sequence: The sequence below is what I wove from the base of the skirt to the top. Each band is different and there will be some variation in how the sequences weave.
For visual rhythm, keep the distance between pick-up-loop rows consistent.

BAND 1. Alternate 1 pick 10/2 pearl bleached cotton and 1 pick 16/2 linen.

BAND 2. Three picks bleached cottolin, 1 pick 16/2 natural linen, 3 picks bleached cottolin, 2 picks 16/2 natural linen, 3 picks natural cottolin, 1 pick 16/2 natural linen, 3 picks natural cottolin, 2 picks 16/2 natural linen.

BAND 3. Two picks 10/2 pearl cotton, 2 picks natural cottolin, 2 picks hemp, 2 picks natural cottolin.

BAND 4. Alternate 3 picks of hemp with 3 picks of 10/2 pearl cotton.

BAND 5. Alternate ½" (1.3 cm) stripes of natural and bleached cottolin.

BAND 6. Four picks bleached cottolin, 2 picks 16/2 linen, 4 picks bleached cottolin, 1¼" (3.2 cm) alternating natural cottolin and bleached cottolin, ¾" (2 cm) bleached cottolin.

NOTES

To avoid twists in the warp behind the heddles, use the indirect warping method.

Use three double-pointed knitting needles end to end to pick up the loops across the width of the cloth.

For the warp, I alternated unmercerized 10/2 cotton and 10/2 pearl cotton, but you could use just one of these with good results. For weft, I used undyed cotton and linen yarns that I had on hand. Feel free to mix and match yarns that are about 20 wraps per inch.

For shaft looms, thread plain weave on a straight draw (1, 2, 3, 4). For the picked-up loop rows, just raise shaft 1, picking up loops in every space.

Skirt

STEP 1. Weave 2" (5 cm) with 10/2 pearl cotton for hem.

STEP 2. Weave 1 pick of the paper yarn used singly, weave 1 pick of 10/2 pearl cotton, 1 pick of paper yarn, and 4 picks of 10/2 pearl cotton.

STEP 3. Using the paper yarn doubled on a shuttle for the loops, raise Heddle I only and pick up a loop in every space and place it on a knitting needle, skipping 4 spaces at the beginning and end of the row (to be folded under later for hem).

STEP 4. Leaving the knitting needles in place, weave 2 picks of 10/2 pearl cotton, carefully remove the needles, beat well, weave 2 more picks of 10/2 pearl cotton, and beat well again.

STEP 5. Repeat Steps 3 and 4 once.

STEP 6. Weave 2 rows with 10/2 pearl cotton followed by 2½" (6.5 cm) of stripes according to the stripe sequence on page 223.

Repeat Steps 2–6 for pattern. After weaving Band 6, repeat Steps 2–5 and then weave 5" (12.5 cm) with pearl cotton for top of apron.

Waistband and Ties

Alternate 4 picks bleached cottolin with 1 pick of paper yarn for 12" (30.5 cm). Be sure to beat consistently for even stripes.

Finishing

Remove fabric from loom and machine zigzag ends to prevent fraying. Handwash in warm water and mild detergent. Rinse well, squeeze out excess water, and lay flat to dry. Steam-press on the wrong side with a steam iron and pressing cloth (this will flatten the loops, which is part of the design).

Assembly

Skirt

Hem the sides of the skirt by folding ¼" (6 mm) to the wrong side and machine stitching. Fold under ¾" (2 cm) hem on the lower edge of the skirt and handstitch in place, avoiding the loops on the right side of the fabric. To gather the top edge, baste along the edge, then pull the basting threads to gather the top to 18" (45.5 cm) across. Fold the skirt in half and mark the center of the top edge.

Waistband/Tie

Divide the waistband/tie fabric into three equal pieces (count the weft threads between cuts so that the stripes will align when the pieces are sewn together) and mark for cutting. Before cutting, zigzag on each side of the marked lines to prevent raveling. Alternatively, use an anti-fray product such as June Tailor Fray Block. Test the product on a sample of the fabric first, then cover two threads on each side of the marked lines and allow it to dry completely before cutting.

With right sides together, match the stripes and sew the short ends of three strips together to make one long piece for the waistband. Fold the waistband in half widthwise and mark the center. Fold the long edges ¼" (6 mm) to the wrong side and press. Fold the waistband in half lengthwise, right sides together. Sew the short ends of the ties, pivoting at the corners and sewing a couple of inches along the long edge of the ties, unfolding the long edges while sewing. Press the ends. Trim each corner, then turn right side out using a point turner for tidy corners, and press again.

Place the waistband on the skirt right sides together, matching the centers and pinning. Flip over the waistband so wrong sides are together and enclosing the top edge of the skirt. Matching the folded edges of the band, stitch along the entire length.

Doubleweave
TABLE RUNNER

Designed and woven by Jane Patrick.

Double weave is useful for making a thick and sturdy fabric. This is why I especially like to use double weave for a table runner—a fabric thick enough to protect the table without too much bulk. I used three different sizes of pearl cotton for this runner. In the warp, I used 3/2 in charcoal and blue and doubled 5/2 chartreuse for the green accent stripes. I like the slight difference in texture between the two yarn sizes. In the weft, to create a solid pink border at either end, I used hot pink in 10/2 pearl cotton. By using a smaller yarn and beating it in with a hand beater to completely cover the warp, I was able to make a bright border to punctuate both ends.

Finished Size
About 11" (28 cm) wide and 33" (84 cm) long, after about 10% shrinkage in length and 12% shrinkage in width.

Weave Structure
Double weave.

Yarn
Warp and Weft: *3/2 Pearl Cotton* (100% cotton; 1,280 yd [1,170 m]/lb): #78 Charcoal, 675 yd (617 m); #109 Bermuda, 120 yd (110 m). *5/2 Pearl Cotton* (100% cotton; 2,100 yd [1,920 m]/lb): #152 Pistachio, 180 yd (165 m). *10/2 Pearl Cotton* (100% cotton; 4,200 yd [3,840 m]/lb): #129 Fruit Punch, 80 yd (73 m).

Equipment
Rigid heddle loom with at least 13½" (34.5 cm) weaving width and two-heddle capability; two 10-dent rigid heddle reeds; four pick-up sticks; three stick shuttles.

Number of Warp Ends
264.

Warp Length
2 yards (1.8 m), which allows 28" (71 cm) for take-up and loom waste.

Warp Width
13¼" (33.5 cm).

EPI
20 (10 per layer).

PPI
20 (10 per layer).

The blue blocks within the gray background are produced by bringing the stripes of blue in the lower layer to the top gray layer. Each blue block is accented with a thin line of doubled chartreuse beat firmly into place. On the reverse side, the greens intersect in the gray stripes, leaving solid blue blocks. Turn the pink ends to the inside of the runner where they will be hidden and stitch the ends closed to make the runner fully reversible.

NOTES

The top layer will have all gray warp threads.

Instead of carrying the weft up the edges, leave about 3" (7.5 cm) ends hanging when changing colors. After weaving, thread the ends in a tapestry needle and hide them between the two layers.

This weave wants to draw in. Be sure to angle the weft at least 45 degrees when inserting it in the shed.

To help keep track of the weaving sequence, always begin and end weft colors at the same selvedge edge.

To help identify the proper warp ends to pick up with the second set of pick-up sticks in the gray areas, transfer the current pattern to a second pick-up stick in front of the heddle and use this as a guide for the next pick-up sequence.

Warping

Warp Color Order

															Total
Charcoal	32		1			1	28		1			1	28		1			1	32	180
Blue		1			1			1			1			1			1			60
Chartreuse*				8						8						8				24*
		10X			10x			10X			10X			10X			10X			264

*Doubled ends (total doubled ends is 48).
Use this guide to measure your warp on the warping board. When threading the rigid heddle loom, you'll see that the threads that alternate in the chart above will be paired when threaded in the heddles. Shaft loom weavers will alternate the colors.

Threading the heddles

Follow the directions for warping two heddles on page 178. Thread the colors as follows:

Heddle I: Thread a charcoal in all of the holes, except in the chartreuse stripes where you'll have chartreuse. There will be three charcoal in the slots in the solid charcoal areas and two blue and one charcoal in the slots in the two-color block areas.

Heddle II: Thread the blue threads in the holes. There will be two charcoal and one blue in the slots in the two-color areas.

Preparation

Weave about an inch of plain weave to align the warp threads so you can see them better when commencing with the pick-up. At the fell of the cloth with the heddles in the down position, with pick-up stick A pick up the rightmost of the paired threads. Transfer this pattern to the back of the loom. For pick-up stick B place both heddles in the up position and slide pick-up stick A flat up to behind the heddles and insert pick-up stick B behind the heddles into the lower of the two sheds.

To prepare for the exchange of layers, place both heddles in the down position and at the fell of the cloth pick up every left thread of the paired threads with pick-up stick C (transfer to behind the heddles). Now, raise both heddles and slide pick-up stick C flat up to behind the heddles and slide pick-up stick D into the lower shed.

Since you will need to remove both of these pick-up sticks after each sequence, you might consider saving the C pattern with string heddles on a heddle rod (see page 98). You can easily insert pick-up stick C into this shed and use it to create your D shed.

Weaving

You will be weaving tubular doubleweave for this runner, exchanging layers to create the blue blocks within a gray background punctuated with thin warp and weft chartreuse stripes.

STEP 1. With pink and weaving sequence A, weave hem for 1" (2.5 cm) at about 48 ppi to completely cover the warp. A hand beater will help pack in the weft.

STEP 2. With charcoal and weaving sequence A, weave 18 picks on each layer for a total of 36 picks for both layers.

STEP 3. With charcoal and weaving sequence B, weave 10 picks on each layer for a total of 20 picks for both layers.

STEP 4. With chartreuse (used single) and weaving sequence B, weave 2 picks on each layer for a total of 4 picks for both layers.

STEP 5. Repeat Step 3.

STEP 6. Repeat Steps 2–5 for a total of 12 repeats.

STEP 7. Repeat Step 2.

STEP 8. With pink and weaving sequence A, weave 1" (2.5 cm) at about 48 ppi to completely cover the warp for the hem.

Finishing

Remove fabric from loom. Machinestitch ends to prevent fraying. Correct any errors and weave in all ends. Handwash in warm water with mild soap. Rinse well, squeeze out excess water, and lay flat to dry. Steam-press. Fold the hems inside the weaving, leaving a ⅜" (1 cm) border. Handsew hem and press again.

Weaving Tubular Doubleweave

Weaving Sequence A
Step 1. Pick-up stick B (lower layer).
Step 2. Heddle II up (upper layer).
Step 3. Heddle I down (lower layer).
Step 4. Pick-up stick A (upper layer).
Repeat these 4 steps for pattern.

Exchange layers.

Weaving Sequence B
Step 1. Heddle II down (lower layer).
Step 2. Pick-up stick C (upper layer).
Step 3. Pick-up stick D (lower layer).
Step 4. Heddle I up (upper layer).
Repeat these 4 steps for pattern.

Draft for Shaft Looms

If you use a loom with only 4 shafts, use a direct tie-up. That is, tie up only one treadle to each shaft and use both feet to lift three shafts when needed.

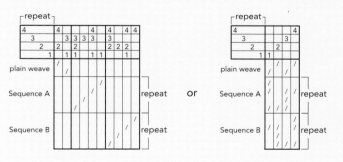

For this treadling, weave a row on the upper layer and then a row on the bottom layer, and then the other shed on the upper layer and then the lower layer, 4 picks per repeat.

Glossary of Weaving Terms

apron bars. The rods or sticks, connected to both the cloth beam and warp beam with apron cords, to which the warp is tied.

balanced weave. Fabric in which the number of warp ends per inch is the same as the number of weft ends per inch.

beat. To push the weft threads into place with the rigid heddle reed or by hand with a hand beater.

butterfly. A figure-eight tied bundle of yarn used for weaving.

clasped weft (also meet and separate). A technique in which a shuttle passes through the shed and encircles a loop of yarn and draws it into the shed to create a tapestry-like effect.

cross. The figure eight made at one end of the warp when measuring. It keeps the warp ends in order and helps prevent tangles.

direct-peg warping. A method of warping the loom in which the warp is measured around a single peg and threaded through the reed in the same step (see page 232).

discontinuous weft. A weft that does not travel from selvedge to selvedge, but rather several wefts that weave short distances across the web to create a pattern, as in tapestry.

draw in. The tendency of the web to narrow during weaving.

end. One warp yarn (or thread).

epi (ends per inch). The number of warp ends in 1" (2.5 cm).

fell line. The place on the loom where unwoven warp and web (or woven warp) meet.

felt. A thick, fuzzy, insulating fabric, usually made of wool.

felting. The irreversible process of binding fibers together, usually made of wool.

fiber. The substance, such as wool, from which yarn is spun.

ghiordes knot. A knot used to make pile, also called a rya knot.

heddle. On a rigid heddle loom, the device that holds the warp, determines sett, and beats the weft into place, also called a rigid heddle reed. Also a loop of yarn that holds a warp thread, as in a heddle rod and string heddles.

heddle block. The notched area on the inner face of the loom sides. Holds the heddle or heddles in the upper, lower, and neutral positions.

loom. A frame that holds the warp for weaving.

loom waste. Any yarn that is not woven at the beginning and end of a warp.

loop pile. A method of making protruding loops by looping weft yarn over a rod, with a tabby or plain-weave ground.

meet and separate. See clasped weft.

novelty yarn. Generally, a fancy, complex yarn that has different twists, irregularities, and fibers.

pick (also shot). One row of weaving.

pick-and-pick. A pattern in which two colors alternate in plain weave rows (for example, 1 row of white, 1 row of red, 1 row of white, 1 row of red, and so on).

pick-up. The technique of manipulating warp threads to create warp or weft floats in weaving.

pick-up stick. A narrow stick used to pick up patterns. Also can be turned on edge to form a shed.

plain weave. The simplest of all weaves—an over, under, over, under interlacement.

pile. A weft-faced weave in which yarns protrude from the surface, often made of knots or loops with a tabby or plain-weave ground.

plied yarn. A yarn that is composed of several single strands of yarn twisted together.

ppi (picks per inch). The number of weft rows, or picks, in 1" (2.5 cm) of weaving.

selvedge. The edge threads in weaving.

sett. Number of warp ends in one inch.

shed. The space between raised and lowered warp threads through which the shuttle passes during weaving.

shed stick. Narrow stick used to make a shed, also called a pick-up stick.

shot. See pick.

shuttle. The tool that holds yarn for weaving.

singles yarn. A yarn made of one strand; not a plied yarn.

sley. To thread the warp threads through the rigid heddle reed, generally with a threading hook.

stick shuttle. Flat narrow stick with grooves on the ends used for holding weft for weaving.

tabby. A plain-weave ground that binds pattern picks.

take-up. The amount of warp and weft length "lost" during weaving. Instead of going in a straight line, the warp and weft yarns actually curve over and under each other, and therefore extra yarn is required.

tapestry. A weft-faced weave woven of discontinuous wefts.

threading hook. A long flat metal hook with a handle used to thread the rigid heddle reed.

warp. noun: The set of threads held taut by a loom. verb: to put the warp threads onto the loom.

warp-dominant: A fabric in which the warp is predominant but does not completely cover the weft.

warp-faced. Cloth in which only the warp shows.

warping. The process of putting the warp onto the loom.

warping board. A rectangular frame fitted with dowels that is used to measure the warp.

warping peg. A single peg that is clamped to a table and used to measure warp in the direct-warping method.

weaving. Crossing one set of threads with another. The warps are those threads that are held taut by a loom. The weft threads cross the warp.

web. On the loom, the warp that has been already woven. Woven fabric.

weft. The threads that cross the warp.

weft-dominant. A fabric in which the weft is prominent but does not completely cover the warp.

weft-faced. Cloth in which only the weft shows.

yarn. Continous fibers that have been spun or constructed.

Direct, Single-Peg Warping

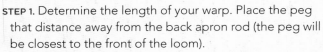
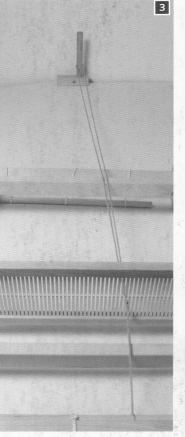

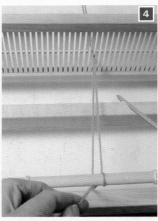

STEP 1. Determine the length of your warp. Place the peg that distance away from the back apron rod (the peg will be closest to the front of the loom).

STEP 2. Place the loom on a table with the back facing the edge. Clamp it as necessary.

STEP 3. Place the yarn source on the floor under the back beam of the loom. Place the heddle in a neutral slot.

STEP 4. Determine the edge of the weaving width (divide the weaving width by two and measure out that distance from the center).

STEP 5. Bring the apron rod up and over the back beam. Tie on the warp end to the apron rod in line with one edge of weaving width (**Figure 1**).

STEP 6. Insert the heddle hook from the front side to the back, grab the warp yarn and draw it through the slot (**Figure 2**).

STEP 7. Place this loop around the warping peg. There will be 2 warp ends through the slot (**Figure 3**).

STEP 8. Continue to draw loops through the slots, around the apron rod, and then around the warping peg for the desired total number of warp ends (**Figures 4** and **5**).

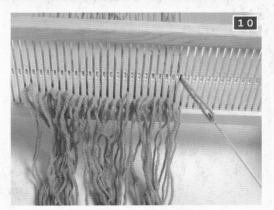

STEP 9. Cut off the yarn from the yarn source and tie the end to the apron rod (**Figure 6**).

STEP 10. Remove the loop of warp from the warping peg, cut the end of the loop (**Figure 7**), and tie it in a loose overhand knot (**Figure 8**).

STEP 11. Wind the warp onto the back cloth beam between layers of heavy paper or corrugated cardboard until about 10" (25.5 cm) remain in front of the heddle (**Figure 9**).

STEP 12. Working at the front of the loom, take 1 warp end out of a slot and thread it in the adjacent hole (**Figure 10**).

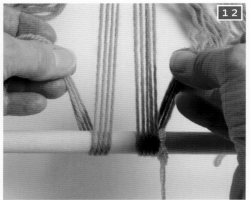

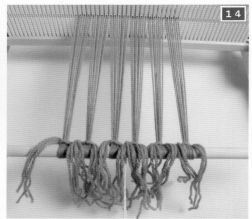

STEP 13. When all of the slots and holes have been threaded, check your work that there is one thread through each slot and each hole across the weaving width (Figure **11**).

STEP 14. Bring the apron rod up and over the front beam. To tie the warp onto the front apron rod in a surgeon's knot, pull a 1" (2.5 cm) bundle over the top of the apron rod, divide it in half (Figure **12**), loop the ends around each other twice, and pull tight (Figure **13**). Repeat across the entire warp (Figure **14**). I like to start the knots in the middle of the warp and work back and forth from side to side. Adjust each knot as necessary until the warp tension is even all the way across. When the tension is even, tie the ends of the surgeon's knots in bows (Figure **15**) to secure them.

STEP 15. Now you are ready to weave.

Rigid Heddle Project Record Sheet

Project Name: _____

WARPING

WarpYarn _____

Slots:	
Holes:	

Warp Color Order _____

Total Warp Ends _____

Ends Per Inch _____

Width in Reed _____

Rigid Heddle Dent _____

Warp Length _____

WEAVING

Weft Yarn _____

_____

Weft Color Order _____

Picks Per Inch _____

Pick-up Stick Pattern _____

Woven Width _____

Woven Length _____

Finishing _____

Finished Size _____

Bibliography and Resources

BOOKS ON RIGID HEDDLE WEAVING

Davenport, Betty Linn. *Hands On Rigid Heddle Weaving*. Loveland, Colorado: Interweave, 1987.

———. *Textures and Patterns for the Rigid Heddle Loom*. Battle Ground, Washington: self-published, 2008, revised edition; distributed by Fine Fiber Press.

Gipson, Liz. *Weaving Made Easy*. Loveland, Colorado: Interweave, 2008.

Hart, Rowena. *The Ashford Book of Rigid Heddle Weaving*. Ashburton, New Zealand: Ashford Handicrafts, 2002.

Howard, Sarah, and Elisabeth Kendrick. *Creative Weaving: Beautiful Fabrics with a Simple Loom*. Ashville, North Carolina: Lark Books, 2008.

Iwamura, Misao. *Plain Weaving: Try Creating Original Textiles Using Plain Weaving*. Tokyo: Bunko Publishing, 2002. English translation distributed in the U.S. by Habu Textiles.

Lamb, Sara. *Woven Treasures: One-of-a-Kind Bags With Folk Weaving Techniques*. Loveland, Colorado: Interweave, 2009.

McKinney, Rev David B. *Weaving With Three Rigid Heddles*. Greeley Hill, California: self-published, 1985.

Xenakis, Athanasios David. *The Xenakis Technique*. Sioux Falls, South Dakota: Golden Fleece Publications, 1978.

BOOKS ON COLOR

Itten, Johannes. *The Elements of Color*. New York: Van Nostrand Reinhold, 1970.

Menz, Deb. *Color Works*. Loveland, Colorado: Interweave, 2004.

Stockton, James. *Designer's Guide to Color*. San Francisco: Chronicle Books, 1984.

BOOKS ON COLOR-AND-WEAVE

Sutton, Ann. *Colour-and-Weave Design Book: A Practical Reference Book*. England: Sterling Publishers, 1985.

———. *Ideas in Weaving*. Asheville, North Carolina: Lark Books, 1982.

BOOKS ON FOLK TRADITIONS

Collingwood, Peter. *The Maker's Hand*. Loveland, Colorado: Interweave, 1987.

BOOKS ON KNOTS AND BRAIDING AND FINISHES

Ashley, Clifford. *The Ashley Book of Knots*. Reissue edition. New York: Doubleday, 1944.

Baizerman, Suzanne, and Karen Searle. *Finishes in the Ethnic Tradition*. St. Paul, Minnesota: Dos Tejedoras, 1978.

Budworth, Geoffrey. *The Complete Book of Decorative Knots*. New York: Lyons Press, 1998.

McEneely, Naomi. *Compendium of Finishing Techniques*. Loveland, Colorado: Interweave, 2003.

Pawson, Des. *The Handbook of Knots*. New York: DK Publishing, 1998.

Owen, Peter. *The Book of Decorative Knots*. New York: Lyons and Burford, 1994.

Shaw, George Russell. *Knots: Useful and Ornamental*. New York: McMillan Publishers, 1972.

West, Virginia. *Finishing Touches for the Handweaver*. Loveland, Colorado: Interweave, 1988.

BOOKS ON TEXTILE DESIGN

Aimone, Katherine Duncan. *The Fiberarts Book of Wearable Art*. Asheville, North Carolina: Lark Books, 2002.

Braddock, Sarah E., and Marie O'Mahaony. *Techno Textiles*. New York: Thames and Hudson, 2001.

Koumis, Matthew, ed. *Art Textiles of the World: USA Vol. 1*. Winchester, England: Telos Art Publishing, 2000.

Takekura, Masaaki, publisher. *Suke Suke*. Tokyo: Nuno Corporation, 1997.

BOOKS ON WEAVING

Alderman, Sharon. *Mastering Weave Structures*. Loveland, Colorado: Interweave, 2004.

Allen, Heather. *Weaving Contemporary Rag Rugs: New Designs, Traditional Techniques*. New York: Sterling, 2001.

Atwater, Mary Meigs. *Byways in Handweaving: An Illustrated Guide to Rare Weaving Techniques*. Coupeville, Washington: Shuttlecraft Books, 1992, distributed by Unicorn Books.

Chandler, Deborah. *Learning to Weave, revised edition*. Loveland Colorado: Interweave, 1995.

Collingwood, Peter. *The Techniques of Rug Weaving*. New York: Watson-Guptill Publications, 1972.

Dixon, Anne. *The Handweaver's Pattern Directory*. Loveland, Colorado: Interweave, 2007.

Drooker, Penelope B. *Embroidery with the Loom*. New York: Van Nostrand Reinhold, 1979.

Held, Shirley. *Weaving: A Handbook for Fiber Craftsmen*. New York: Holt Rinehart and Winston, 1973.

Ligon, Linda, and Marilyn Murphy. *The Weaver's Companion*. Loveland, Colorado: Interweave, 2001.

Meany, Janet, and Paula Pfaff. *Rag Rug Handbook*. Loveland, Colorado: Interweave, 1996.

Patrick, Jane. *Time to Weave: Simply Elegant Fabrics to Weave in Almost No Time*. Loveland, Colorado: Interweave, 2006.

Redman, Jane. *Frame-Loom Weaving*. New York: Van Nostrand Reinhold, 1976.

Sutton, Ann. *The Structure of Weaving*. Asheville, North Carolina: Lark Books, 1982.

Tidball, Harriet. *Surface Interest: Textiles of Today: Shuttle Craft Monograph Two*. Lansing, Michigan: The Shuttle Craft Guild, 1961.

———. *Two-Harness Textiles: The Loom-Controlled Weaves: Shuttle Craft Monograph Twenty*. Santa Ana, California: HTH Publishers, 1967.

———. *Undulating Weft Effects: Shuttle Craft Monograph Nine*. Freeland, Washington: HTH Publishers, 1963.

WEAVING AND TEXTILE ART MAGAZINES

Fiberarts
fiberarts.com
Interweave
201 East Fourth St.
Loveland, Colorado 80537

Handwoven
handwovenmagazine.com
Interweave
201 East Fourth St.
Loveland, Colorado 80537

Selvedge
selvedge.org
PO Box 40038
London N6 5UW
United Kingdom

Shuttle, Spindle, and Dyepot
weavespindye.org
Handweavers Guild of America
1255 Buford Hwy, Ste. 211
Suwanee, GA 30024

Textilforum
ETN-net.org
Friedenstr 5
PO Box 5944
D-30059 Hannover
Germany

Vav Magasinet
vavmagasinet.se
Westmansgatan 37
582 16 Linkoping
Sweden

Weaver's Craft
weaverscraft.com
Plain Tabby Press
4945 Hogan Dr.
Fort Collins, CO 80525

Weavezine
weavezine.com
Warp Thread Media
PO Box 860
North Bend, WA 98045

Index

abrasion of warp threads, testing for, 18, 19
apron project, 222–225

bags, see Rag Bag Threesome
balanced weave, 14, 16
bands, warp-faced, 169–173
basket weave, modified, 184, 195
beads, in Danish medallions, 50
Blue Star Ghiordes Knot design, 144
Brook's bouquet, 59–63, 212
butterflies, winding, 159
buttons, Chinese knot, 39

candlewick pattern, 45
Chinese knot button, 39
clasped weft technique, 164–165
clutch bag, 34, 41
coasters, 141, 174–175
color-and-weave effects
    double weave, 213
    with floats, 119, 120–123
    log cabin, 27–29
    sampler, 24–26
    two-heddle weaving, 189
color, designing with
    Brook's bouquet, 59, 61, 63
    Danish medallions, 50
    in double weave, 215–218
    in plain weave, 21, 24–26
    two-heddle weaving, 189, 200
    warp floats, 114–119
    see also color-and-weave effects
confetti cut pile, 147, 150
cord, making, 38–39, 40
Country Girl/City Girl Apron, 222–225
cross, making, 180–181
crow's feet, 51
cut loops, 46
cut pile techniques
    Blue Star design, 144
    confetti pile, 147, 150
    Desert Cacti design, 146

fill-in, weaving, 148–149
    ghiordes knots, 141, 143–144
    Philippine edges, 145
    Rya Butterfly design, 148
    tips, 142

Danish medallions, 47–52, 57
deflected warps, 129
deflected wefts, 124–125
dents, 9
Desert Cacti design, 146
design considerations
    designing in the reed, 21
    drafts, translating patterns to, 119
    graphing designs, 147
    plain weave, 15–18, 21–23, 120
    see also color, designing with; texture, designing with
    differential shrinkage, 127–128
direct, single-peg warping, 178, 232–234
double weave
    basic instructions, 203
    color and texture, 215–220
    finger-controlled techniques, 212
    fixing errors, 217
    pick-up techniques, 205, 213–214
    reversible fabric, 219–220
    sampler, 206–211
    threading, 204
    tips, 204
    window screen fabric, 219
Double Weave Table Runner, 226–229
drafts, translating patterns to, 119

embroidery, 200–202

Felted Pin-Striped Wrap Skirt, 130–131
Felted Scarf in Beige, 30–31
felting, 19
Fiberworks software, 119

fill-in, for cut pile, 148–149
finger-controlled weaves
    advantages of, 43, 73
    with double weave, 212
    see also specific techniques
Flip Loom, 10
floats, see warp floats; weft floats
flossa rugs, 146
fringe accents
    fringe loops, 47
    weft floats, 110–113

ghiordes knots, 141, 143–144
graphing designs, 147

handspun yarns, 19–20
headers, weaving, 67
heddle rods, 98–99
heddles, 9, 10
hemstitching
    beginning of work, 69
    end of work, 70
    functions of, 68
    Italian, 71
    ladder, 70
    needle weaving, 72–73
    as trim, 72
    zigzag, 72
honeycomb patterns
    with two heddles, 197–198
    warp floats, 119
    weft-faced fabrics, 167–168
    weft floats, 113
Honeycomb Pillow Pair, 132–135

Incredible Rope Machine, 40
indirect warping, 178–181
inkle looms, 169
inlaid patterns with weft floats, 108–109
Italian hemstitching, 71

krokbragd, 161–164

lace structures
    Brook's bouquet, 59–63, 212
    embroidery on, 202
    Spanish lace, 64–68
    spot lace, 91, 92, 94
    two-heddle weaving, 186
    weft floats, 83–84, 86, 89–90
    see also leno
ladder hemstitching, 70
leno, 53–58, 212
Linen Placemats with Leno and Spanish Lace Borders, 76–77
log cabin, 27–29
looms
    Flip Loom, 10
    heddle positions, 9, 80, 82
    inkle, 169
    rigid heddle, 9–10
loop pile, 44–47, 150–154

Mexican lace, 56
mock waffle weave, 100

needle weaving, 72–73
novelty yarns, pick-up techniques with, 124–129

pattern weft, see supplementary weft
Philippine edges, 145
picks per inch, effects of changing, 16
pick-up techniques
    basic instructions, 81–82
    color-and-weave effects, 120–123
    with double weave, 205
    heddle positions, 80, 82
    heddle rods, 98–99
    lace structures, 83–84, 86
    novelty yarns, 124–129
    selvedges, managing, 87
    spot lace, 86, 91, 92, 94
    sticks, 80
    translating to drafts, 119

twills, 189, 190, 191–193
  with two-heddle warps, 187, 188, 189–193
warp-faced fabrics, 171–173
warp float sampler, 96–98
weft-faced fabrics, 166–168
weft float sampler, 88–95
  see also warp floats; weft floats
pile, see cut pile techniques; loop pile
pillows project, 132–135
placemats project, 76–77
plaid effects
  pick-up patterns, 122
  as texture, 22–23
  see also color-and-weave effects
plain weave
  basics, 13–14
  design considerations, 15–18, 21, 120
  fine setts, 178, 196–199
  samplers, 24–26, 27–29
  sett, determining, 15
  spaced warps and wefts, 19
  stripes and plaids, 22–23
  with two heddles, 180, 184, 189, 195
  see also double weave
Project Record Sheet, 235
Pulled-Thread Scarf, 32–33
purse with shoulder strap, 34, 37–40

Rag Bag Threesome
  clutch, 34, 41
  purse with shoulder strap, 34, 37–40
  tote, 34, 35–37
reversible fabric, double weave, 219–220
rigid heddle reeds, 9, 10
rope machine, 40
Rya Butterfly design, 148
rya rugs, 146

sampling, 23
scarves
  Felted Scarf in Beige, 30–31
  Pulled-Thread Scarf, 32–33
selvedges, 87
sett
  determining, 15
  for double weave, 204
  fine setts, 178, 196–199
Shrug in Leno, 74–75
shuttles, 11
skirt project, 130–131
soumak, 155–160
spaced designs
  Danish medallions, 52
  warps, 19
  wefts, 19
spacers, 19, 72
Spanish lace, 64–68
spot lace, 91, 92, 94
stripes
  with leno, 58
  as texture, 22–23
  threading on two heddles, 182–183
  warp floats, 117, 118
Summertime Coasters, 174–175
supplementary weft
  basics, 85
  with double weave, 214
  with lace, 106–107
  two-heddle weaving, 186–187
  weft floats and, 92–93, 95, 125–126

table runner project, 226–229
tapestry effects with weft floats, 105
texture, designing with
  Danish medallions and, 50
  with double weave, 215–220
  in plain weave, 21–23
  stripes and plaids, 22–23
  two-heddle weaving, 183–190, 194–195

Textures and Patterns for the Rigid Heddle Loom (Davenport), 124
threading
  for double weave, 204
  single heddle 10, 15
  two heddles, 178–179, 200
tools, 10–11, 98–99
tote bag, 34, 35–37
tubes, double weave, 210–211
twills, 189, 190, 191–193
two-heddle weaving
  basic instructions, 180
  for fine setts, 178, 196–199
  indirect warping, 178–181
  striped warps, 182–183
  textures and patterns, 183–190, 194–195
  twills, 189, 190, 191–193
  see also double weave

waffle weave effects, 117
warp-faced fabrics, 14, 169–173
warp floats
  combined with weft floats, 87, 100–103, 127–128, 184
  heddle position, 82
  honeycomb, 119
  1/3 and 1/5 floats, 84–85
  samplers, 96–98, 114–119
  stripes, 117, 118
  two-heddle weaving, 184–185
  waffle weave effects, 117
warping
  color order with two heddles, 200
  determining sett, 15
  direct method, 178, 232–234
  indirect method, 178–181
  winding the warp, 180–181
warps
  deflected, 129
  spaced, 19
weft-faced fabrics
  basics, 14, 138–139
  clasped weft technique, 164–165

cut-pile techniques, 141–150
krokbragd, 161–164
loop pile, 44–47, 150–154
  with pick-up patterns, 166–168
  sampler, 139–140
soumak, 155–160
weft floats
  basic instructions, 83–84
  columns, 106
  combined with warp floats, 87, 100–103, 127–128, 184
  fringy and fuzzy accents, 110–113
  heddle position, 82
  honeycomb, 113
  inlaid patterns, 108–109
  lace, 83–84, 89–90
  with multiple pick-up sticks, 94–95
  with plain weave, 90–91, 104
  sampler, 88–95
  solid bands, 103
  spot lace, 86, 91, 92, 94
  with supplementary weft, 85, 92–93, 95, 106–107, 125–126
  tapestry effects, 105
  3/1, 5/1, and 7/1 floats, 83, 91, 92–93
  two-heddle weaving, 190
  weft-emphasis fabrics, 166–168
wefts
  contrasting, 17
  deflected, 124–125
  spaced, 19
windowpane patterns
  color-and-weave plus floats, 121
  with two heddles, 199
  warp and weft floats, 100–102
window screen, 219

zigzag hemstitching, 72

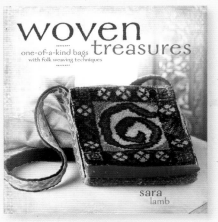